IMAGES
of America

TALKEETNA

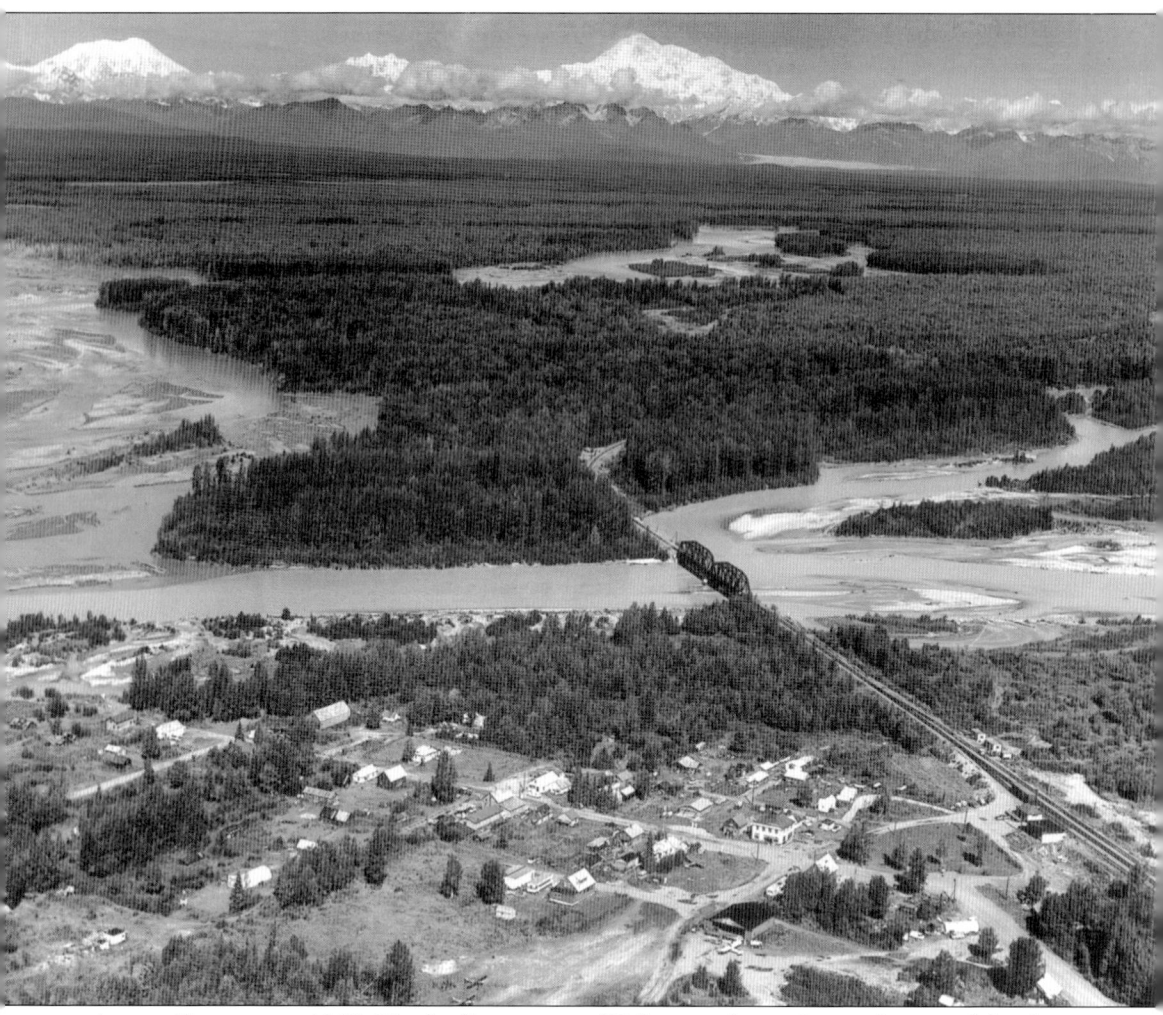

AERIAL TALKEETNA, 1965. This bird's-eye view of Talkeetna shows the confluence of the three rivers, the Talkeetna, Susitna, and Chulitna, along with the railroad bridge at milepost 227. The original village dirt runway, which is still in use today, can also be seen, as can the Alaska Range peaks of Mount Foraker, Mount Hunter, and Denali (Mount McKinley). (Courtesy of the Talkeetna Historical Society.)

ON THE COVER: LANDING. This classic view of Talkeetna captures the essential elements of the special village, including Don Sheldon in a Supercub plane on final approach, landing on the village airstrip; Sheldon's classic 1940 Jeep pickup; the Fairview Inn; the US Commissioners Building; Nellie Carlson's log cabin; and the Sheldon home. A corner of the B&K Trading Post can be seen on the right, along with several 55-gallon fuel barrels. (Courtesy of Talkeetna Historical Society, Roberta Sheldon.)

IMAGES of America
TALKEETNA

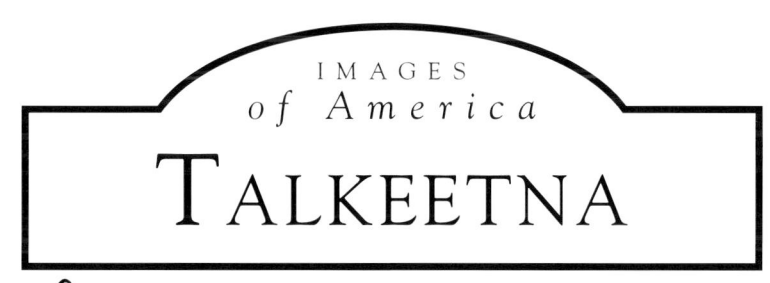

Thanks for supporting the THS.
Tom Sisul
Joy Keniston-Longrie

The Talkeetna Historical Society,
Tom Sisul, and Joy Keniston-Longrie

Foreword by Roberta Sheldon

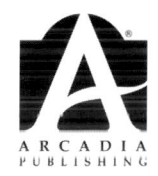

ARCADIA
PUBLISHING

Copyright © 2013 by the Talkeetna Historical Society, Tom Sisul, and Joy Keniston-Longrie
ISBN 978-0-7385-9628-0

Published by Arcadia Publishing
Charleston, South Carolina

Printed in the United States of America

Library of Congress Control Number: 2012950528

For all general information, please contact Arcadia Publishing:
Telephone 843-853-2070
Fax 843-853-0044
E-mail sales@arcadiapublishing.com
For customer service and orders:
Toll-Free 1-888-313-2665

Visit us on the Internet at www.arcadiapublishing.com

*Dedicated to past, present, and future people (Dena'ina)
who make Talkeetna such a unique place*

Contents

Acknowledgments		6
Foreword		7
Introduction		8
1.	Dena'ina	9
2.	Rivers and Rails	15
3.	Trappers, Prospectors, and Miners	29
4.	Historic Talkeetna	47
5.	Bush Pilots	85
6.	Denali	93
7.	Fun—Talkeetnan Style	111
8.	Future Legacy	123

Acknowledgments

Special thanks go to the following: Annie Duquette and Lisa Roderick (Talkeetna Air Taxi); Maureen McLaughlin, Roger Robinson, and Jay Katzen (NPS); Aaron Leggett (Anchorage Museum of History and Art); Pat Beaver Pratt; Eleanor Trepke and Spunky; Marne Gunderson (Fairview Inn); Roberta Sheldon; Joe Eagle; Brian Okonek; Pam Rannals; Wendy Battino; Nancy Trump (Latitude 62); Mar Chilcoat; Pat McGee; Ollie Hudson; Connie Twigg; Jonathon Durr; JoEllen Bye, Jayme Spires, and Lauren Evans (THS); Trisha Costello (Roadhouse); Lori Stec and Dennis Freeman (Nagley's); Violetta Wolfe (Boston Museum of Science); Tony Decaneas (Decaneas Archives, Revere, Massachusetts); Ken Marsh, Trapper Creek Museum; Jim Kari, UAF, Alaska Native Language Center; Amberose Longrie; Leah Falk; John Scarlett; and Brian T. Wygar (Adelphi University).

The following organizations have been abbreviated within this book:
ADN	*Anchorage Daily News*
ASA	Alaska State Archives
AMAH	Anchorage Museum of Art and History
ANHM	Alaska Native Heritage Museum
AT	*Anchorage Times*
BMS	Boston Museum of Science
DAC	Denali Arts Council
DCL	Dartmouth College Library
NPS	National Park Service
UAA	University of Alaska, Anchorage
UAF	University of Alaska, Fairbanks
TCM	Trapper Creek Museum
THS	Talkeetna Historical Society
USGS	United States Geological Survey
USLOC	United States Library of Congress
VN	*Valley News*
WSU-MASC	Washington State University-Manuscripts, Archives, and Special Collections

Foreword

As a lifelong Alaskan and a Talkeetna resident for more than 48 years, it is a pleasure to pen this book's foreword. When I arrived here in 1964, there were around 150 people in the village, including about 10 wonderfully unique old-timers of much advanced age. These distinctive gentlemen, who had led exceedingly tough but gratifying lives in Alaska, wore wool pants, wool shirts, tough, seasoned footwear, and red felt hats, which, at the time, were a popular new novelty available at the B&K store. On those occasions when I was on Main Street, several would kindly greet me with a mannerly tip of the hat, which so touched me. But, within four or so years, most had quietly passed away. It was only sometime later that I fully realized I had witnessed the end of an era in Talkeetna.

Talkeetna is a special place indeed, with ongoing devoted community values, a proud appreciation for its historical heritage, and people who are fiercely protective of the well-being and environment of the simple village lifestyle, its people, and its surroundings. Rich scenic beauty; powerful and productive wild rivers; and healthy, thriving wilderness contribute to the transcendental aura of this village. A love for the wild and natural, the "integrity of place," and things that can challenge our mettle have long existed here. One old-timer, Jim Beaver, now gone, liked to say, "The tougher it gets, the better I like it!" It is important to note here that we are also savvy and totally plugged into the 21st century.

This book contains a wealth of photographs that have long been archived, many of which have never seen publication until now. Thanks to Joy Keniston-Longrie and Tom Sisul, the researchers and authors of this book, and to the many local residents who contributed their memories, stories, and pictures to share this wonderful account of Talkeetna. The authors' thoroughness and hard work have resulted in this sterling contribution to Talkeetna, the place we treasure because it is real. A longtime local resident named Art said it all when he once earnestly proclaimed, "Talkeetna is really real!"

—Roberta Sheldon, local Talkeetna historian

INTRODUCTION

There is something magical, almost mystical about Talkeetna that is hard to describe. Is it the spiritual shadow effect of Denali? Or is it the sense of timelessness resulting from the relative isolation of this remote natural setting? Could it be the international flavor brought by visitors from around the world, which creates a feeling of a global community? Is it the sense of a village community and acceptance of unique lifestyles not found in larger towns and cities? It certainly is not tropical weather. It is perhaps best articulated by geologist Leslie White in a letter he wrote to the Talkeetna Historical Society:

> In September of 2001, I stepped into the bar of the Fairview and could detect no change since 1958. I, like others I am sure, went to Alaska and fell in love. I have not been successful in articulating exactly what it is about the place that grabs you by the heart; but, as a certainty, it is something . . . and this time, just as 43 years ago, when I left Alaska, I left a part of my heart behind.

Located at the end of the road in the land of the midnight sun, the historic village of Talkeetna has played a significant role in native Alaskan history, and more recently in trapping, mining, railroad, and mountaineering history. The literal translation of *K'Dalkitnu* (Talkeetna), "he is keeping food cache-river," reflects the role the area has had since before Europeans entered this region, which continues today—it is a gathering place by the junction of three rivers where good food, drink, and comfortable accommodations can be found.

Just as the Athabascan Susitna Valley *Dena'ina* ("the People") were always on the move, seeking food, dictated by seasonal cycles based on weather, bird/animal migration patterns, and growing seasons, the nonnative population continues this seasonal cycle of activity—providing food and shelter to people who come and go. The official population of Talkeetna peaked during the construction of the Alaska Railroad, from 1916 to 1923, at nearly 1,000 residents. The population dipped to its low, just 150, in 1964. Today's population hovers around 950 permanent residents. The annual spring breakup of ice signals the beginning of the next cycle, as the daylight lengthens and people start moving into the surrounding area. There continues to be a seasonal influx of an estimated 200,000 visitors who gather in Talkeetna for food, rest, and socialization each year before and after traveling to remote areas for fishing, sightseeing, recreating, and mountain climbing. They gather afterwards in Talkeetna to eat, drink, and rest before returning via train or car to their permanent homes. When the leaves change color, daylight hours shorten, the rivers and lakes begin to freeze and visitors go south. Locals reclaim Talkeetna, where the cache of food, beverage, shelter, and strong bonds of friendship are ever-present.

This book is a pictorial history of Talkeetna. Each image has its own amazing story of people, their work ethic, character, strength, and integrity. The authors refer the reader to the many books written about this area for a more in-depth understanding of the Talkeetna people and stories behind these images. We hope you enjoy this journey through time, and maybe you too will leave a part of your heart in Talkeetna, or perhaps take a part of its spirit with you.

One

Dena'ina

The first people who lived in the Talkeetna area were Dena'ina, which means "the People" in the Athabascan language. Prior to European contact, Talkeetna was named after the river known as K'dalkitnu, which is commonly believed to mean "where three rivers join" or "river of plenty." A more literal translation is "he is keeping food cache-river." The K'dalkitnu area—at the confluence of the K'dalkitnu (Talkeetna), Suyitnu (Susitna), and Ts'ilutnu (Chulitna) Rivers—was an important location for trading, fishing, and caching food. In the Dena'ina language, nu means "river," Suyitnu means "Sandy River," and Ts'ilutnu translates to "Forearm River."

Dghelay Teht'ana, or "the Mountain People," were a band of Dena'ina who considered K'dalkitnu part of their accustomed hunting, fishing, and gathering grounds. The seasons dictated their activities, and they were always on the go. Family units worked together throughout the seasons to gather, hunt, fish, preserve, and prepare foods. Each year, when the frozen rivers broke up and birds made their annual migration back to K'dalkitnu, it was time to trap beavers, geese, and ducks. During the summer months, when the days were filled with light, smaller family groups would set up temporary camps for fishing and gathering berries. The leaves turning yellow signaled the season to hunt moose and caribou. It was important that the Dena'ina had their caches full by mid-fall to last through the frigid winter months.

As the days grew shorter and colder, rivers and lakes began to freeze, signaling time for the Dghelay Teht'ana family groups to gather at their winter camps. The long, dark, cold winter months were filled with the sounds of drums, singing, dancing, ceremonies, and storytelling. Elders shared stories and legends teaching traditional values, which have been passed from generation to generation since time immemorial. Traditionally, elders teach the importance of respect for all living things, of hunting only for what is needed and using every animal part, and of sharing with the entire village. This seasonal rhythm of life continued for nearly 10,000 years, but was significantly disrupted after first contact with nonnatives, resulting in cultural and health impacts.

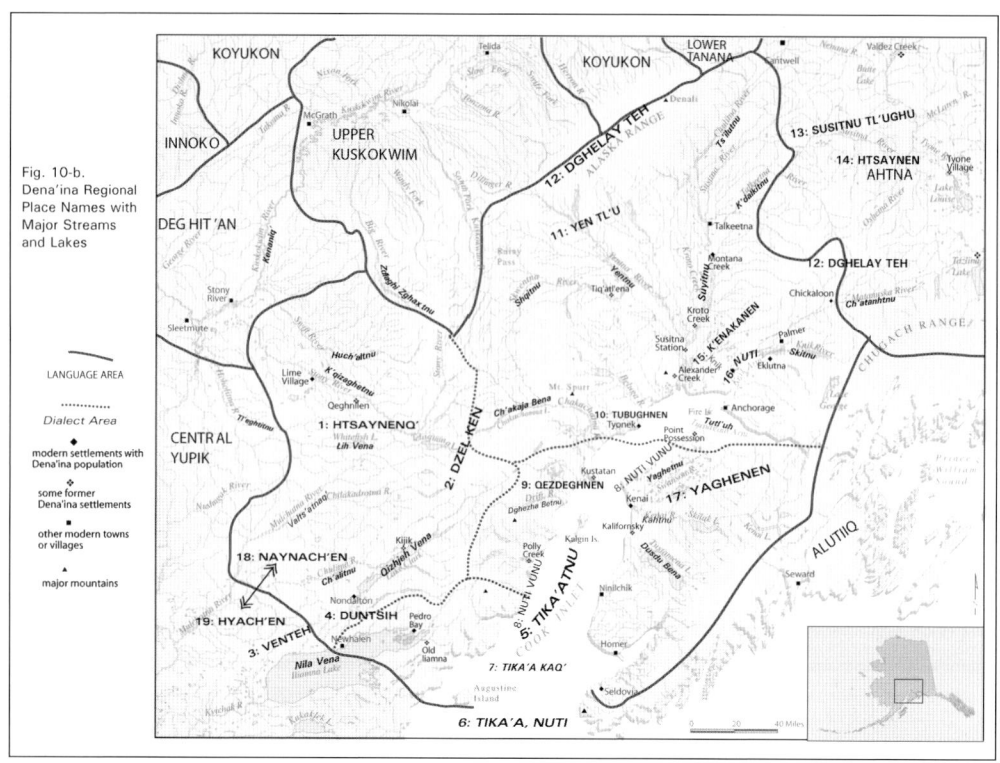

ATHABASCAN DENA'INA REGION MAP. The Dena'ina Athabascan-language area roughly demarks a horseshoe shaped area of approximately 41,000 square miles. Dena'ina ełnena, "the Dena'ina homeland," encompasses Cook Inlet and the southern part of the Alaskan Range, including Dghelay Ka'a, better known as Deenaalee (Denali), meaning "the High One" or "the Tall One." The mountain people were bilingual, speaking both the Dena'ina and Ahtna languages. (Courtesy James Kari, UAF.)

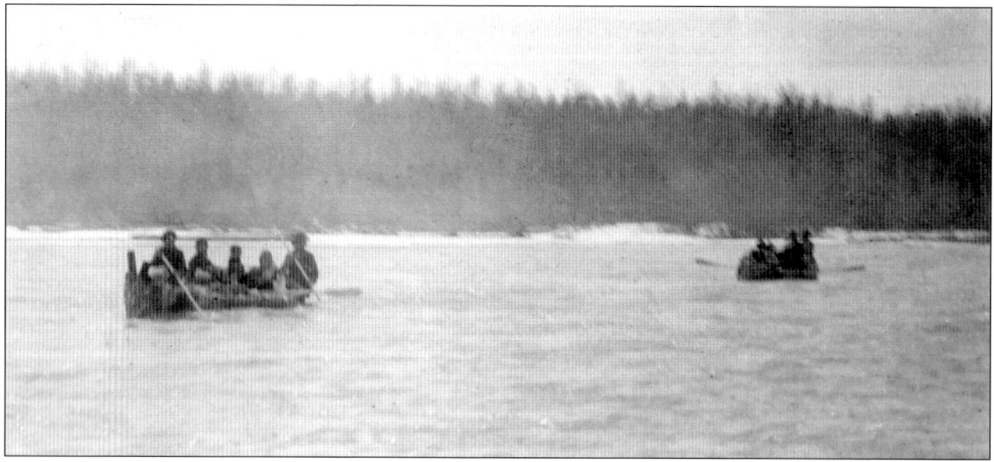

BADI (CANOE). The primary mode of transportation during warmer months was the *badi*, of which there are three types: the *baqay* (birch bark) canoe and two types of *elgheji* (hide boats)—one made with tanned moose or caribou hide and another made from untreated skins sewn together to make a temporary canoe for floating meat to the winter camp after hunting large game. In this photograph, taken by Belmore Browne in 1910, the Dena'ina use untreated-skin elgheji. (Courtesy DCL.)

***Ush Duch'Elashi* (Making Snowshoes).** In *A Dena'ina Legacy*, Peter Kalifornsky writes, "You cut soft birch into strips for the snowshoe frame. Then you carve it . . . You put in cross braces . . . When it's dry you drill the frame holes. Then you lace through frame holes with leather rope. Then you lace the footpieces up . . . And then you put them on and go hunting in them." (Courtesy DCL.)

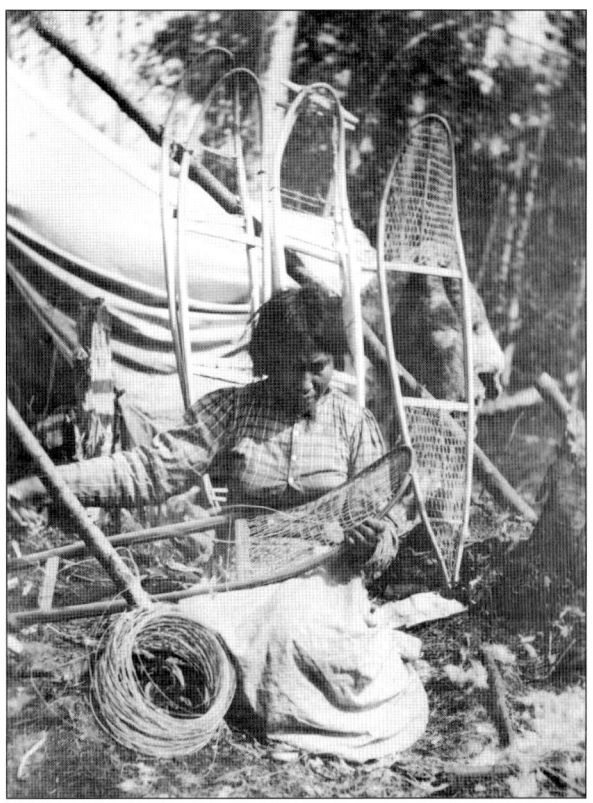

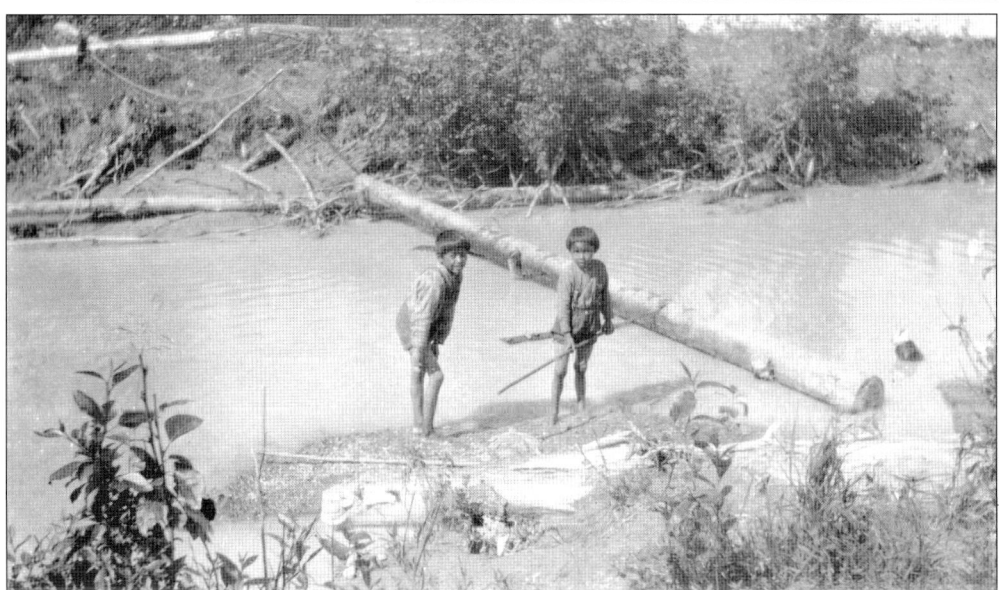

***Kił gga* (Young Boys).** These two *Kił gga* are playing in a shallow portion of K'dalkitnu (Talkeetna River) in approximately 1915. The Dena'ina population was heavily impacted by the flu pandemic that hit the area in 1918. After the epidemic, many remaining Dena'ina left K'dalkitnu and Tsar'ukegh (Susitna Station) and moved to Knik or other areas, although the Dena'ina still consider K'dalkitnu to be their ancestral home. (Courtesy UAF.)

11

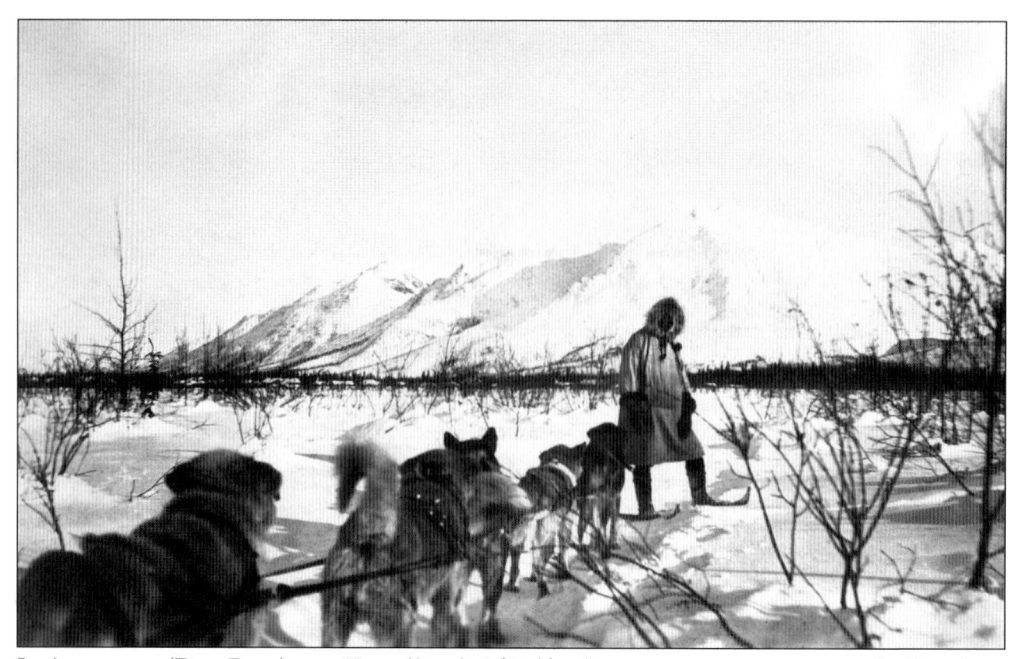

ŁIK'A HAŁ YESA (DOG PACK) AND HETL (SLED). Łik'a (dogs) were an important asset to the Dena'ina. They were trained to help hunters chase large game, such as *dnigi* (moose) or *ghenuy* (caribou) and were used to pack supplies. The hetl was initially pulled by a woman with a line wrapped around her shoulders. After the European Americans arrived in the area, the łik'a were used to pull the hetl. (Courtesy UAF.)

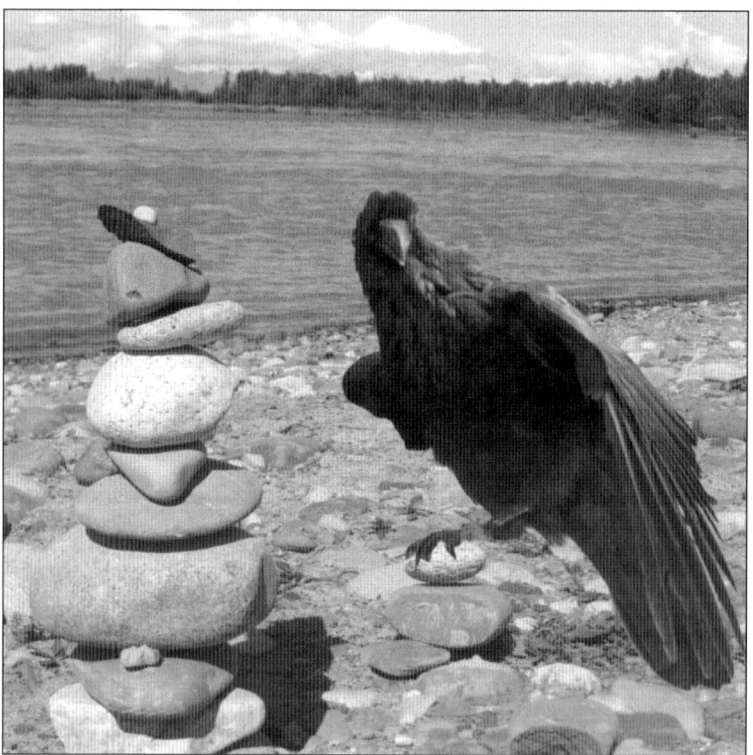

CHULYIN OR DELGGA (RAVEN). A frequent character in Dena'ina legends, *Chulyin* directly translates as "the one that eats feces" and "the one that caws." Chulyin is almost always looking for food and is very noisy. Chulyin is often portrayed as a trickster, never to be trusted. He is very clever and has the ability to transform himself into other forms. Raven gave Dena'ina songs and stories. (Courtesy Amberose and Leah Falk.)

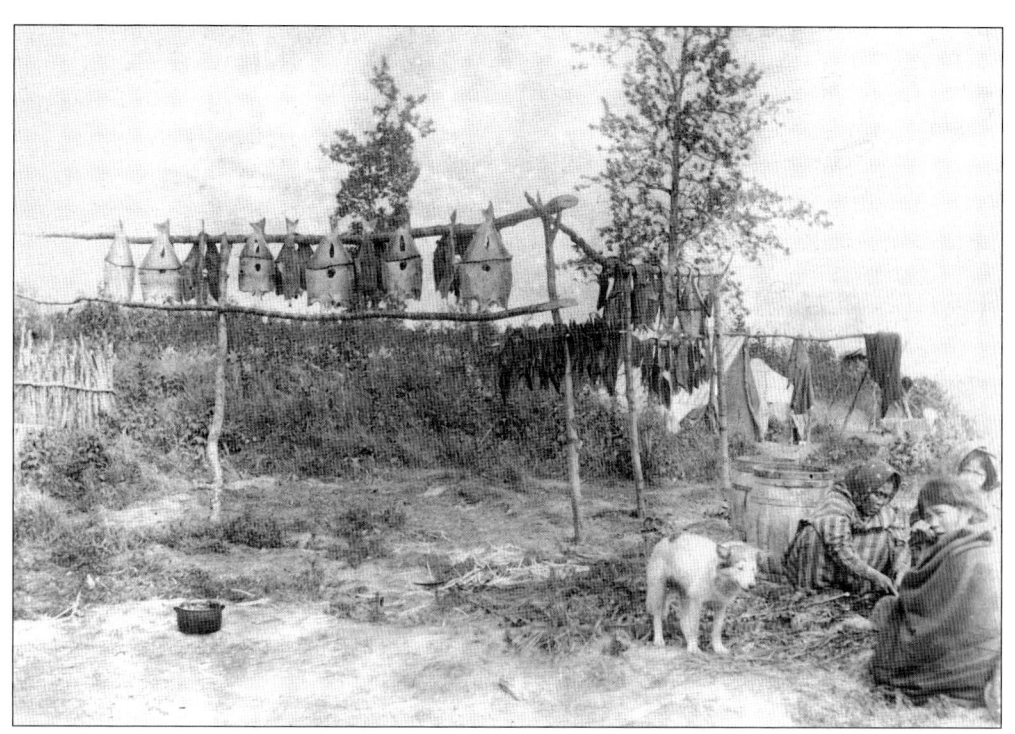

BABA (DRYING FISH). Baba was very important to the Dena'ina and their łik'a for sustenance. The salmon's seasonal migration dictated the activities of Dena'ina who lived in the area, and the catching and preparation of the baba was a team effort. It was the principal food for the dogs, who consumed twice as much as did the humans, and it was important not to have too many łik'a for the baba food supply. (Courtesy UAF.)

CHAQILIN Q'A (UNDERGROUND FISH CACHE). Food was preserved and stored where animals could not reach it. One type of cache was an elevated structure. However, the *chaqilin q'a* was the most common type used by the Dena'ina to store fish by taking advantage of permafrost conditions underground. The chaqilin q'a was created by digging a hole in the ground, lining it with birch bark, layering fish and fireweed leaves, and sealing it airtight. This chaqilin q'a near K'dalkitnu (Talkeetna) was recently excavated by archaeologists. (Fran Seager-Boss, Brian T. Wygar

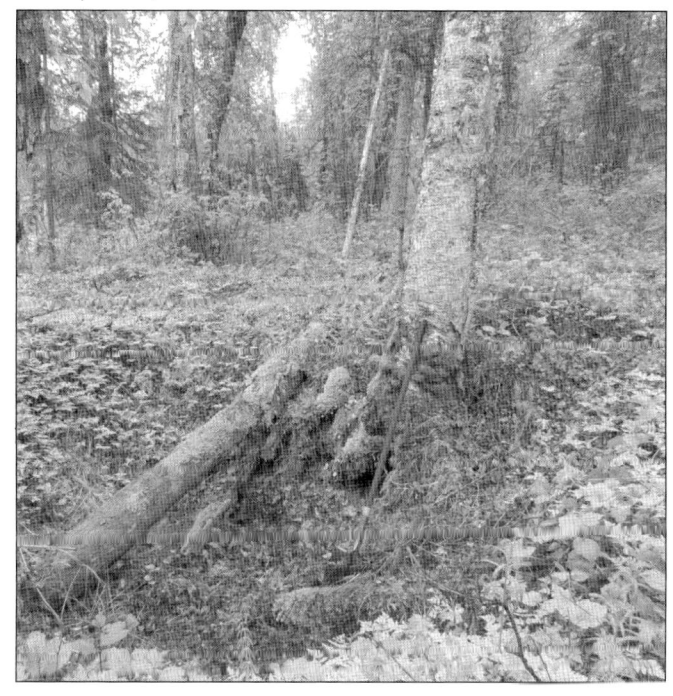

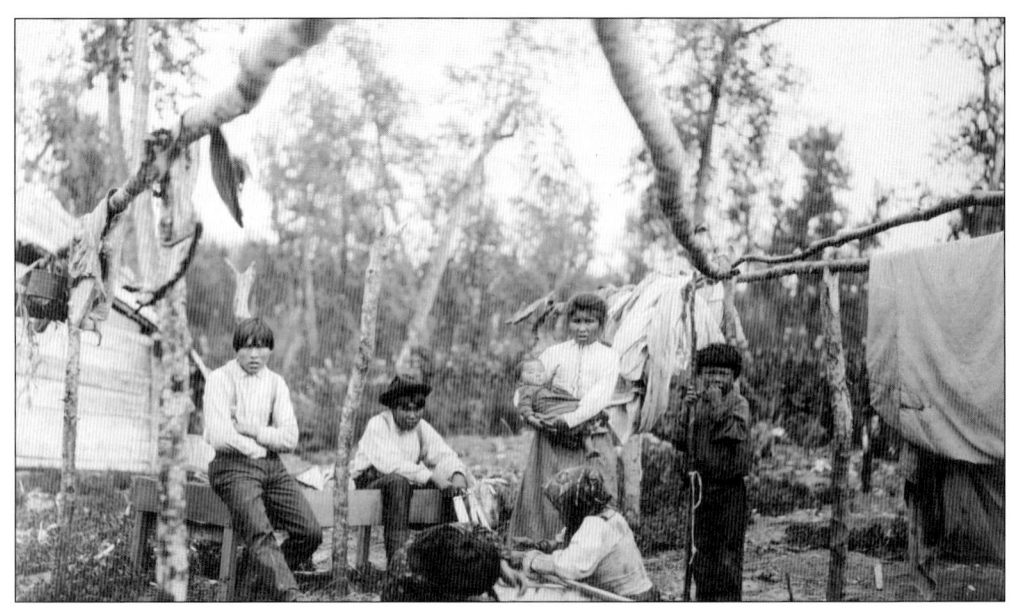

DGHELAY TEHT'ANA (THE MOUNTAIN PEOPLE). When the Belmore Browne Expedition to Denali passed through K'dalkitnu (Talkeetna) in 1910, they met this Dghelay Teht'ana family, believed to be part of Chief Nicolie's band. Dghelay Teht'ana suffered greatly from disease brought by Europeans beginning in the 19th century. A wood home can be seen to the left. Dghelay Teht'ana were often used as guides by early explorers. (Courtesy DCL)

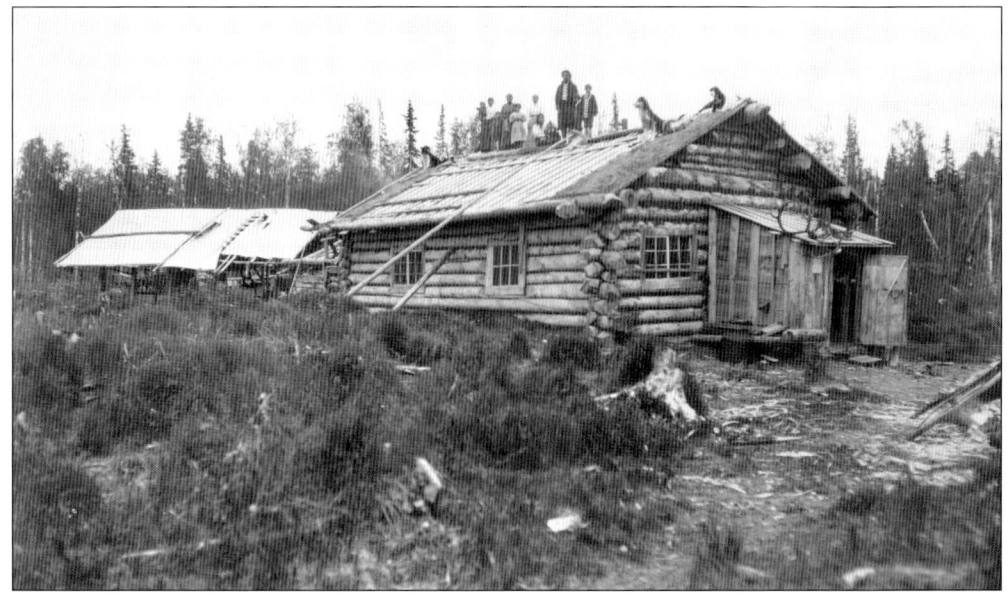

CHIEF OF DGHELAY TEHT'ANA. Ch'k'idetnishen, Talkeetna Nicoli, Chief of Dghelay Teht'ana lived in this log house in Talkeetna in 1915. Standing on the roof are, from left to right, Alec and Joe Nicoli (both sons of Chief Taleetna Nicoli), Ch'K'idetnishen (Chief Talkeetna Nicoli), Ts'ituya (daughter of Chief Talkeetna Nicoli), three unidentified people, Nidina (wife of Chief Talkeetna Nicoli), and an unidentified person. They are also joined by three dogs. In 1917, the railroad moved the family to a new one-acre lot, located half a mile south of the new village of Talkeetna. (Courtesy USLOC.)

Two

Rivers and Rails

The headwaters of the Talkeetna River emerge from the glaciers of the Talkeetna Mountains. The glacially fed Talkeetna meanders 80 miles west before merging with the Susitna and Chulitna Rivers at the village of Talkeetna. The Susitna River is the 15th largest river (based on discharge volume) in the United States and flows 313 miles (504 kilometers) into Cook Inlet. When the first Europeans gained access to the Talkeetna area, the Susitna, Chulitna, and Talkeetna Rivers served as the primary avenues of transportation. When the rivers were not frozen, canoes and flat-bottomed boats were used to transport people and goods to stations located along the river.

As early as 1896, the Susitna River served as the primary transportation link for gold prospectors in the watershed. Talkeetna became a supply station for prospectors and trappers in 1910, but closed after one year. Originally, Susitna Station, located 75 miles to the south of Talkeetna, served as the primary river stop. This changed in 1916, when the Alaska Engineering Commission (AEC) selected Talkeetna as the site of a railroad construction camp and the Alaska Railroad divisional headquarters. Talkeetna reopened in 1916 as a riverboat steamer station. From the river stations, people and goods were transported across rough trails on foot or by horse-drawn teams in the spring, summer, and fall.

During the winter, when the rivers froze, nature created a "frozen highway system" that made transportation easier than it was during the warmer seasons. Snowshoes and sleds drawn by humans, dogs, or horses were used to transport goods and people across the frozen landscape. In 1919, the AEC surveyed the village, held an auction, and sold 80 lots for an average price of $14.25 per lot. Overnight, Talkeetna grew to a community of several hundred residents living in tents. The railroad provided a critical transportation link for both Alaska and Talkeetna, which previously had only foot trails or river traffic via canoes and barges. The railroad, combined with Talkeetna's location—the place where three rivers meet, 60 miles "as the raven flies" from Denali—continue to be key to Talkeetna's unique characteristics.

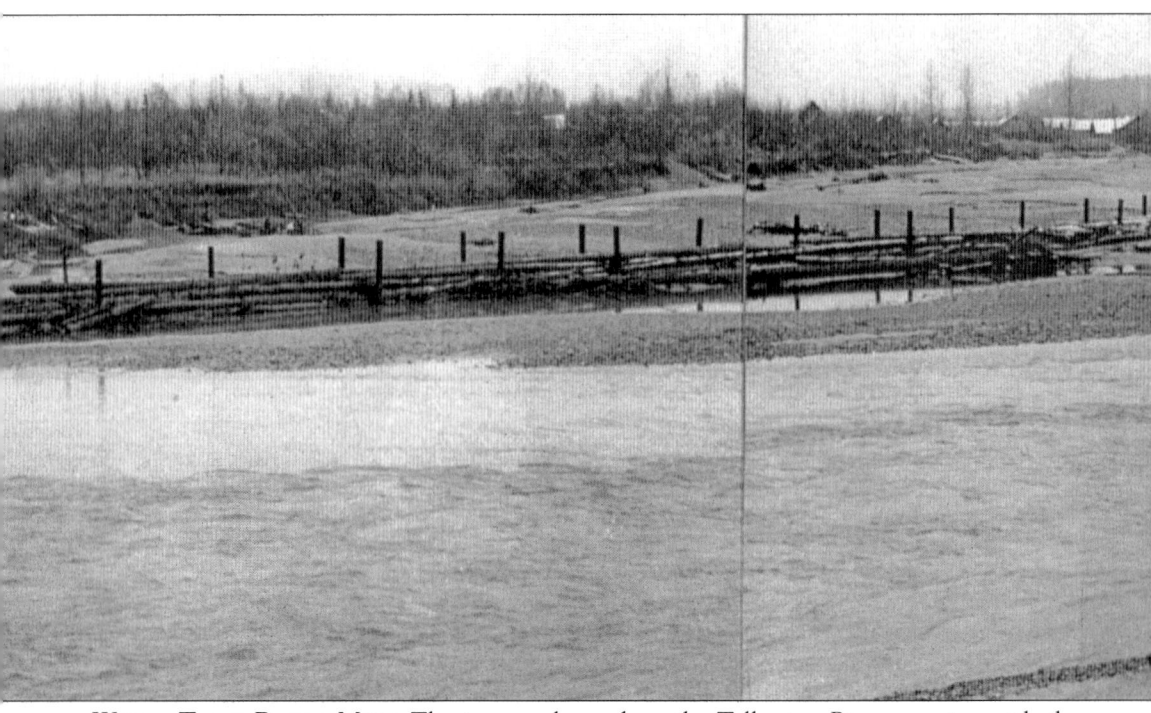

WHERE THREE RIVERS MEET. The images above show the Talkeetna River merging with the Chulitna and Susitna Rivers at the edge of the Village of Talkeetna. Like any wild river, it meanders in its natural floodplain. Sandbars and woody debris change over time and are greatly impacted by the spring breakup of ice-choked rivers and large storms. The Village of Talkeetna is seen on the left. Below, the remains of the shoring constructed by the original settlers along the edge of

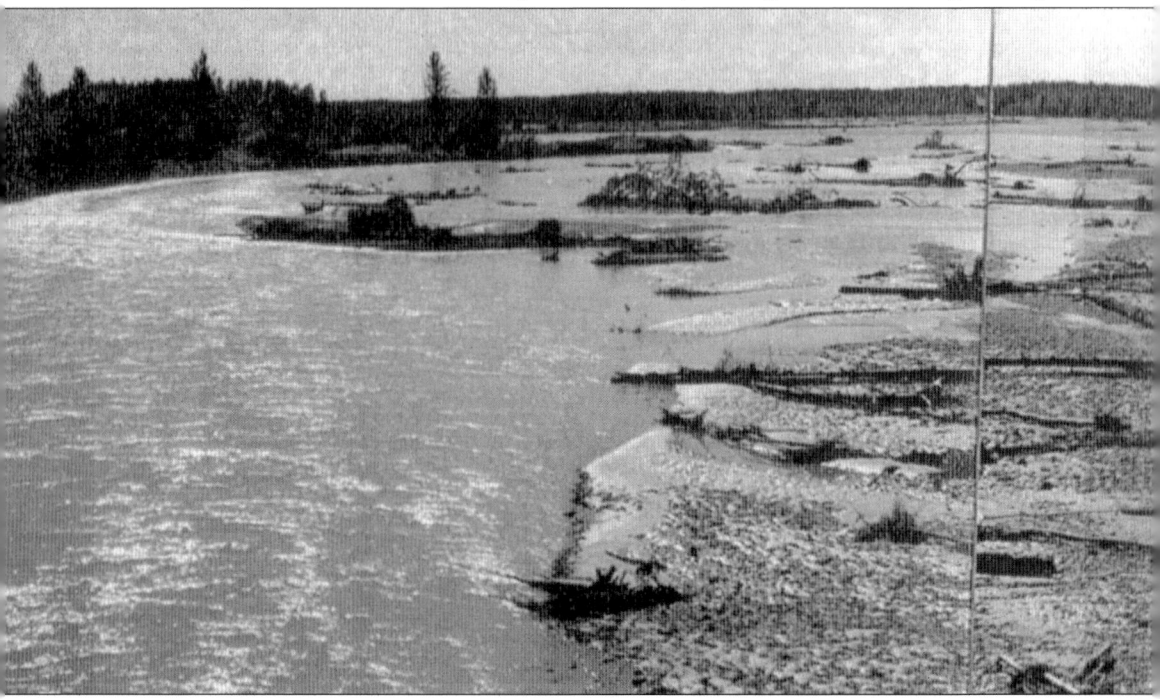

16

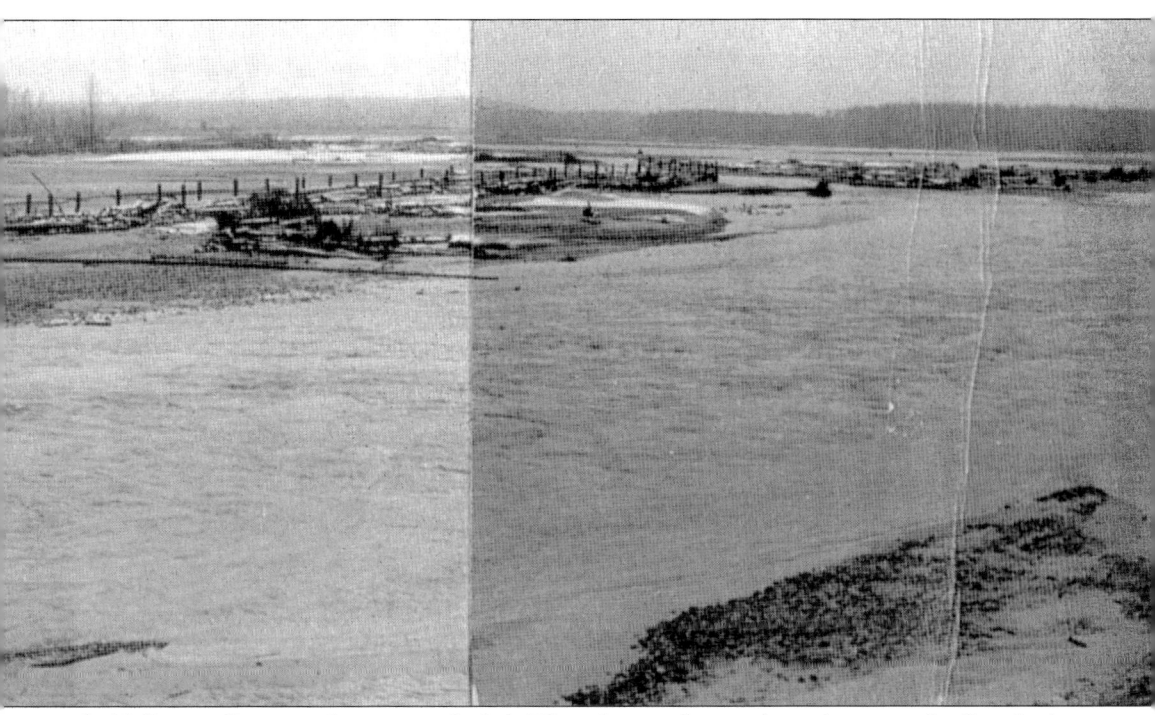

the Talkeetna River can be seen to the left. The pilings indicate where the original village built its rudimentary docks, buildings, and boat landings to support the River Station of Talkeetna. The pilings and shoring were destroyed by floodwaters in 1949, and the portion of the village located on the shoreline was moved inland to the current townsite. (Courtesy THS.)

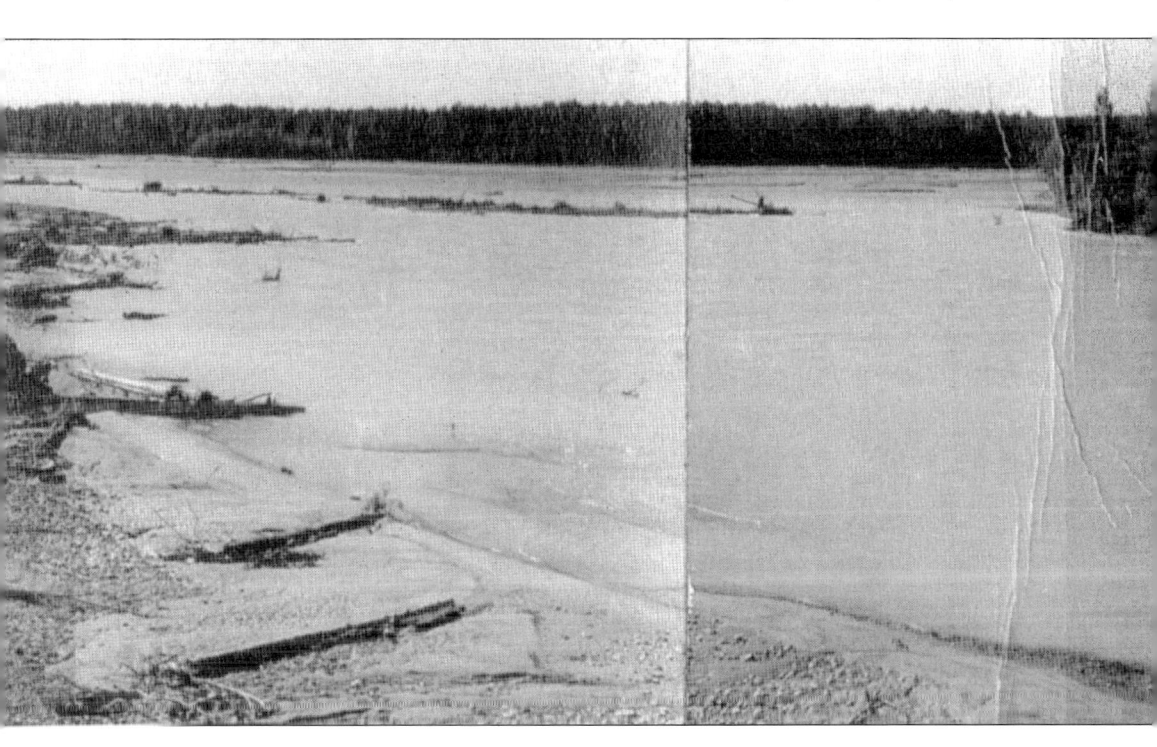

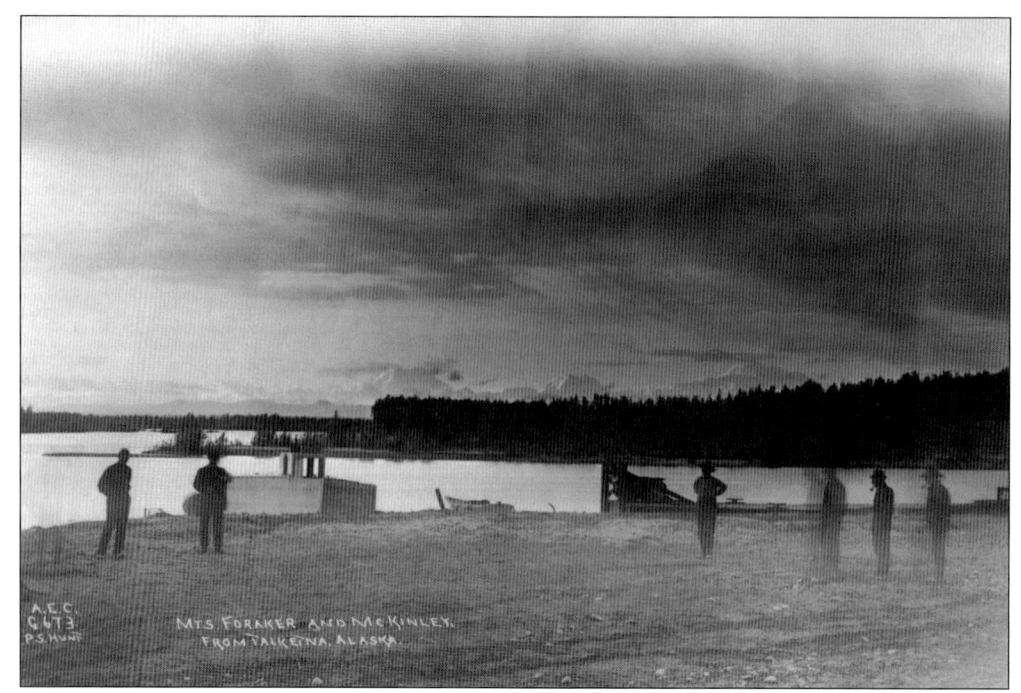

TALKEETNA RIVER STATION. This 1917 cloudy view of Mount Foraker, Mount Hunter, and Denali from the shores of Talkeetna is timeless. The shoreline served as the Talkeetna River steamer station for supplies brought up from Susitna Station and Cook Inlet via steamboats. The station was used extensively by miners and trappers and also facilitated the construction of the Alaska Railroad. The Talkeetna River flows into the Susitna River in this image. (Courtesy AMAH.)

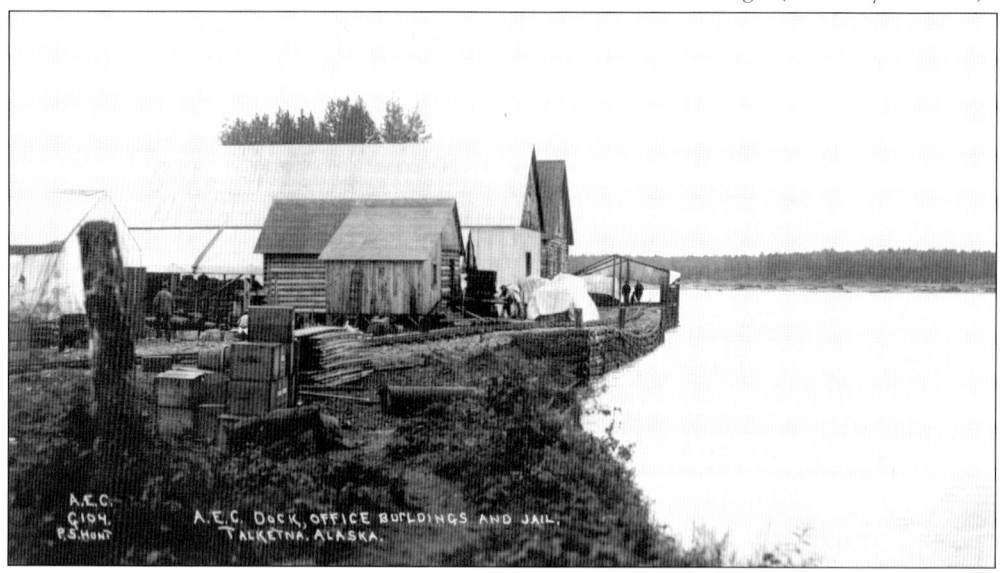

TALKEETNA DOCK. Talkeetna was dependent upon the rivers for supplies and transportation in the early 1900s. The pilings created a bulkhead for buildings. The AEC identifies the structures in this 1917 image as office buildings and a jail. Supplies are visible in the foreground, and in the background, a boat landing. The Talkeetna River can be seen merging with the Susitna River. (Courtesy AMAH.)

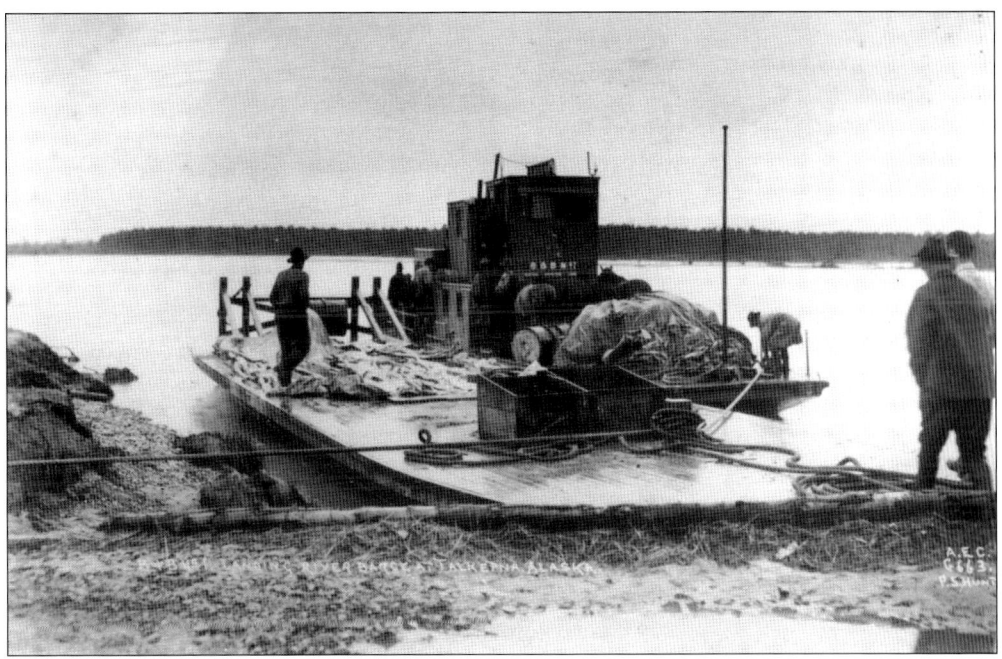

SUPPLIES ARRIVING AT TALKEETNA. Flat-bottomed boats served as the supply line to Talkeetna from Susitna Station and Cook Inlet. The boat was able to dock and unload directly on the bulkhead built along the Talkeetna River shoreline in 1917. Horsepower and manpower were used to unload the supplies, which were used in town or freighted to miners and trappers in outlying areas. (Courtesy AMAH.)

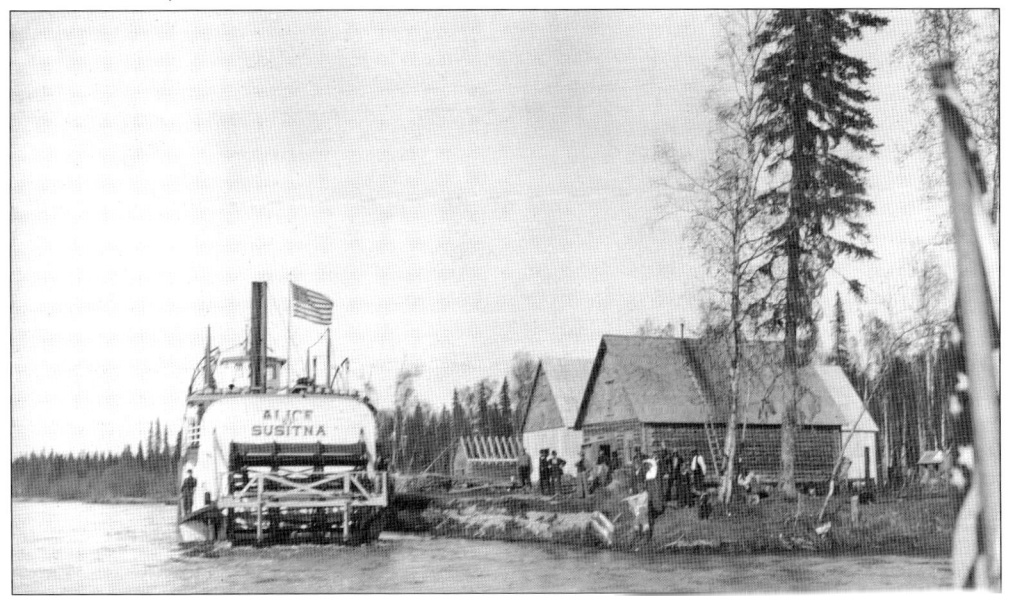

RIVERBOAT ALICE SUSITNA. The 1910 Belmore Browne Expedition to Denali took this picture of the Alice Susitna arriving at Talkeetna. These are the same wood-frame buildings as pictured on the previous page, but seen from a different perspective. In the warmer months, boats were the primary mode of transportation. Horses and human backs augmented the transportation system for overland packing and freighting across rough, muddy trails. (Courtesy DCL.)

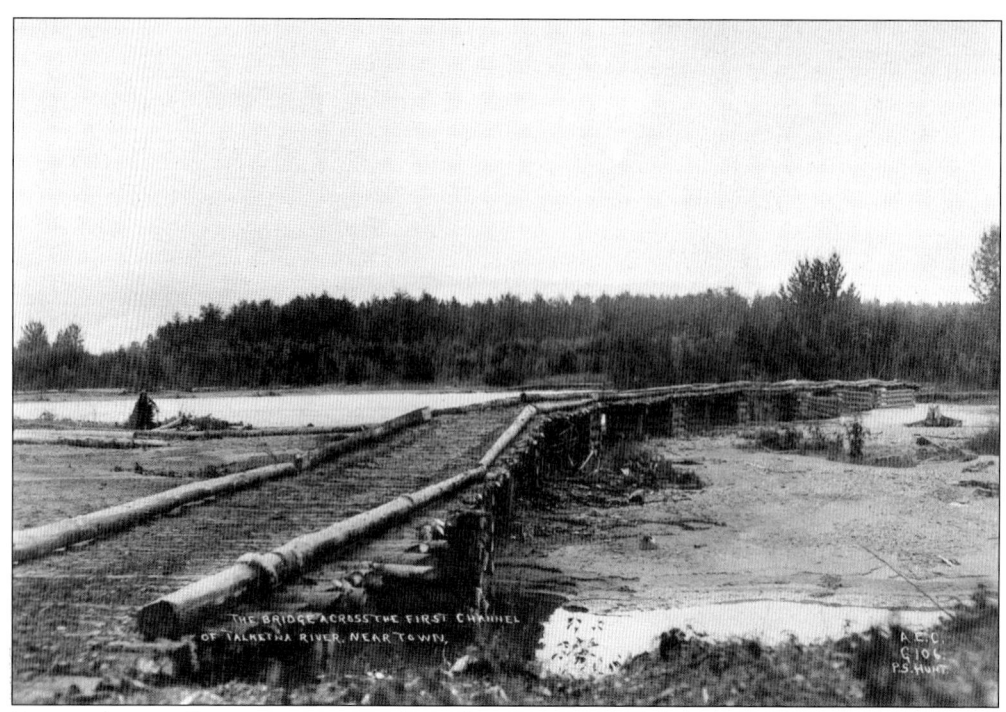

BRIDGE ACROSS TALKEETNA RIVER. The Talkeetna River was a primary transportation corridor and source of food supply. In the warmer months, when it was not frozen, it became a physical barrier to the transportation of supplies to miners and trappers across the river. When the river was frozen, it was much easier to transport goods and people across it. Above, this wooden bridge with extensive log footings was constructed in 1916 to span the main channel of the Talkeetna River. Below is the second bridge built to cross the river after the first was destroyed by swift-moving water, debris, and high floodwaters after only six months of service. (Both courtesy AMAH.)

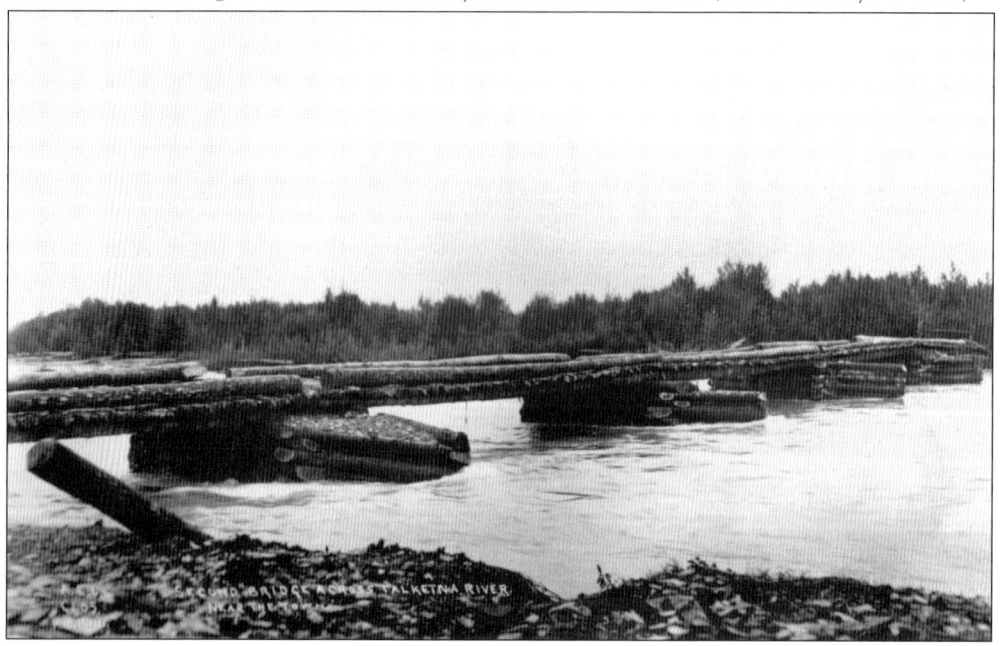

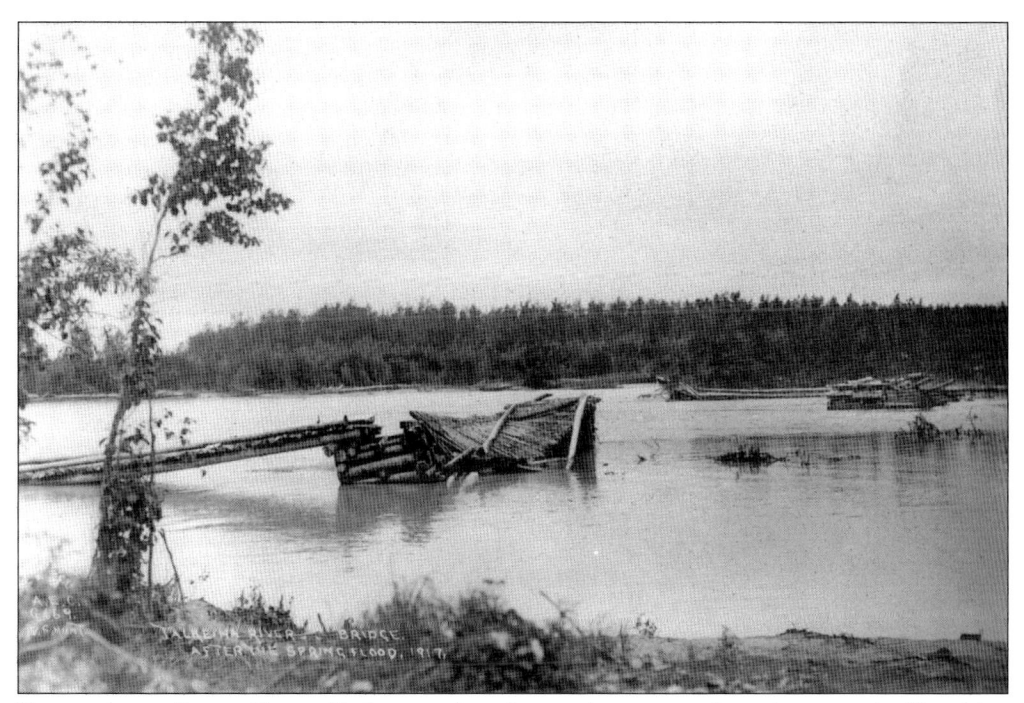

BRIDGE AFTER SPRING FLOOD. Each year, when the weather warms, the unique sounds of breaking ice accompany the thawing of the frozen river. Large and small pieces of ice float downriver, often leaving destruction, including ice dams, in their wake as they meander to the sea. As the glaciers melt and the river ice breaks up, water levels rise, and flooding is common. The potential for damage can be seen with the destruction of the second newly constructed wooden bridge. Below, when the bridge was gone, locals were required to revert back to flat-bottomed-boat transportation to cross the cold river. (Above, courtesy AMAH; below, courtesy THS.)

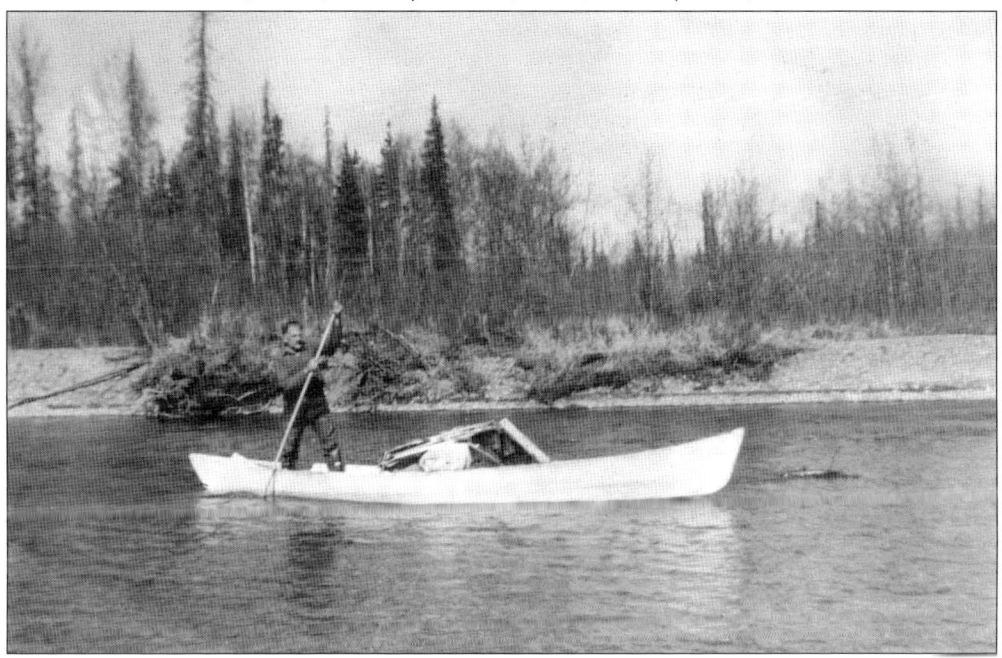

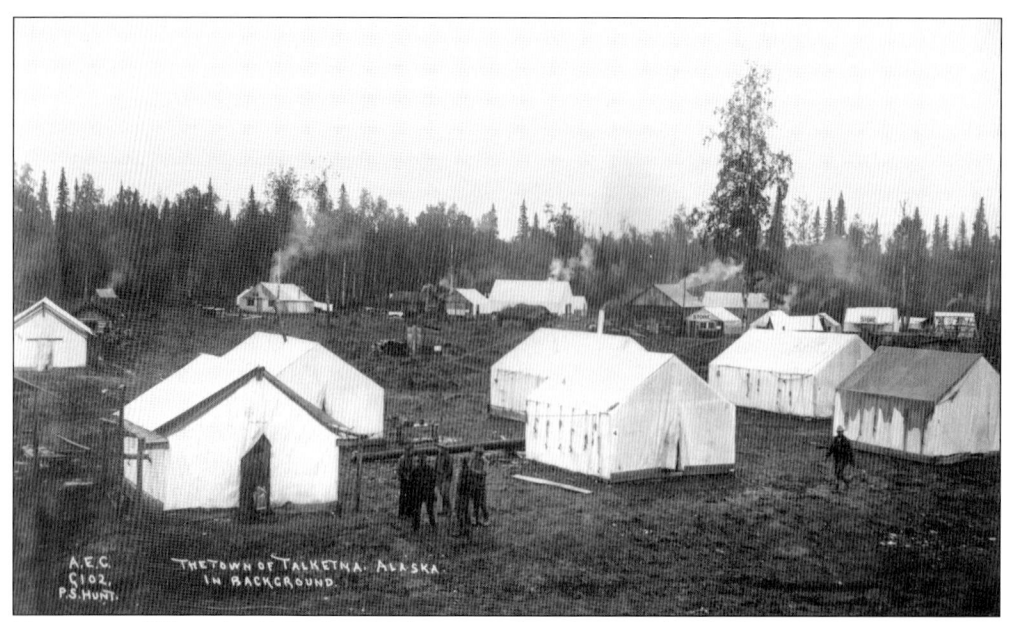

TALKEETNA. When the AEC chose Talkeetna as the Alaska Railroad's divisional headquarters in 1916, a tent city (above) sprang up overnight. It was primarily populated by railroad workers, but it also attracted outfitters, supply stores, miners, and trappers. The village site had been cleared of trees, which were used for framing, heating, and cooking. There was no basic infrastructure, such as drinking water, electricity, or wastewater facilities. Three years later, the US commissioner had improved living conditions, moving from a tent to a wooden building (below). Surprisingly, the poles seen in the background indicate that by 1919 there was telegraph service in Talkeetna. Laundry was hung out to freeze dry in the chilling March weather. (Both courtesy AMAH.)

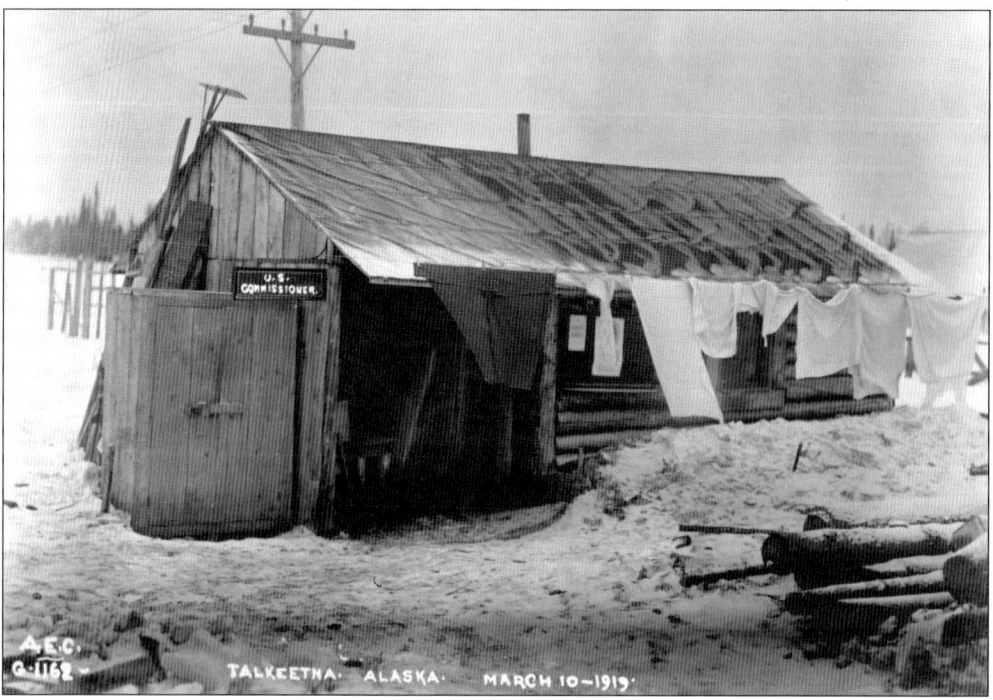

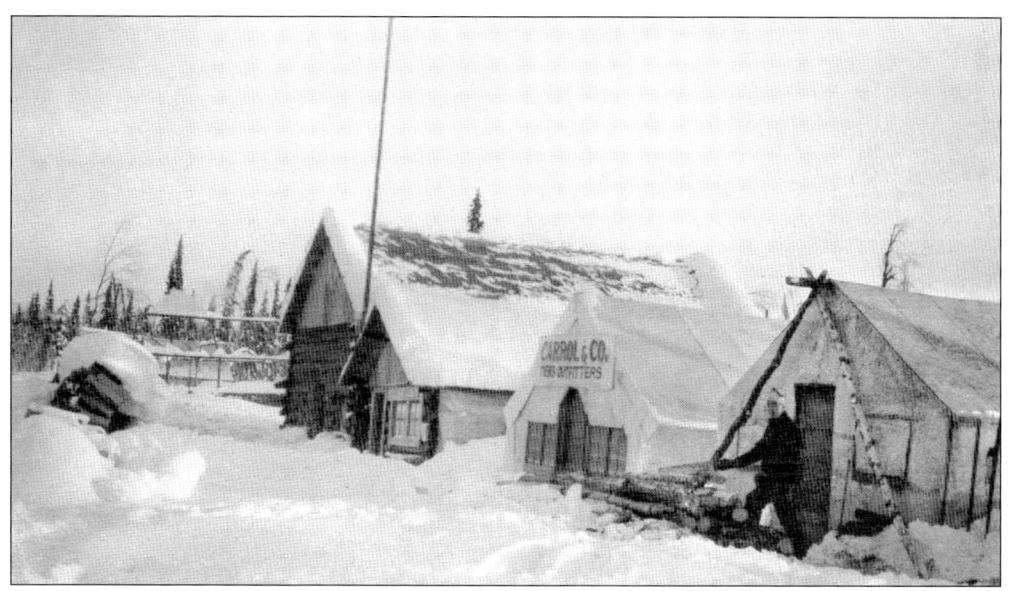

TALKEETNA BUSINESS DISTRICT. By 1917, a thriving business district had been established in Talkeetna, operating seven days a week, 365 days each year as demand required. The 1917 winter scene above shows the business district in various stages of completion. Some of the buildings were bare stick frames, others were wall-framed tents with canvas siding, and yet others were wooden structures with glass windows. The constant demand for firewood to stay warm is evidenced by several snow-covered piles of logs. Gradually, the tent city converted to more permanent-style log buildings, and even some wooden sidewalks are evident near the structure to the right in the c. 1918 image below. The roads were clear of stumps but full of mud, and there continued to be a mixture of buildings in different styles and stages of construction. (Both courtesy AMHA.)

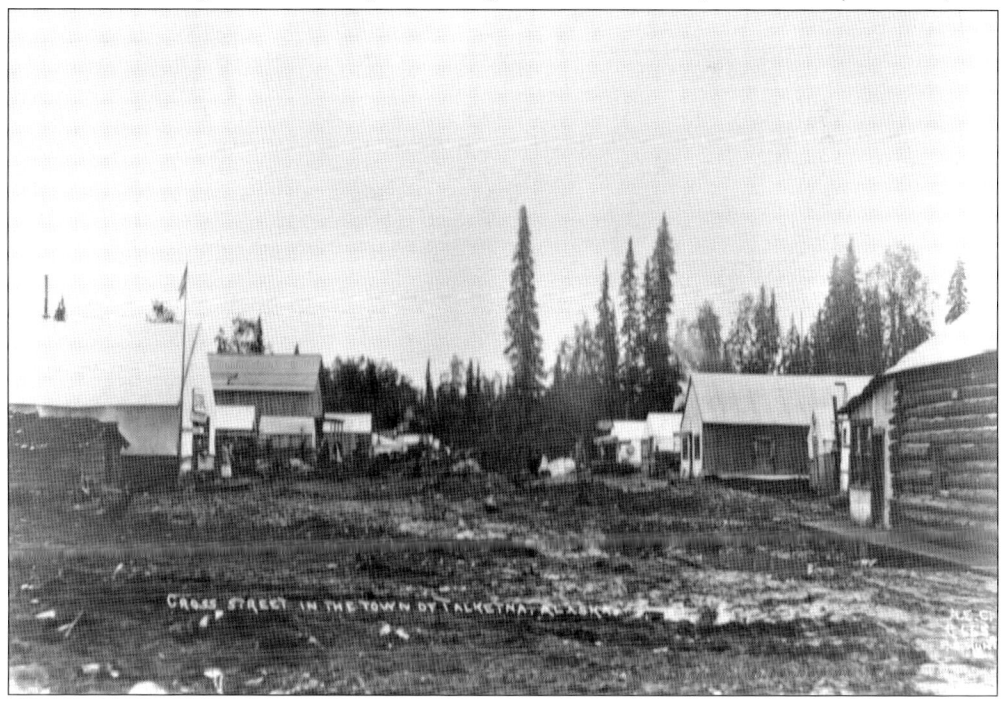

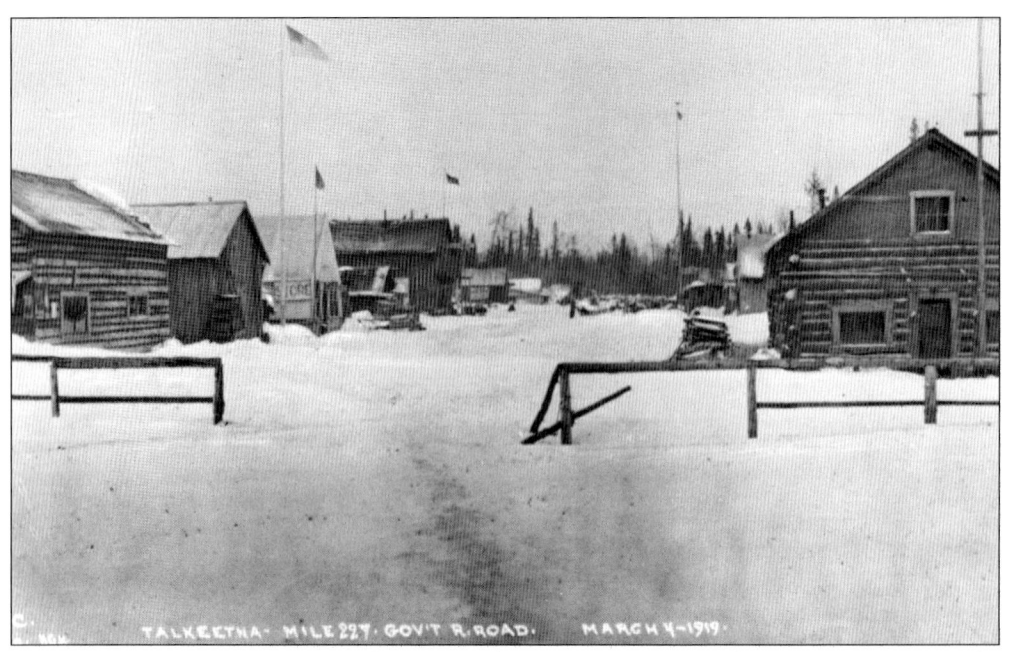

MAIN STREET, TALKEETNA. When the snow and colder weather arrived in the winter of 1919, the streets actually became more pleasant and passable. Flags are flying high, and massive woodpiles are visible on both sides of Main Street. The Bucket of Blood bar is the first building on the left, and Belle McDonald's Trading Post is the first building on the right. (Courtesy AMAH.)

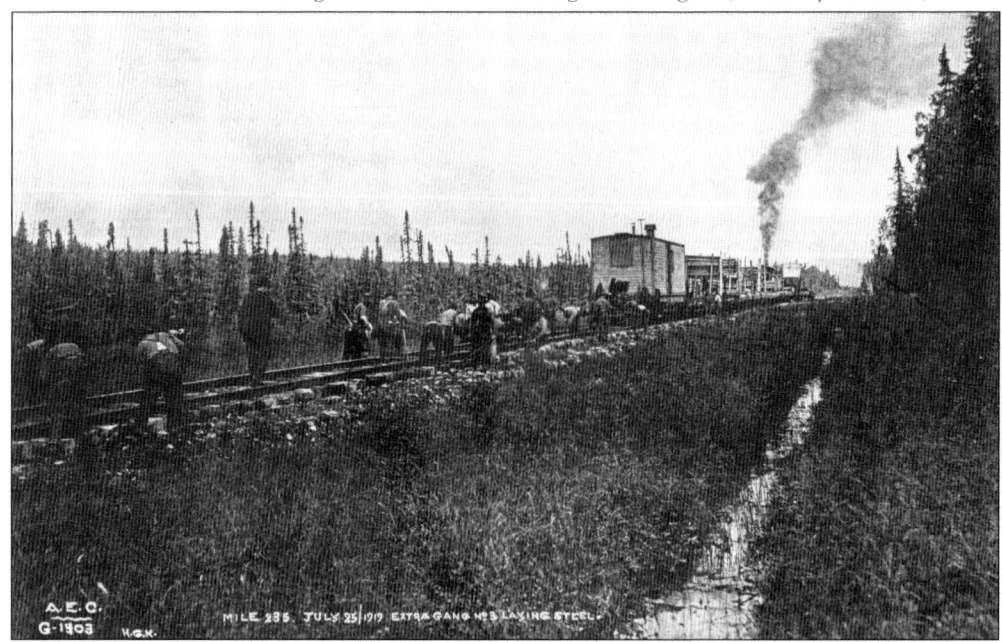

RAILROAD GANG. The ongoing construction of the railroad through Talkeetna created boom years that saw the population rise from a handful of people prior to 1914 to nearly 1,000 people living and working in the area. These men are doing the backbreaking labor of laying steel track on difficult terrain. Closer inspection of the railroad cars reveals that several are full of wood ties used in rail construction (Courtesy AMAH.)

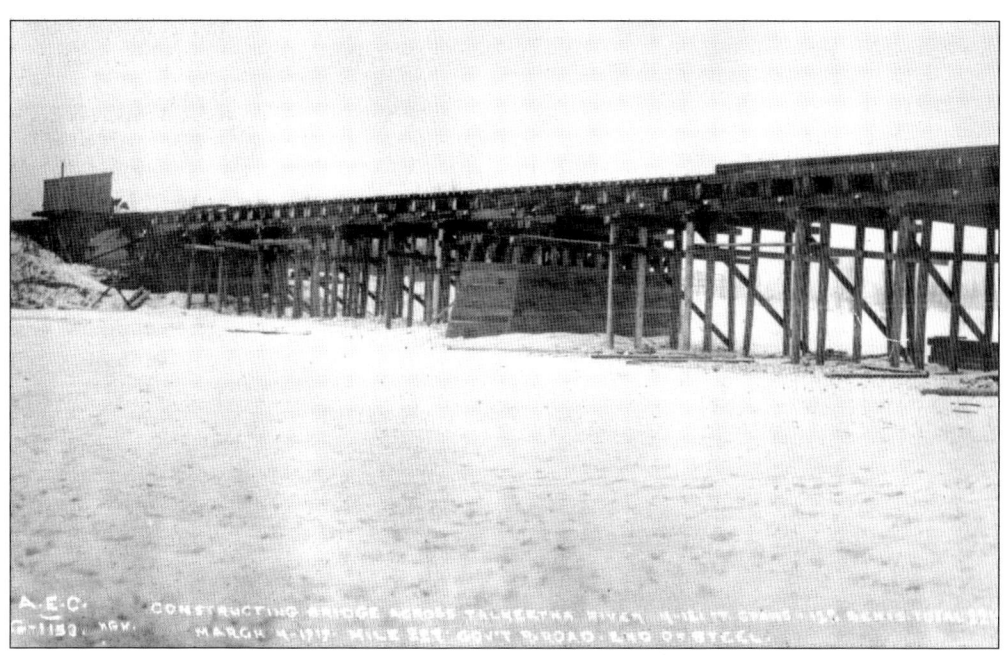

CONSTRUCTING RAILROAD BRIDGE ACROSS TALKEETNA RIVER. The AEC incorporated the lessons learned in the failures of the first two wooden bridges into the design of a new structure, which was built to anticipate the impacts of snow, ice, and breakup. Portions of the bridge were constructed in four 121-foot section spans, supported by 128 bents (support posts). The total length of the bridge, including the approach, was 2,212 feet. (Courtesy AMAH.)

BENT DRIVING. This March 1919 image is of a bent (pile) driver as it completes the 107th bent near the Talkeetna River Bridge. A hydraulic driver was used to pound the bents into the ground to ensure that it was in stable soils. The frozen ground made the work difficult, though such construction conditions may have been preferable to the wet, boggy environment in warmer seasons. (Courtesy AMAH.)

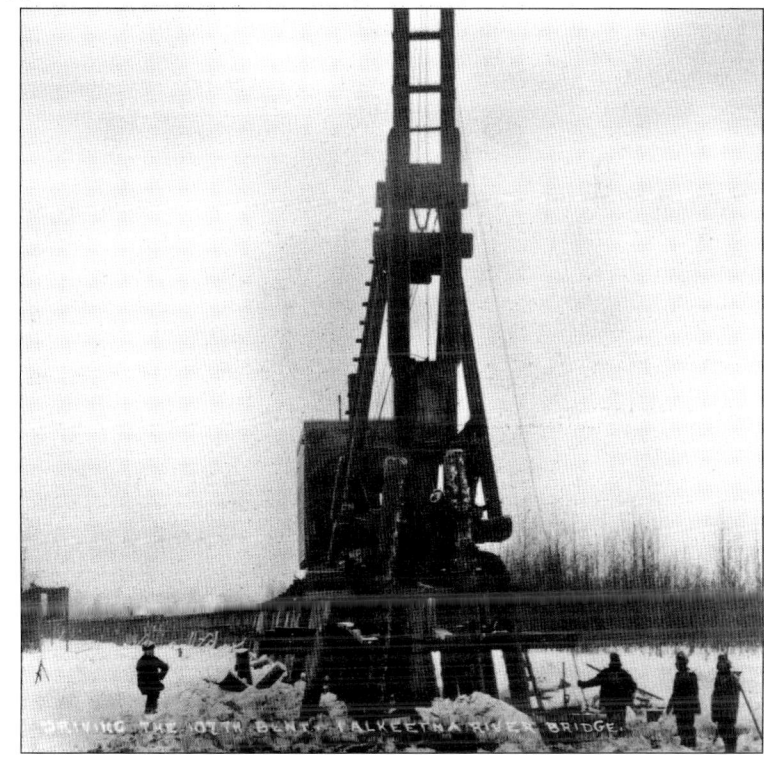

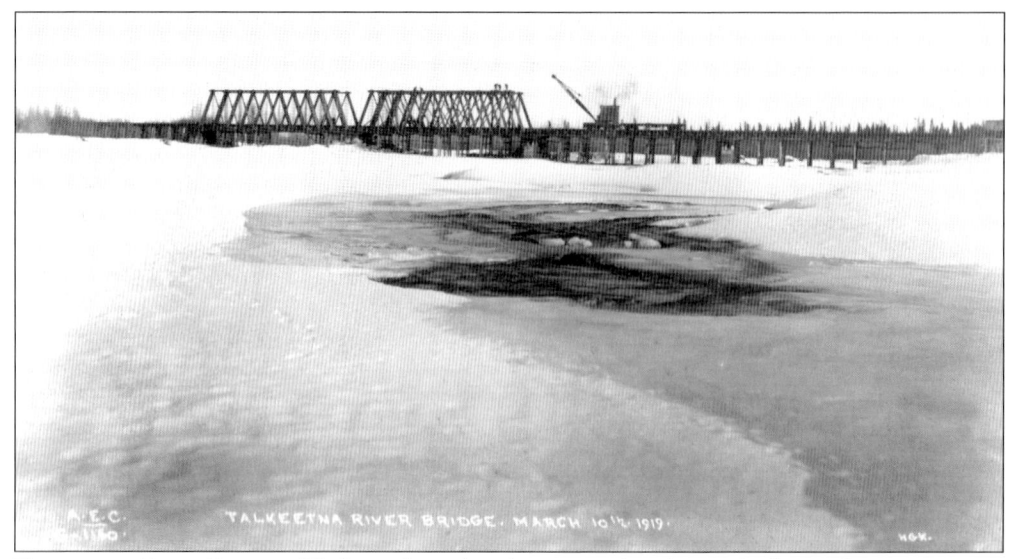

TALKEETNA RIVER BRIDGE. Work on the railroad was completed in multiple simultaneous stages. While the bents were being driven on one end, the tresses to support the rail bed were being constructed concurrently on the bridge itself. This photograph from March 10, 1919, illustrates the construction phase of the Talkeetna Bridge, as well as the frozen condition of the river. (Courtesy AMAH.)

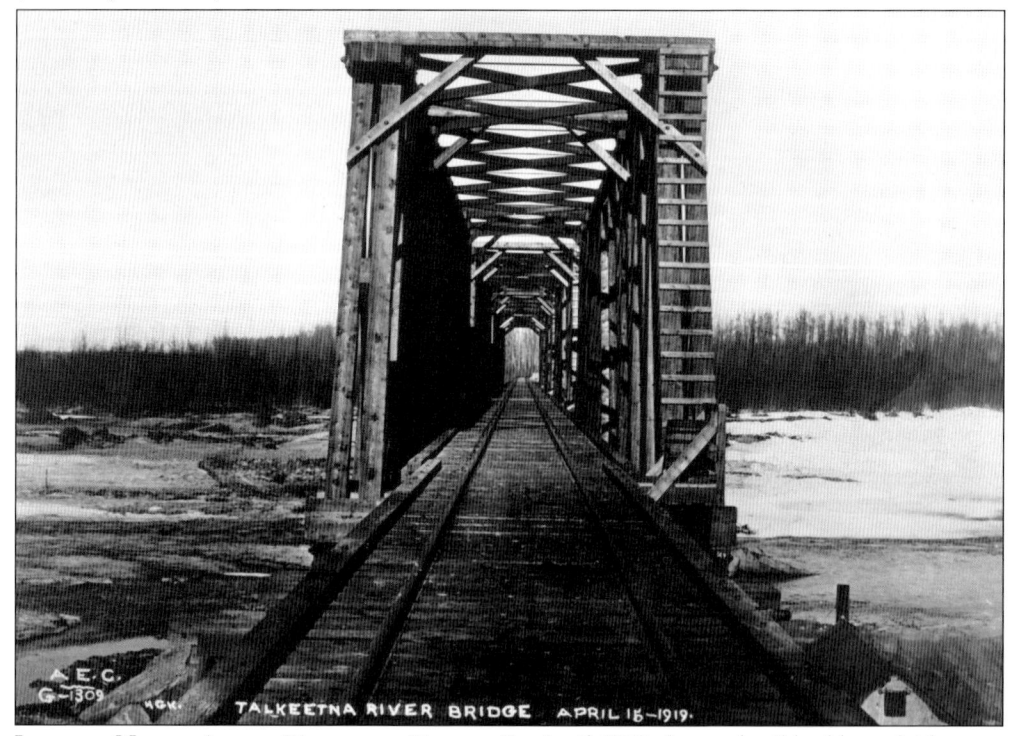

LOOKING NORTH ACROSS TALKEETNA BRIDGE. By April 1919, the steel rail had been laid across the Talkeetna River Bridge at milepost 228, working its way to Fairbanks. It appears that the ice breakup was well underway in the Talkeetna River, although there is still considerable snow on the shoreline. (Courtesy AMAH.)

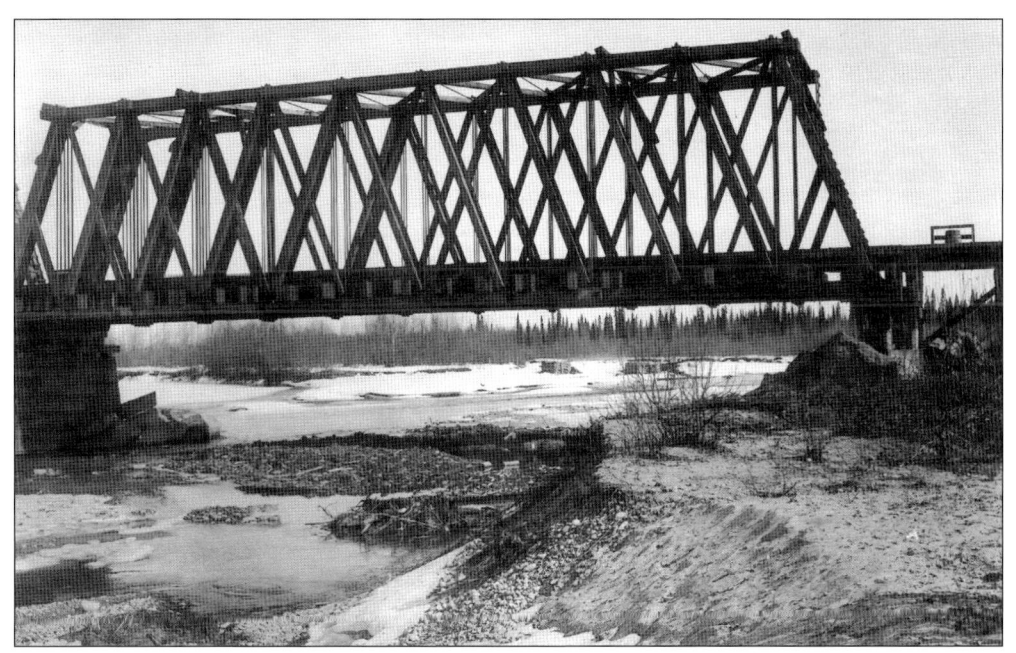

COMPLETED TALKEETNA BRIDGE. This 1919 image shows the completed Talkeetna River Bridge crossing. Spring breakup was in progress. Remnants of the broken wooden bridge can be seen in the background. Once the railroad was completed in 1923, the transportation of goods and people were no longer dependant on the river. (Courtesy THS.)

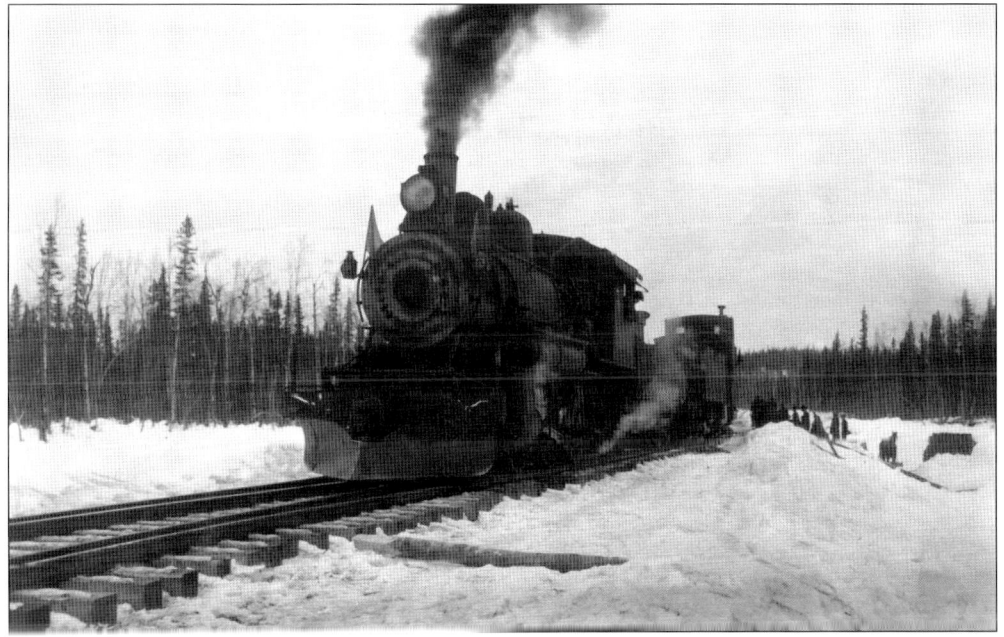

TRAIN ARRIVES TO END OF STEEL. This image from March 1919 was taken when the steel had been laid to mile 227, the location of Talkeetna's original railroad station. The engine hauled supplies, its own fuel, kitchen cars for crews, offices for engineers, and sleeping cars for some of the supervisors. To the right of the train, a horse-drawn sleigh can be seen with a load of logs. (Courtesy AMAH.)

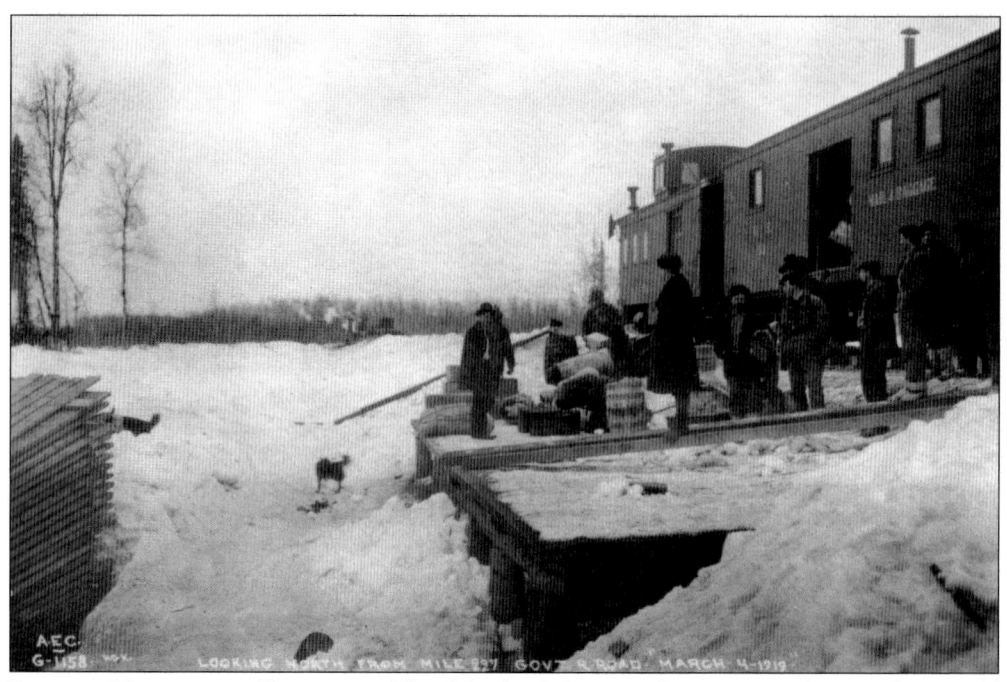

LOOKING NORTH FROM TALKEETNA. This March 1919 image shows a typical scene that would replay on a cyclical basis for the next nine decades—dogs, snow, and people bundled in coats and fur caps unloading supplies at Talkeetna station. (Courtesy AMAH.)

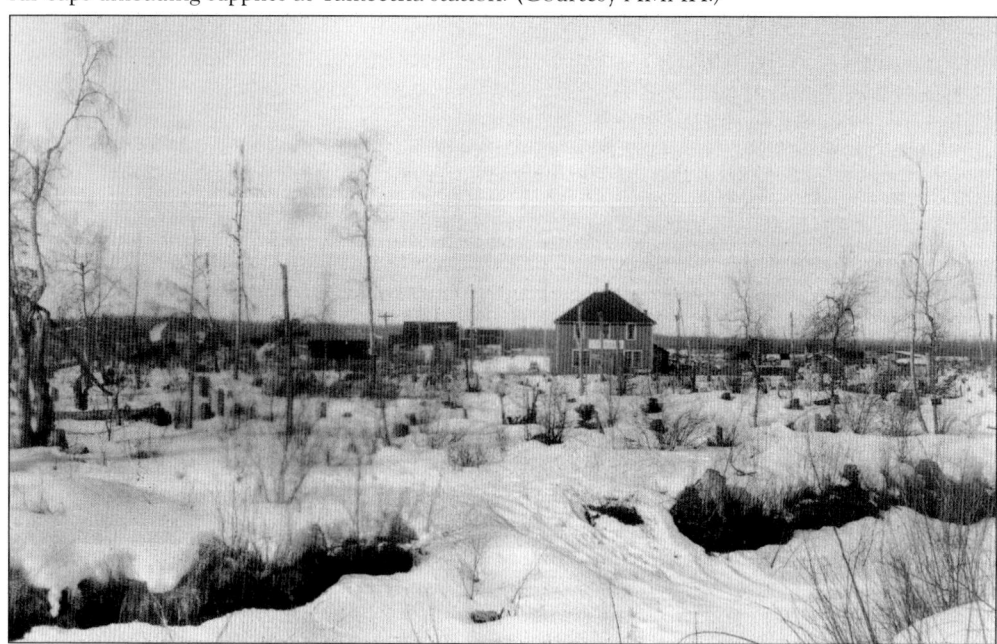

TALKEETNA, 1923. By 1923, the construction of the 480-mile railroad was completed from Seward to Fairbanks, and the need to have a divisional headquarters in Talkeetna no longer existed. This view is of Main Street looking north, toward the railroad bridge. Stumps from clear-cutting are visible, even in the snow. Telegraph lines are evident. The Fairview Inn had been recently completed and opened. (Courtesy AMHA.)

Three

TRAPPERS, PROSPECTORS, AND MINERS

Talkeetna's history is intertwined with the history of trappers, prospectors, and miners. Weather and snow dictated the rhythm of activities of these professions, which complemented each other with their seasonal natures. Placer (hydraulic) and hard rock mining could not be conducted when the ground and rivers were frozen. However, setting traplines is best done during wintertime to obtain the most luxurious furs, which fetched the highest prices. Money received from trapping helped grubstake many a miner's summer activities.

Prospectors first entered the Susitna Region near Talkeetna as early as the 1890s. The Russian fur traders were in Alaska much earlier, however, with the fur trade in the area beginning sometime in the late 1890s or early 1900s. From its inception, Talkeetna served as a supply station for trappers, prospectors, and miners, where they could be outfitted and grubstaked. Talkeetna also served as the initial wholesale market for trappers and miners where some could sell or trade their pelts or pokes of gold, although most took their gold to Anchorage. The living conditions were harsh and isolated, and by necessity each trapper, prospector, or miner was totally self-reliant for shelter, food, water, and warmth. Much like the Dena'ina before them, they were on the go, following the traplines and panning for gold or surface prospecting as the season dictated. Talkeetna served as the staging area for receiving basic goods—flour, sugar, and other supplies—not available in the more remote areas.

The local freighters, such as Dave Lawrence and the Lee brothers, provided a critical supply line to the remote trappers and miners on the other side of the Talkeetna River, including those at Trappers Creek, Peters Creek, Cache Creek, and Dutch Hills. If a prospector or miner survived and was successful, after a few seasons they may have established a home base in Talkeetna. It was not uncommon for a trapper or miner to retire in Talkeetna, and some of their log buildings that have survived the test of time make up the core of present-day Talkeetna's Historic District.

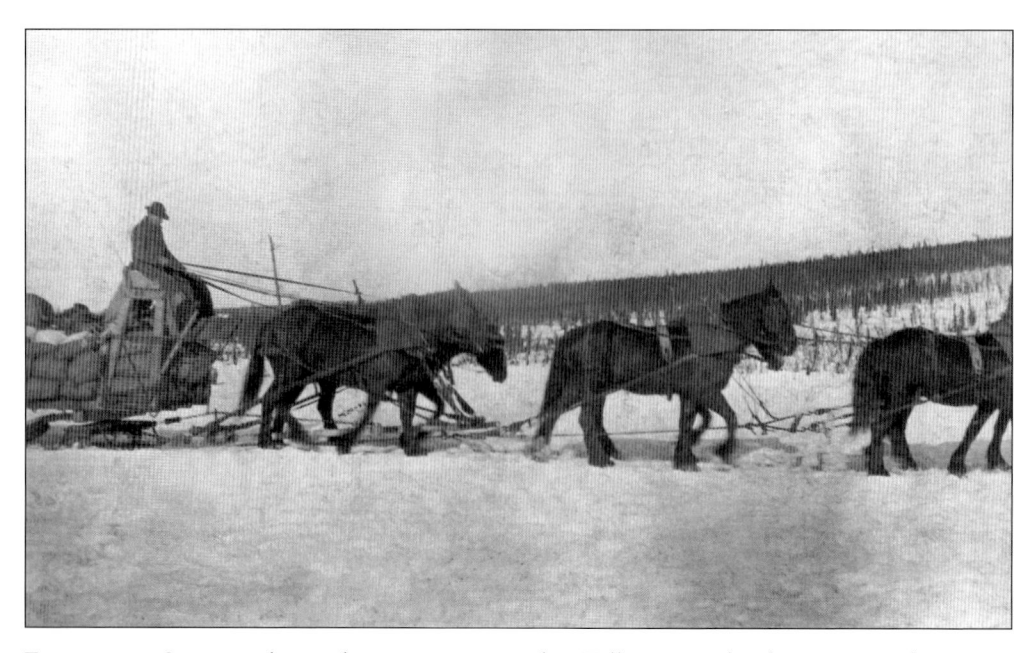

FREIGHTERS. Once supplies and equipment arrived in Talkeetna, either by river or rail, trappers and miners faced the next expensive, difficult, and long leg of the journey—transporting heavy supplies miles into the wilderness over difficult terrain. Overland choices were limited to human backs, horses, or dogs. Freighting business quickly became a mainstay in Talkeetna. Despite the frigid weather conditions, transporting supplies in the winter was easier than in warmer seasons because of the solid footing of the frozen trails and shorter routes. Above, a six-horse team freights supplies on the frozen river. Freighters used snowshoes (both for themselves and, at times, for their horses) to help with the deep snow. Below is an example of how supplies were obtained at the Talkeetna Trading Post and loaded onto a dogsled for transport into the wilderness areas outside of Talkeetna to support trappers, prospectors, and miners. (Both courtesy THS.)

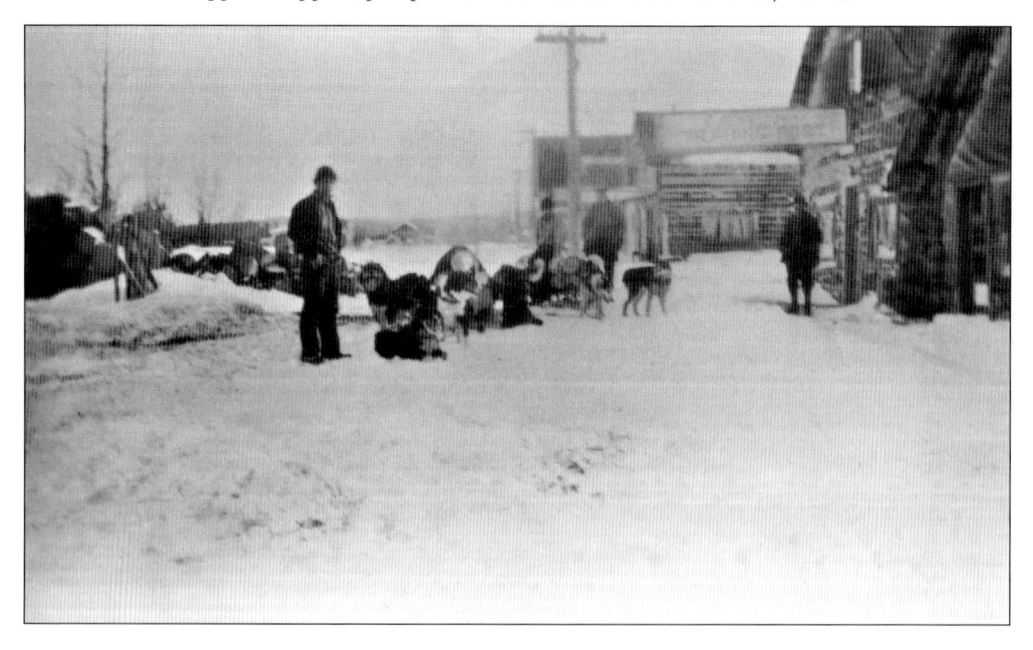

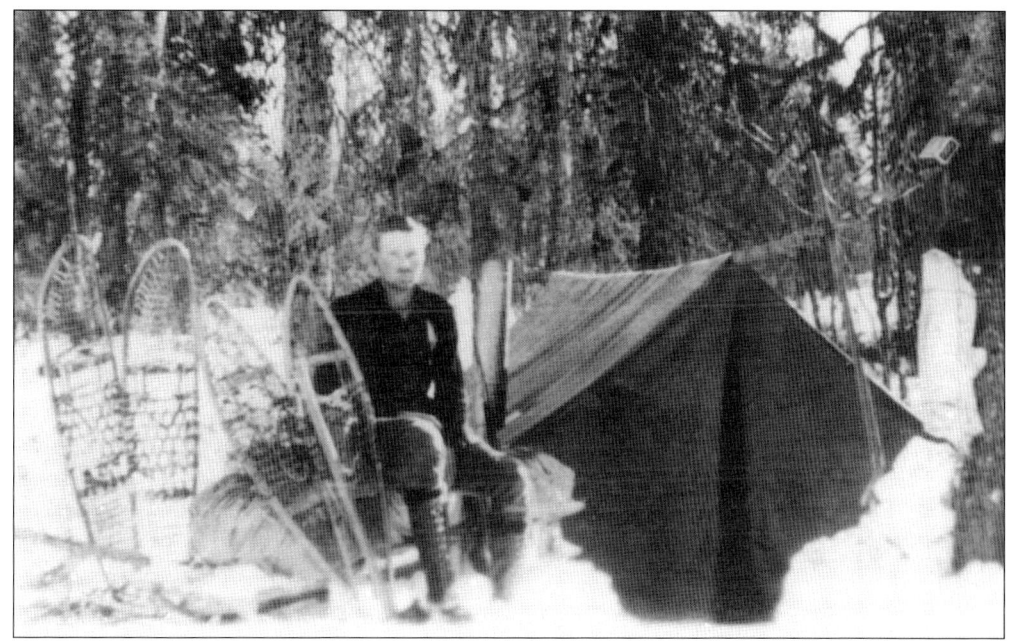

Shelter. Trappers and prospectors were hardy souls, totally self-reliant for every need. Canvas-walled tents were their most commonly utilized type of shelter, be it winter or summer. Above, a man is seen with his snowshoes outside his tent, complete with a chimney for the wood-burning stove used for heating and cooking. Below, trapper Thad Sanford is seen outside his winter trapping cabin on Lane Creek, 15 miles north of Talkeetna. Sanford's loaded sled, snowshoes, and whipsaw (for cutting trees) are all clearly visible. Each of these tools was extremely important for self-sufficiency. Sanford also mined the Lucky Creek and Cache Creek areas from 1937 to 1938 and was involved in Alaska's first strip-coal mining in 1942 at Suntrana. (Both courtesy AMHA.)

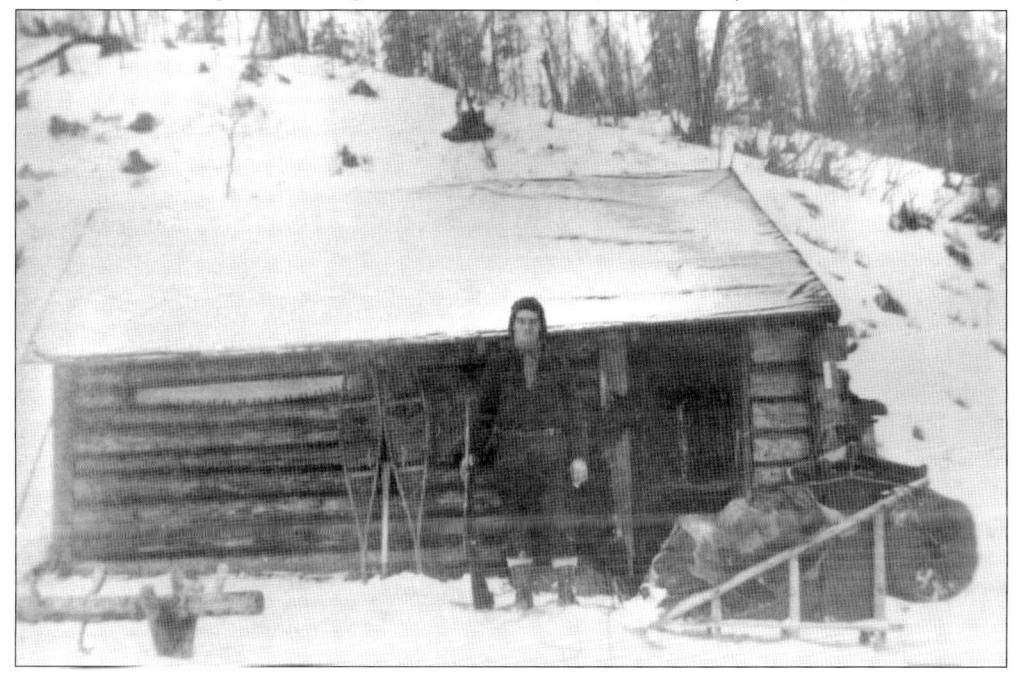

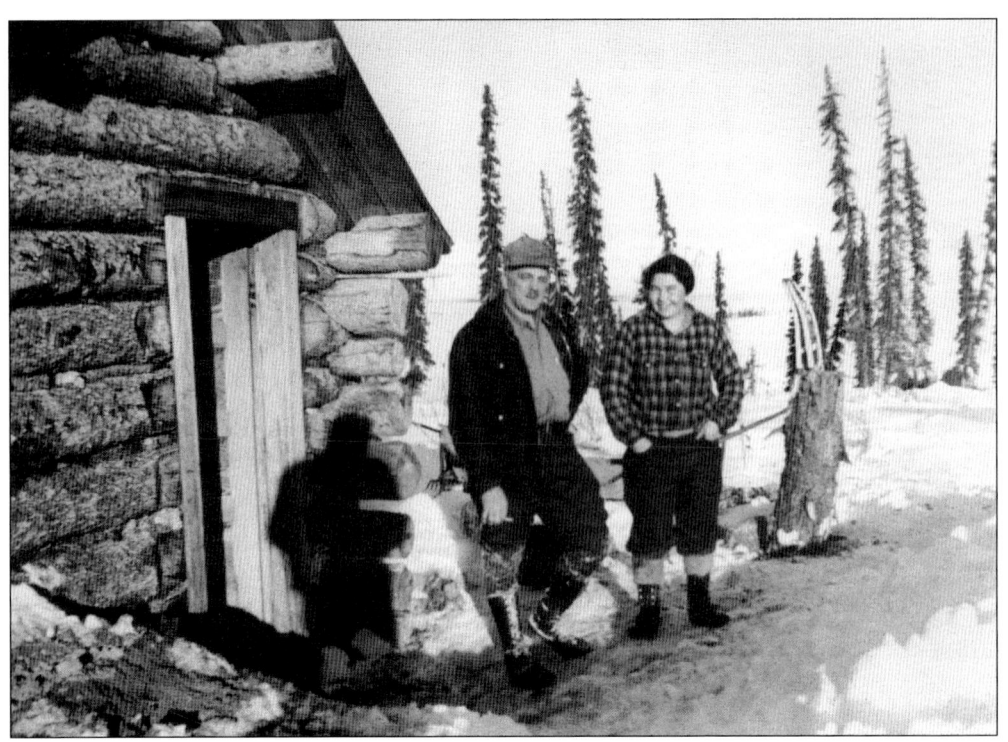

LOG CABIN AND TRAPPING. US commissioner Ben Mayfield and Alice Cantwell are seen outside this remote log cabin. Snowshoes and a sled used for transporting supplies and hides can be seen in the background. Below, Thad Sanford is seen wearing his snowshoes, carrying his rifle, and smoking a cigarette in the (cold) great outdoors near Lane Creek, about 15 miles from Talkeetna, where he tends his traplines. (Both courtesy THS.)

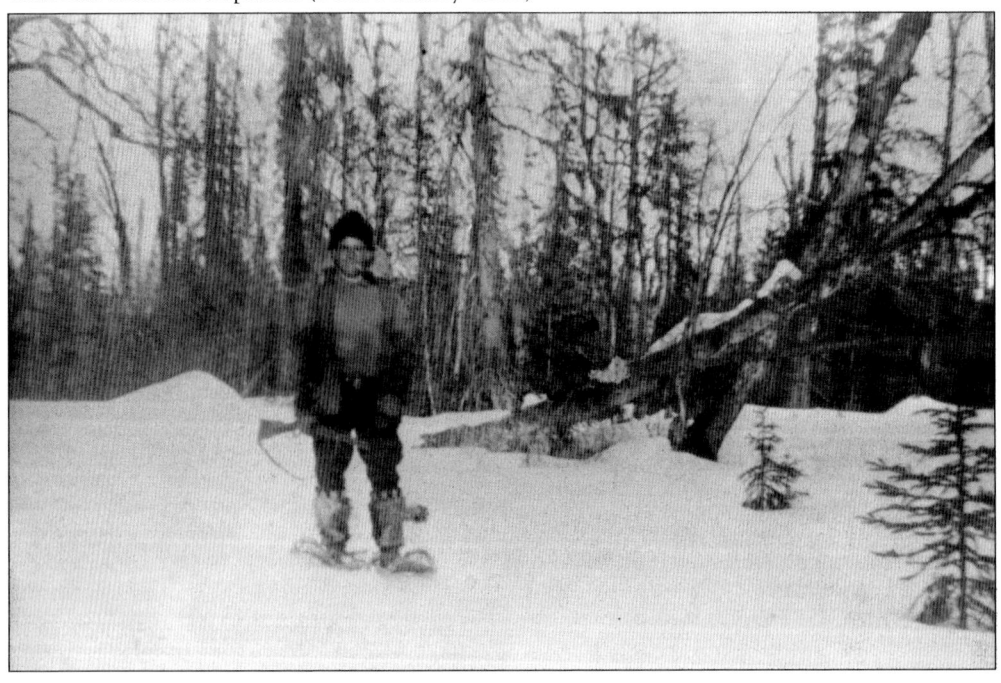

PELTS. Luxurious furs obtained in the wintertime were in highest demand. Here, Hugo Tollefsen holds a distinctive black wolf pelt in a beautiful winter wonderland outside of Talkeetna. In the 1940s and 1950s, Alaska paid a bounty of $50 per wolf pelt. The most commonly trapped furs in the area were marten, mink, fox, lynx, and beaver, which were eventually sold to the Alaska Fur Exchange, located in Seattle, for distribution nationally and internationally. (Courtesy THS.)

BEAVER PELTS. Below, US commissioner Ben Mayfield is seen stretching a beaver pelt over a frame for drying at a temporary summer camp. Scattered cooking and sleeping supplies are also visible. Stretching beaver pelts was customary practice in the fur-trade industry dating back to the Hudson Bay Company days on the Pacific coast from the late 1790s to the 1850s. (Courtesy THS.)

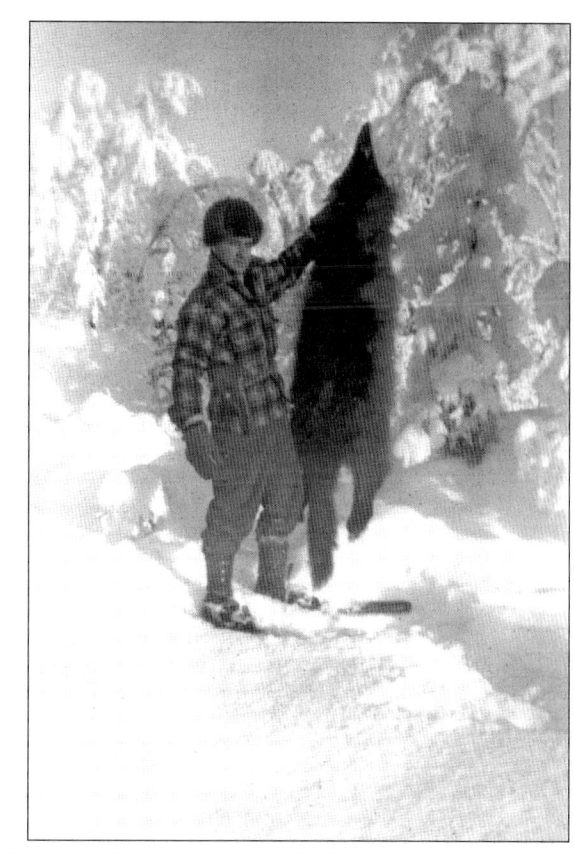

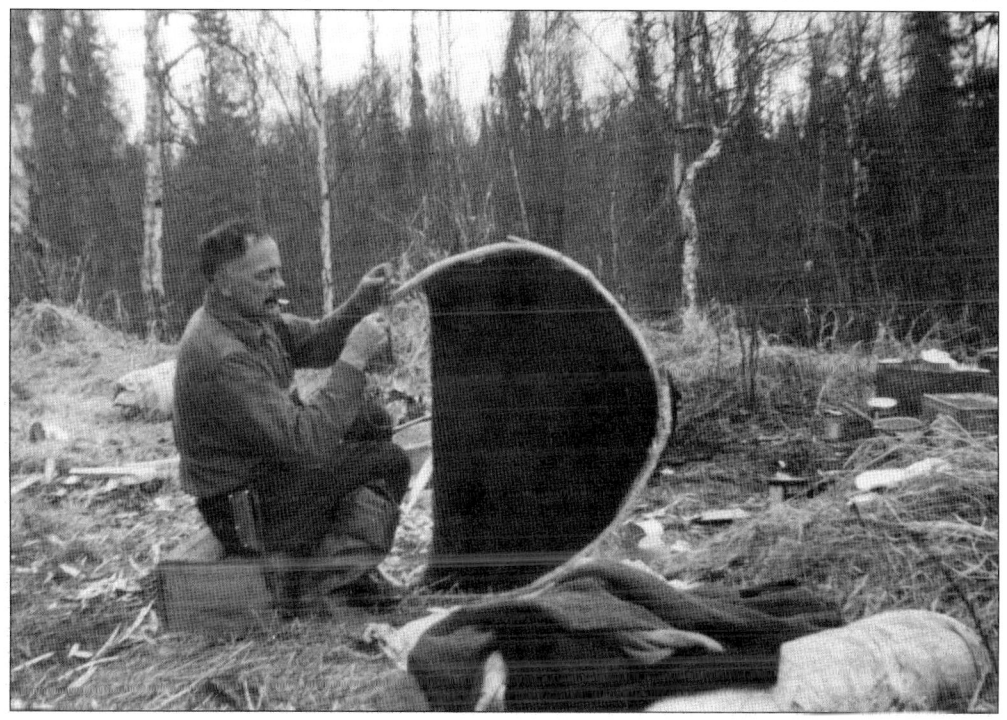

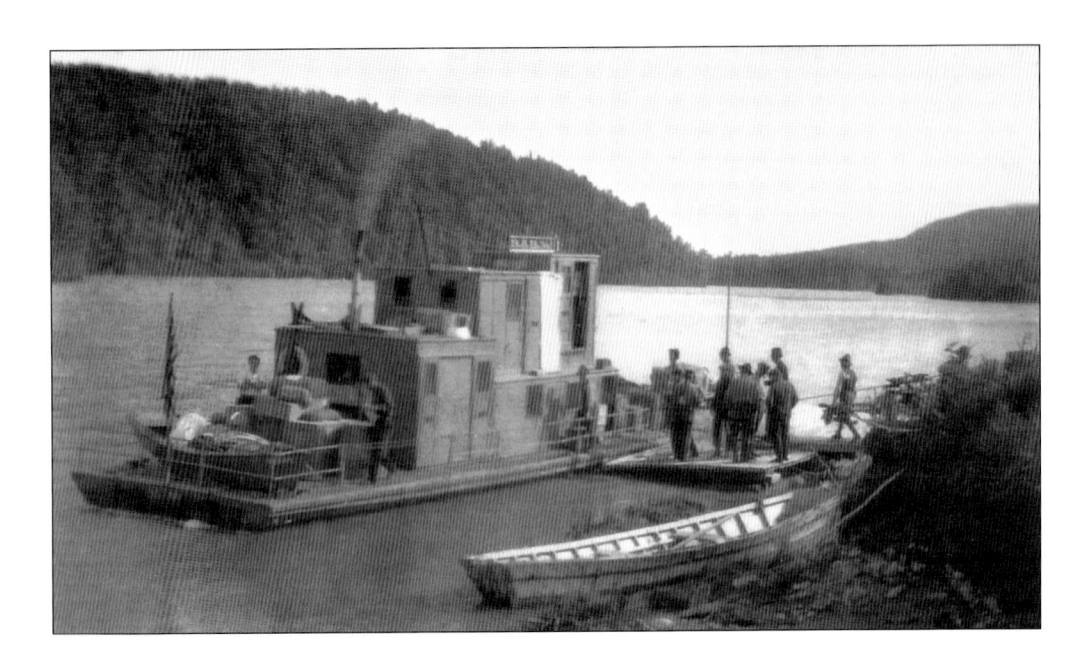

DEAD HORSE LANDING. Nellie Neal operated Dead Horse Roadhouse. The Dead Horse Landing was the halfway point between Seward and Fairbanks, just north of Talkeetna on the Susitna River. It served as the main supply point for railroad construction north of Talkeetna. Dead Horse Hill is named for an incident involving two horses that, spooked by a bear, fell down the hill to their deaths. Above, the flat-bottomed tunnel boat is seen docking at Dead Horse Landing in 1917. Below, Nellie, an excellent big game hunter, poses with her rifle and a display of her hunting trophies outside the Dead Horse Roadhouse around 1918. The business opened in 1917 and closed in 1923, when the Curry Hotel opened up across the tracks. (Both courtesy THS.)

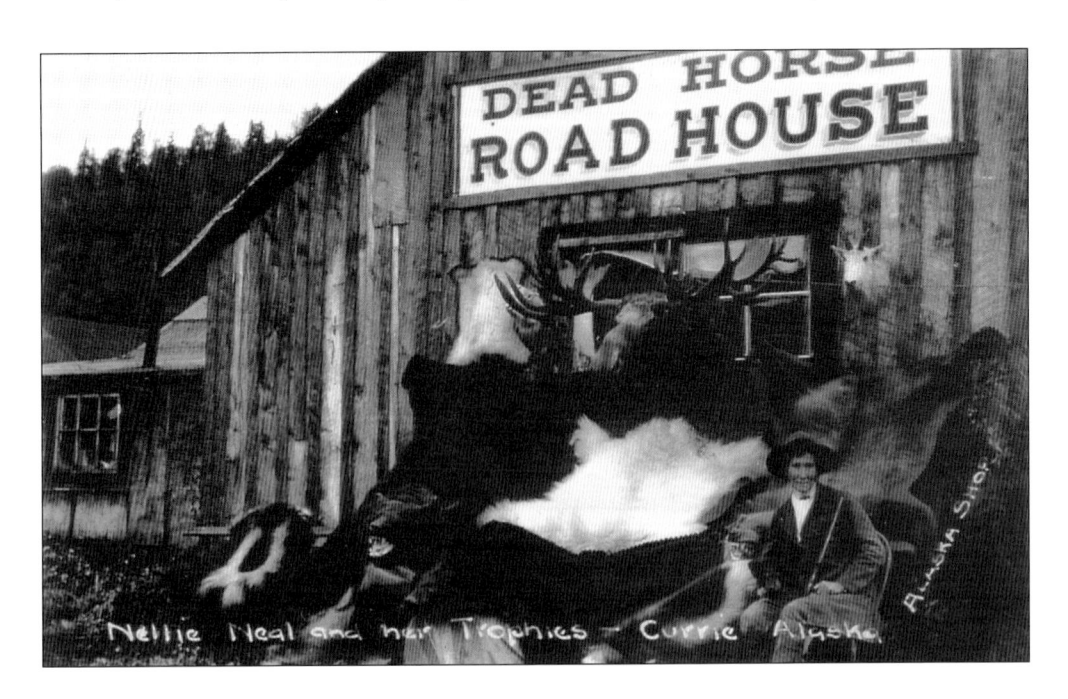

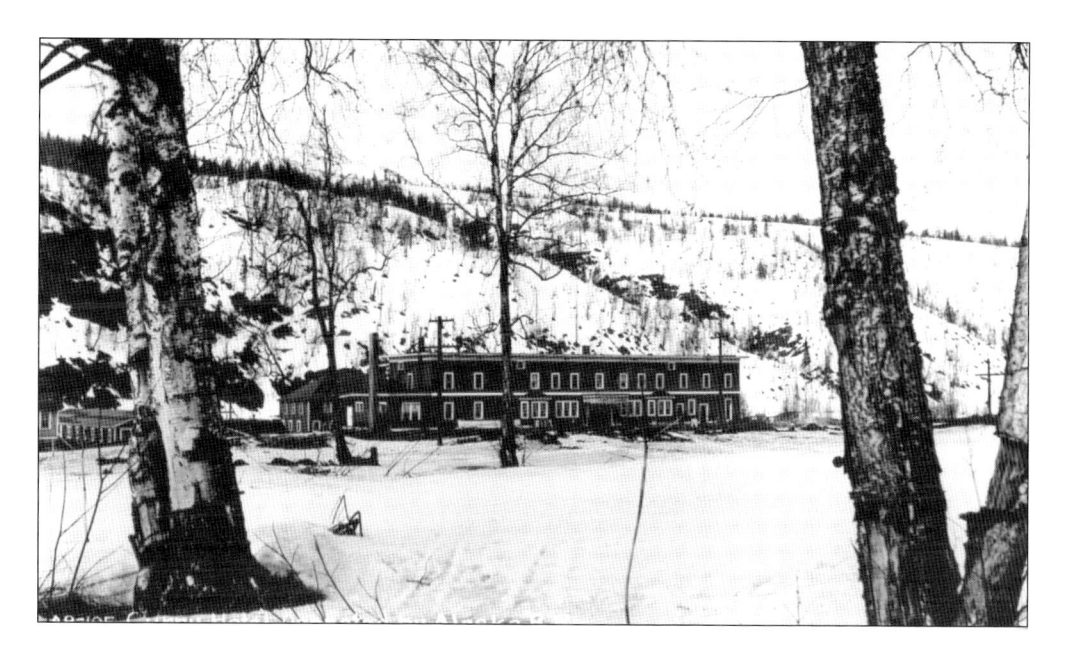

CURRY HOTEL. Completed in 1923, the Curry Hotel was considered extremely luxurious for the time and place. It was located at the midpoint of the Seward-Fairbanks railroad. When the 47-room hotel opened directly across the railroad tracks from the Dead Horse Roadhouse, the one-room log-cabin roadhouse closed. These interior and exterior photographs attest to the opulence of the new hotel. The Curry Hotel baked hundreds of loaves of fresh bread daily for the hotel and the entire Alaska Railroad line. It also operated a full-service laundry for the hotel, the Alaska Railroad, and the Anchorage and Nenana hospitals. Over 13,000 pieces of laundry were sorted, washed, starched, and ironed each month. The hotel operated until 1950 and burned down in 1958. (Both courtesy THS.)

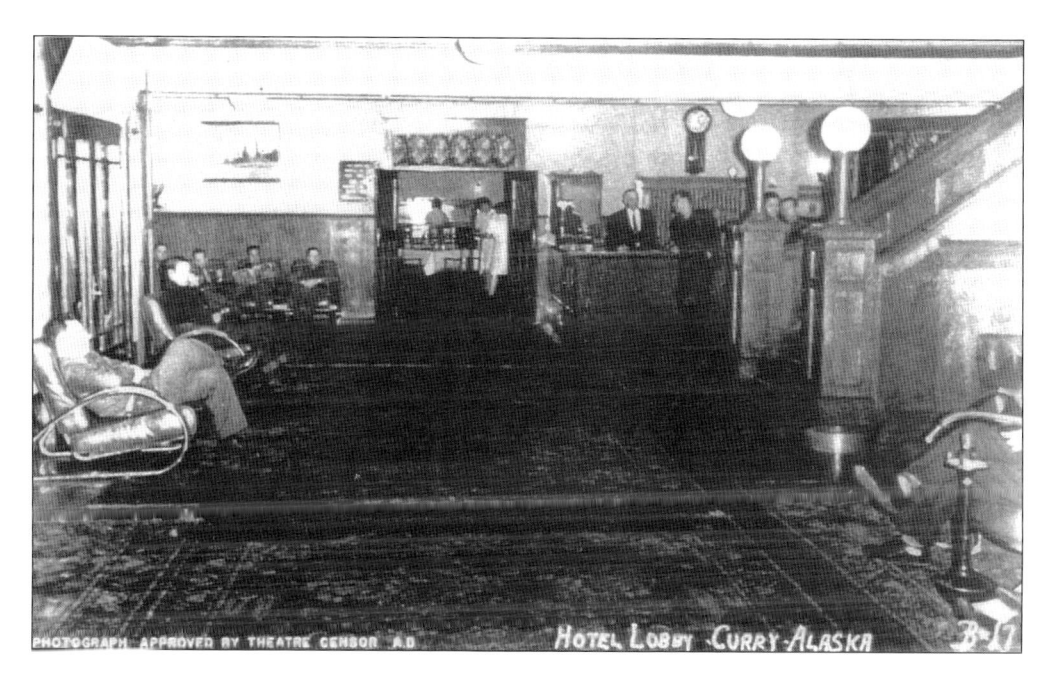

TRAPPER'S DIARY. Adolph J. "Missouri" Taraski (below) gave a rare glimpse into the daily life of a trapper in his 1923–1924 diary (left). His first entry was on June 1, 1923, and in the first week, he spent six days cutting wood and one day panning and cooking. The next week, he was building his cabin, putting moss and earth on his cache, baking bread, and washing clothes. By the end of June, he had built a toilet. Prospecting "assessment" work was completed in July and August, and in August, he killed several caribou and was busy drying meat and packing it to his cache. Rain returned in September. Missouri set snares in extreme cold during November. In January and February 1924, he was laid up for a month due to a sore leg caused by a dog bite. When asked what he did after he retired from prospecting, Taraski replied, "I spend my summers splitting wood and the winter burning it." (Both courtesy THS.)

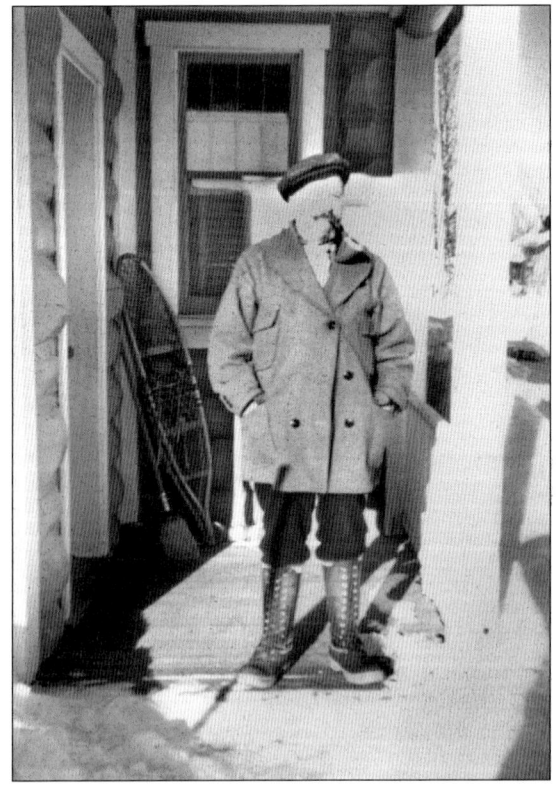

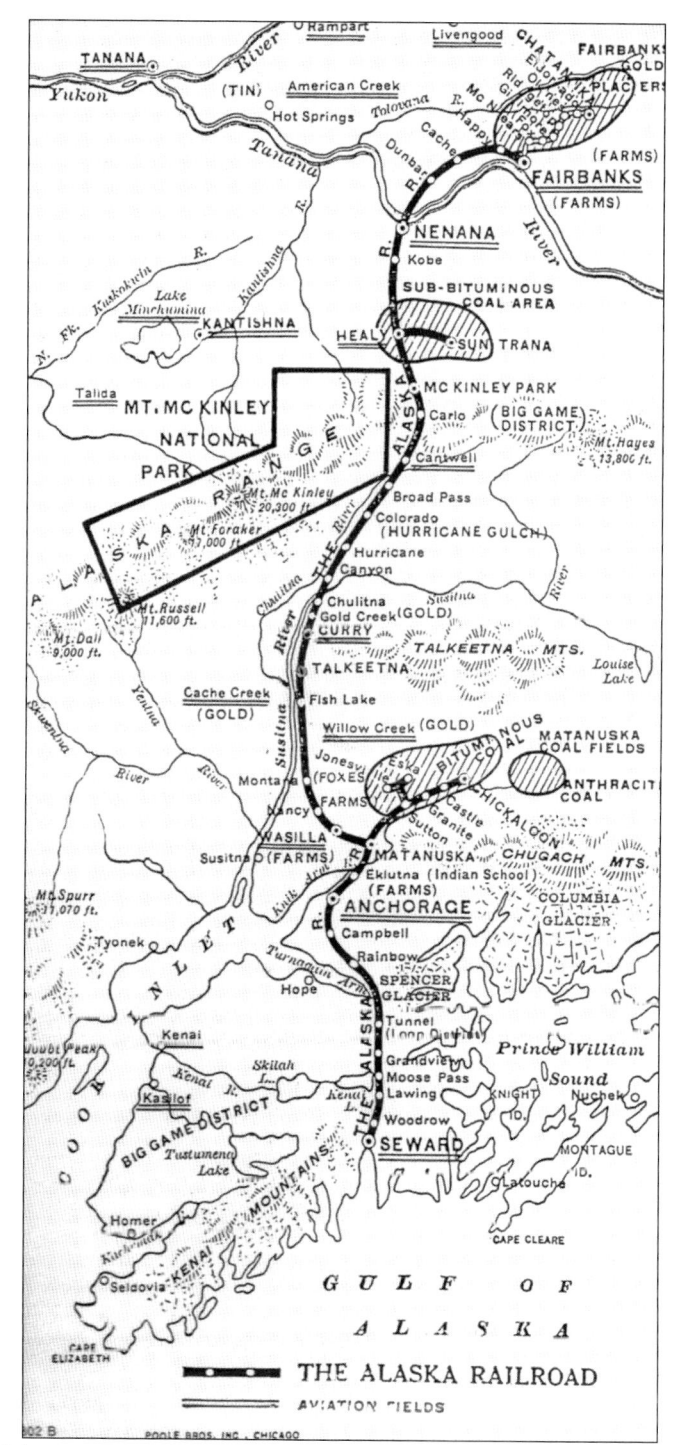

RAILROAD AND MINING MAP. This map shows some of the gold and coal mining in the rural areas outside Talkeetna. The town served as the primary source of supplies freighted to many mining areas, including Cache Creek, Gold Creek, Willow Creek, Peters Creek, Dutch Creek, Trapper Creek, Poorman Creek, Falls Creek, Dollar Creek, and the Patterson mine. (Courtesy THS.)

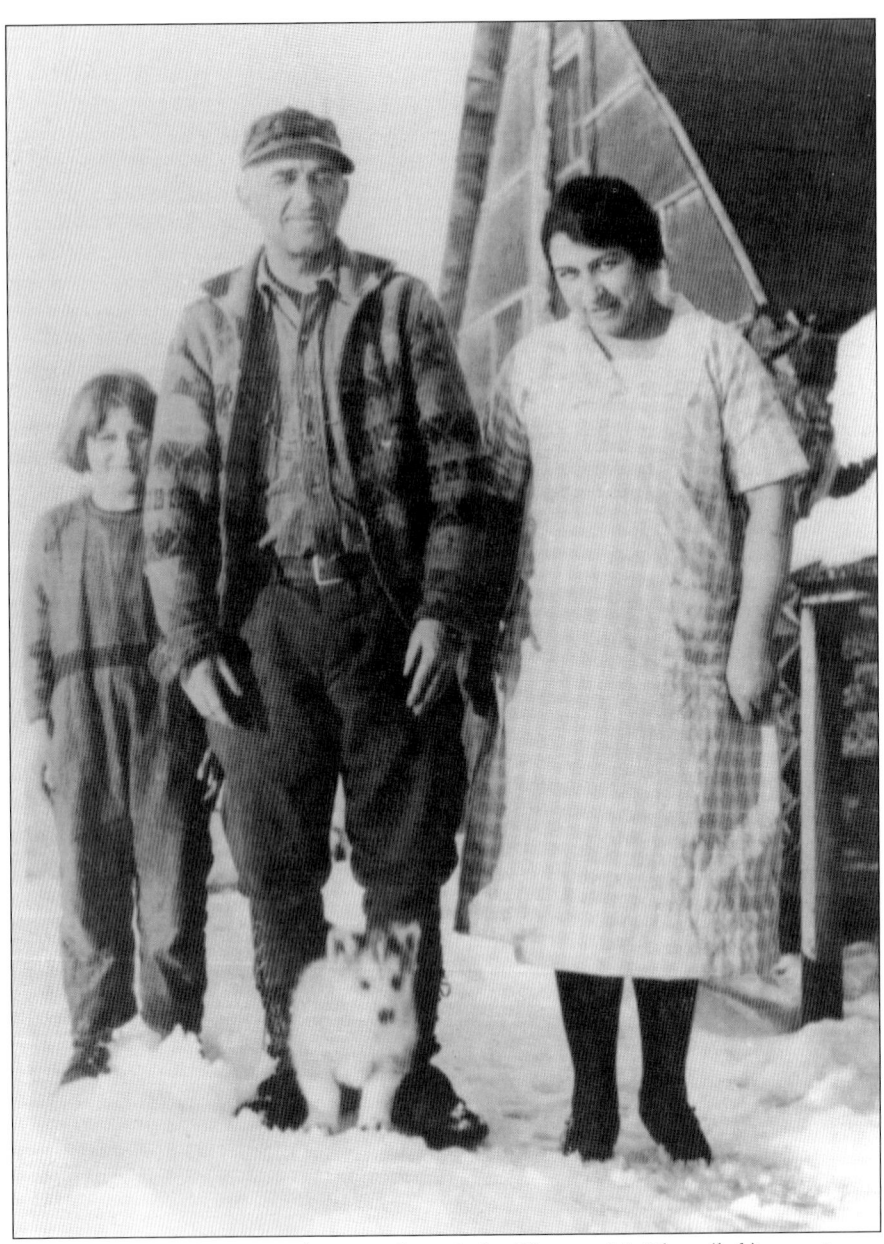

WILDERNESS LIVING. This 1927 photograph includes Eleanor McGhee (left), age six, a puppy named Tuffy, Margueritte Wilkinson (right), age 23, and fur trader and businessman William Dennison, age 44, at Susitna Station. Dennison owned the Johnson Roadhouse at Susitna Station, and Wilkinson managed it. Dennison wanted to marry Wilkinson, but she hesitated due to their age difference. Sadly, Dennison was killed, along with Wilkinson's brother, two years after this photograph was taken in a boating accident on the Yentna River. In 1931, Wilkson married Talkeetnan Mike Trepte, who adopted Eleanor. Growing up in a naturally beautiful setting in remote Alaska was lonely, but Eleanor learned how to hunt, trap, and skin rabbits, mink, and wolverines. She learned to scrape, stretch, and prepare the hides for market. A beaver and dogs were her pets. Eleanor was homeschooled, went to boarding school, and attended the Talkeetna one-room schoolhouse in 1936–1937. (Courtesy THS.)

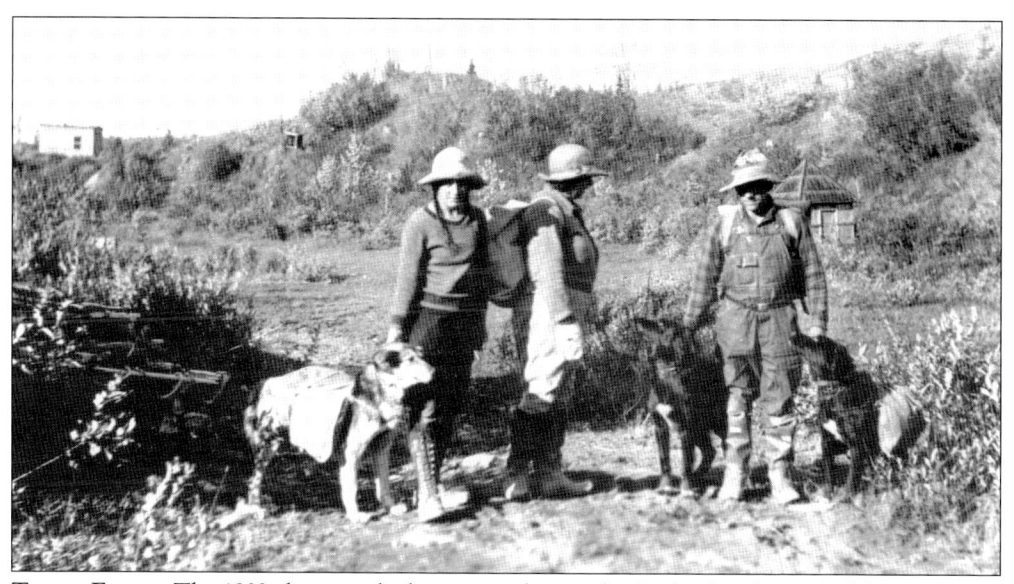

TREPTE FAMILY. The 1932 photograph above was taken in the Cache Creek area and shows Eleanor McGhee Trepte, age 12, Marguerite Wilkinson Trepte, age 29, and Mike Trepte with their three dogs, Tuffy, Shep, and Zip. The Trepte family had just staked mining claims on Dutch Creek, had hiked 17 miles, and had another 37 miles to hike to vote for Tony Diamond for US Congress. Like all miners and trappers, they needed to be totally self-reliant for food and shelter, living in isolated areas and working hard year-round. Many different types of mining techniques were used in this remote area of Alaska. Below, hydraulic mining was used to wash away sediment and to push mining tailings—unused gravel and rocks—away from the sluice boxes in hopes of catching a glimpse of gold. In placer mining, the resulting water-sediment slurry is directed through sluice boxes to remove the gold. (Both courtesy THS.)

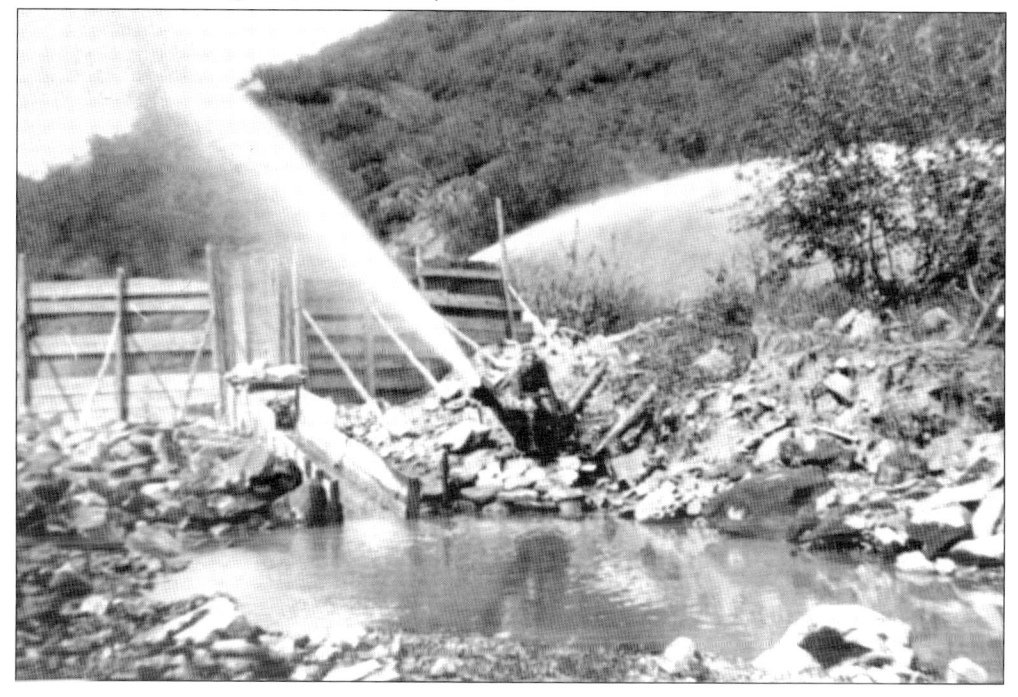

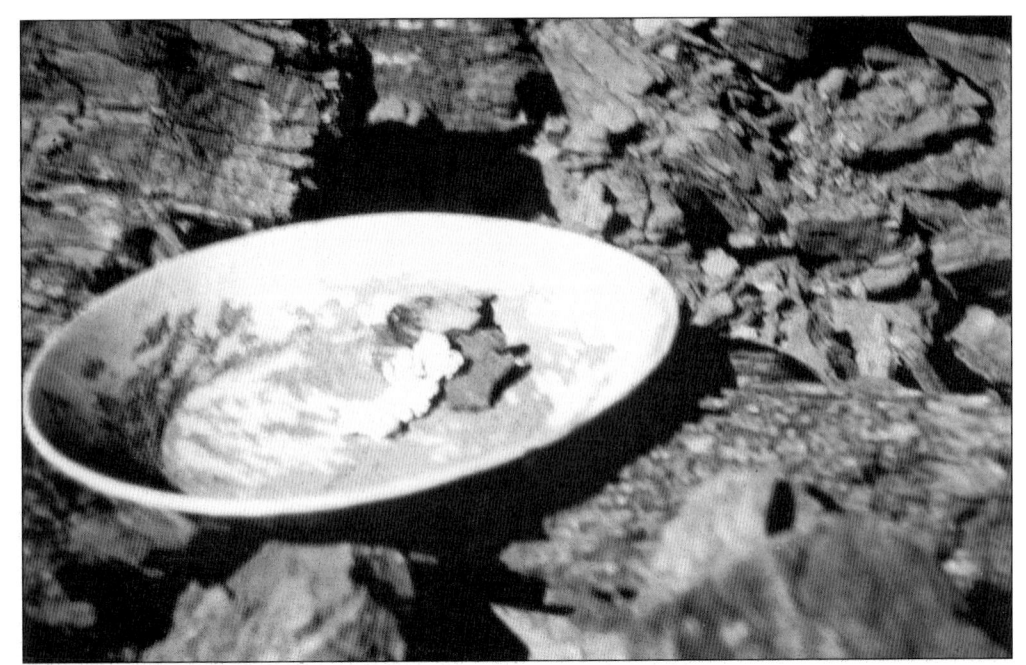

GOLD. It was hard work, but mining for gold paid off for Mike and Margueritte Trepte when they found this large gold nugget on Dutch Creek in 1941. Dutch Creek received its name from an unidentified prospector in 1906. Pokes of gold were commonly brought into Talkeetna at the end of the season. It could be traded there, or the miner could catch the train to Anchorage and sell it to an assay office. (Courtesy THS.)

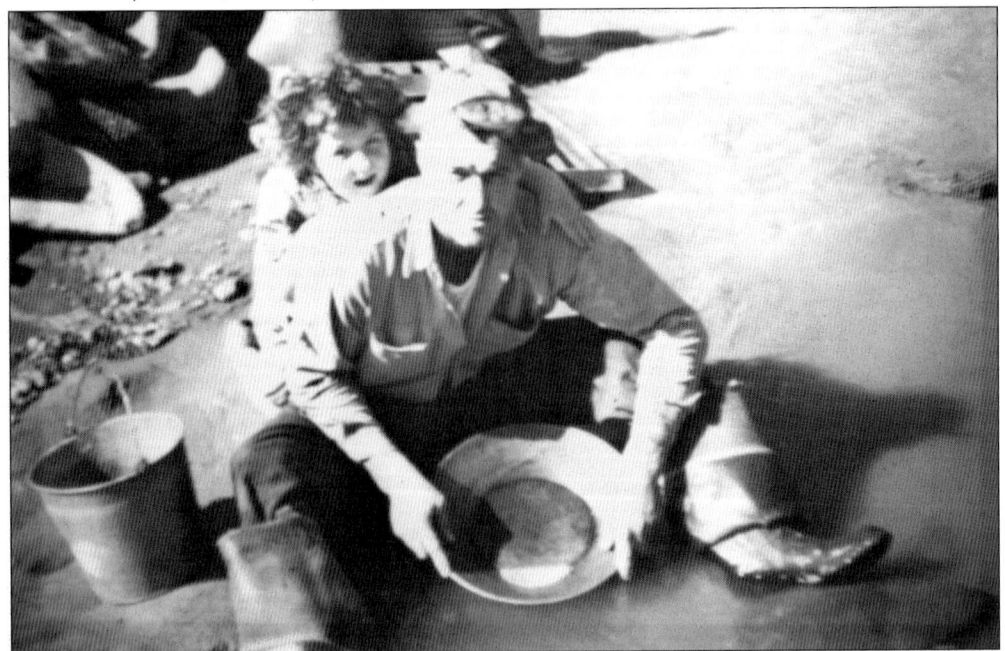

FATHER AND DAUGHTER PANNING FOR GOLD. Pat Beaver (Pratt) sits with her father, Jim Beaver, on Cache Creek with a pan full of gold in the 1940s. The two shared a strong bond and a love for Talkeetna and their cherished Cache Creek. (Courtesy Pat Beaver Pratt.)

Hans Erickson. Miner Hans Erickson is seen here in 1936. He worked the Cache Creek and Falls Creek areas with his partner, Charlie "Smitty" Smith. Erickson was considered one of the best placer miners around. He never married, and eventually came to live in Talkeetna. Sadly, he was trampled by a bull moose in Talkeetna and died shortly thereafter. (Courtesy THS.)

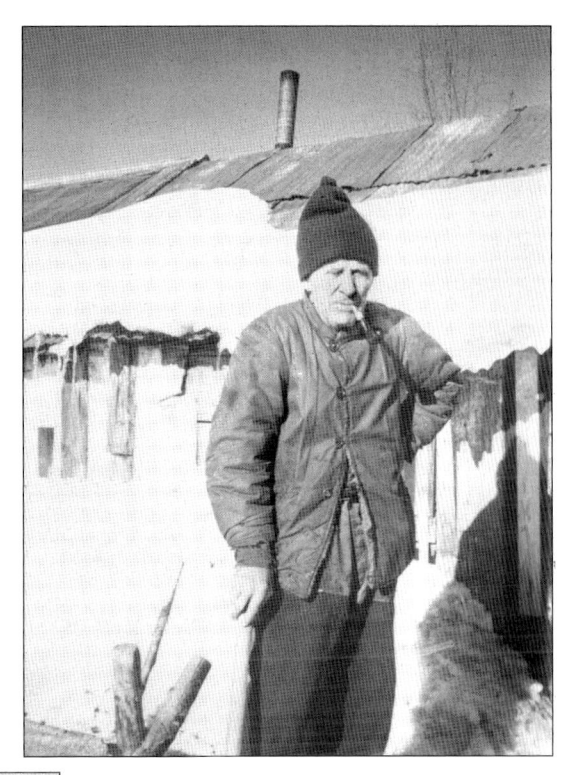

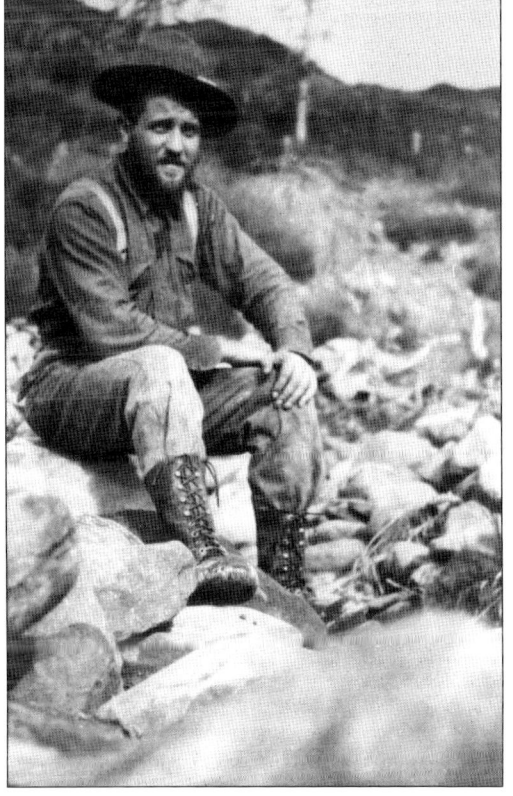

Peters Creek. Tony Meise, a German with bright red hair, worked for the Treptes at Dutch Creek. Meise was one of many young men who came to the rural Talkeetna area in search of ever-elusive golden nuggets. This photograph was taken somewhere on the way to Peters Creek in 1936. (Courtesy Eleanor Trepte.)

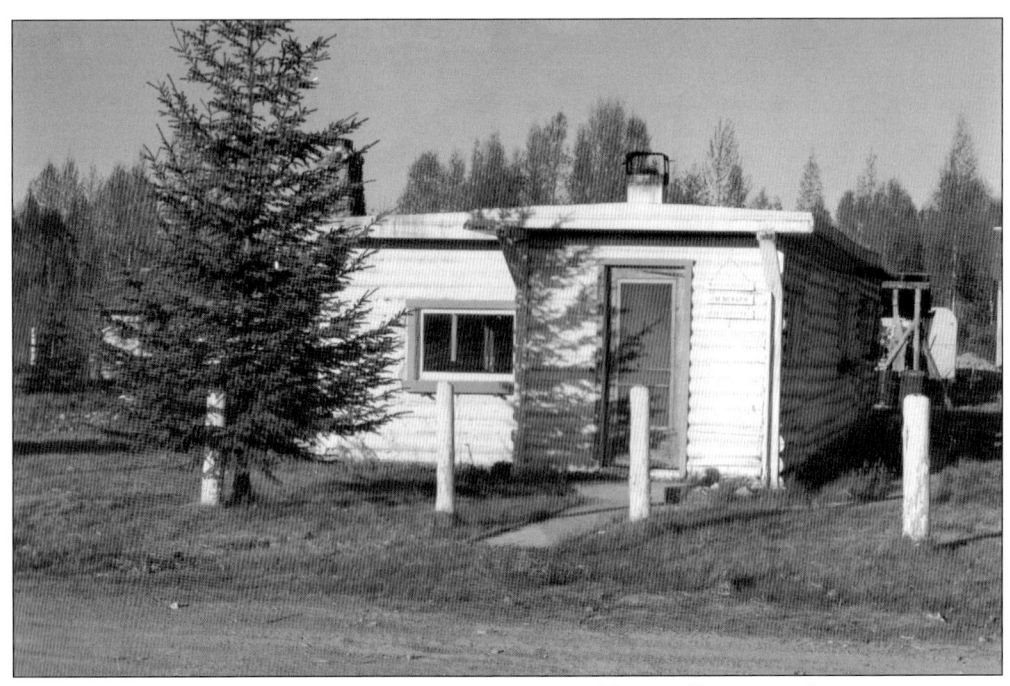

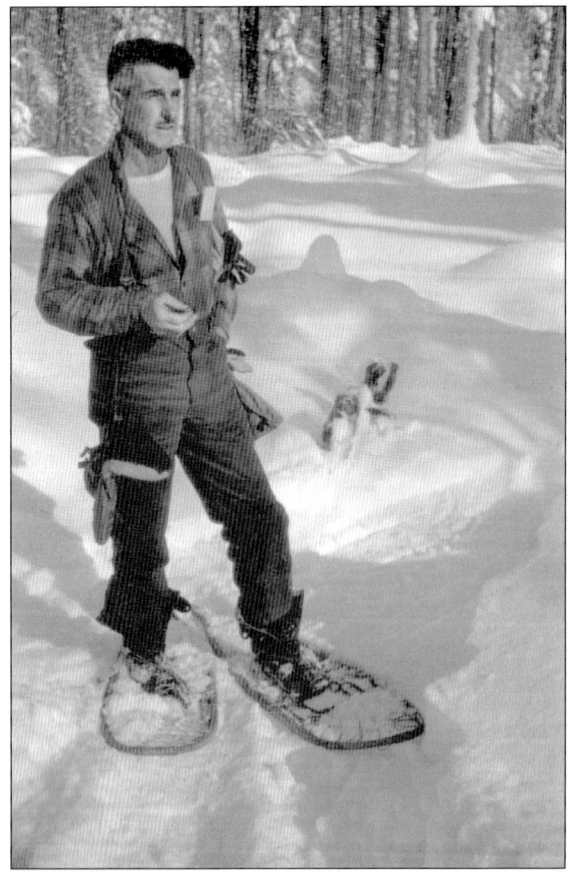

MINING PARTNERS. It was customary in the mining era to have a mining partner. Jim Beaver and Rocky Cummins were mining partners on Cache Creek. Like many miners, they built and maintained log cabins in Talkeetna, and had cabins at their mining claims. The white, flat-roofed log cabin above was built by Beaver. At left, Beaver checks his trap lines with snowshoes on. (Both courtesy Pat Beaver Pratt.)

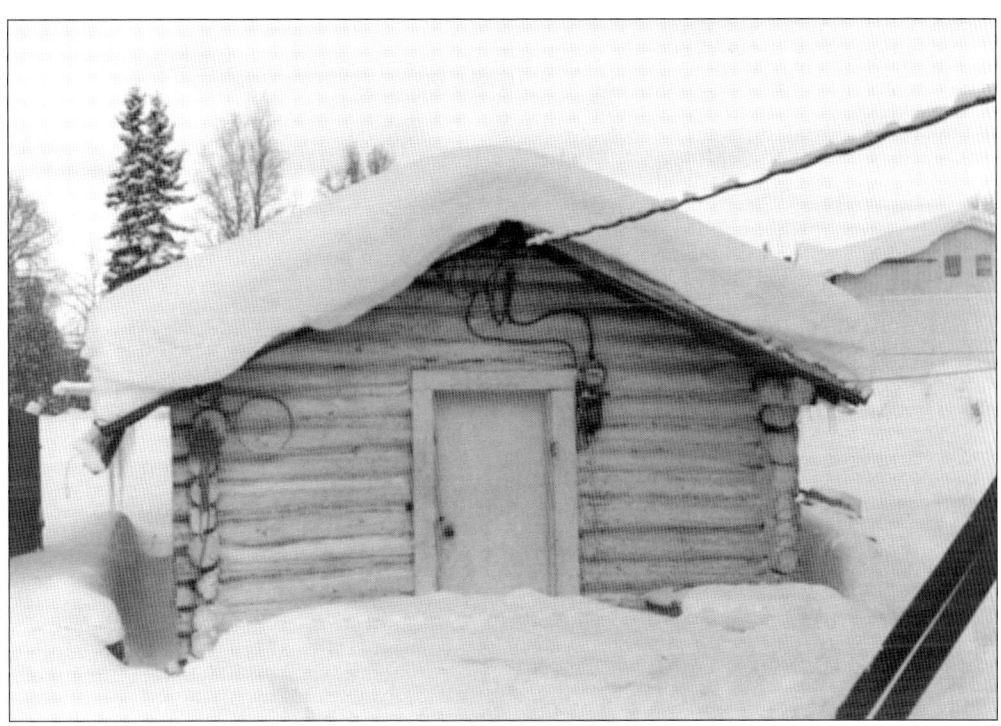

Rocky's Cabin. The cabin above is Rocky Cummins's Talkeetna log cabin, which was next door to the cabin of his mining partner, Jim Beaver. Cummins is seen at right in another miner or trapper's cabin in the 1960s. Both Cummins and Beaver were known for their good cheer and laughter. Cummins's cabin is now a bed and breakfast. (Both courtesy Pat Beaver Pratt.)

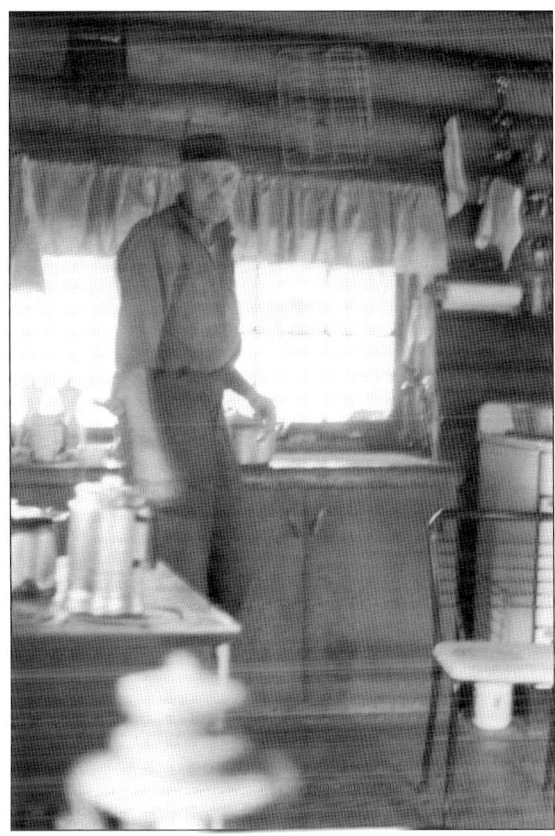

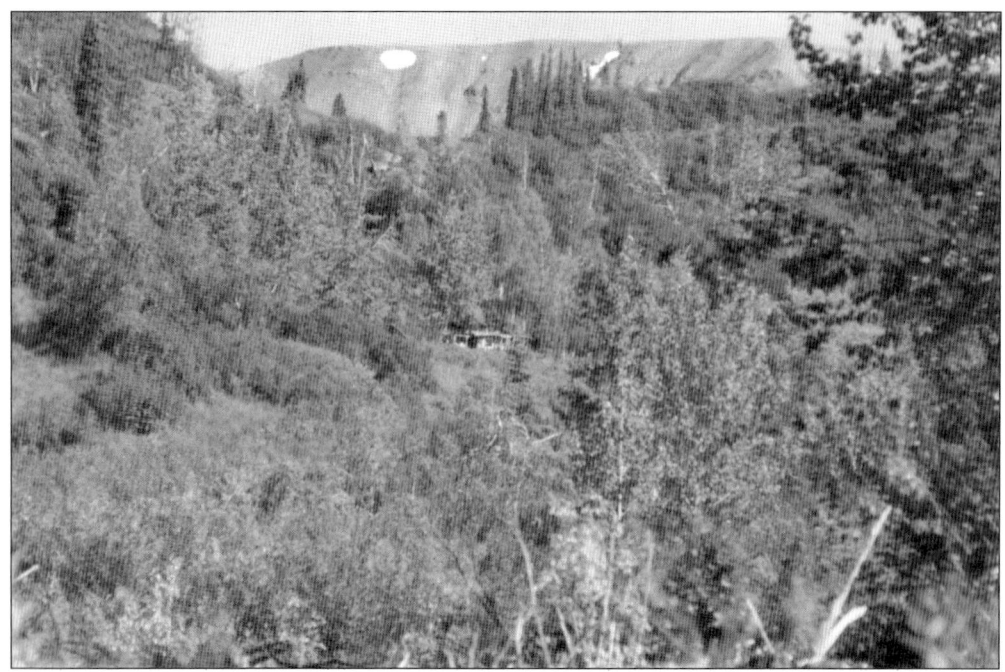

CACHE CREEK. One day in 1969, Pat Beaver, then a college student, was enjoying a cup of coffee in the peaceful wilderness bliss of the Cheechako cabin (above). Her father, Jim Beaver, was out working his mining claim. Pat was preparing to be picked up by bush pilot Don Sheldon later in the afternoon to take her to Talkeetna. While waiting for the bathwater to boil on the wood stove, she sat in her birthday suit with pink rollers in her hair. She looked out the window (below) and was startled to see a big brown bear with a golden hump staring in the window. (Both courtesy Pat Beaver Pratt.)

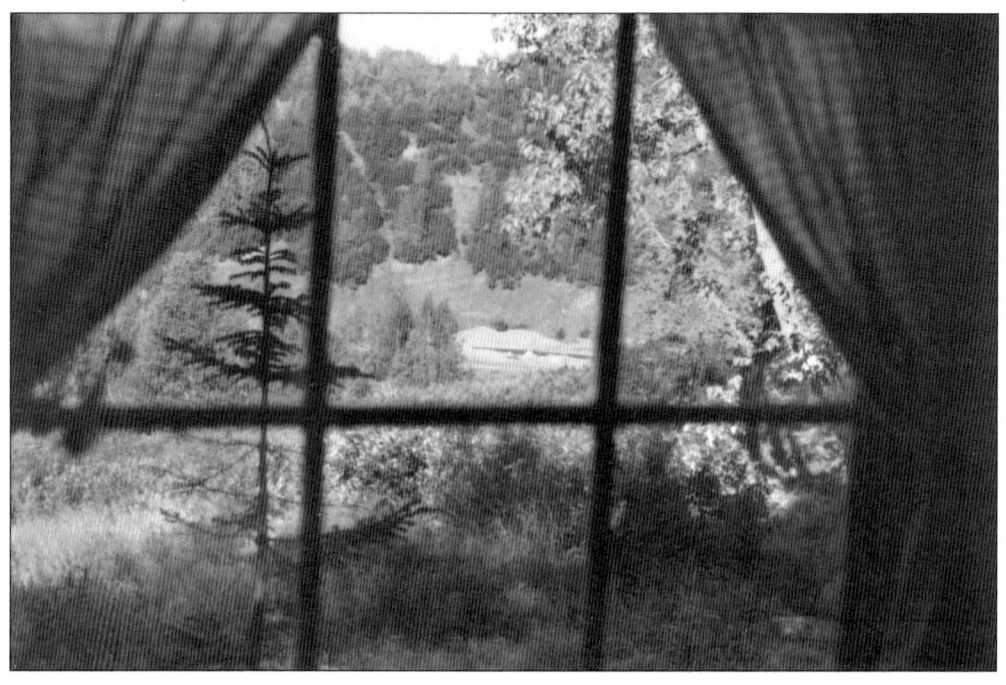

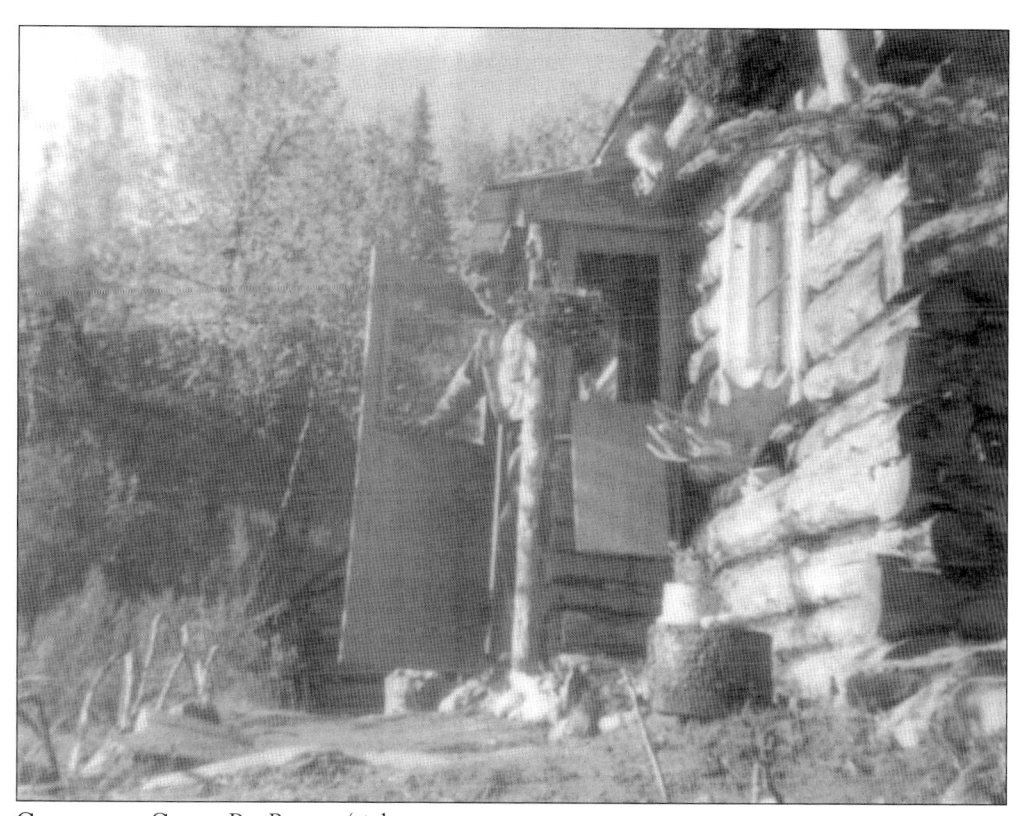

CHEECHAKO CABIN. Pat Beaver (right, on left) tried in vain to scare the grizzly away with noisy pots and pans, throwing things and even firing a gun through the window. But the she-bear wanted in the cabin, so finally, Beaver decided to run for it. She threw on some clothes and ran to the mining pit, leaving a trail of pink curlers. The men grabbed their rifles and came back to find the bear heading straight toward them. The rest is history: the bear-skin (right) still hangs on the wall inside the Beaver cabin in Talkeetna (see page 42). (Both courtesy Pat Beaver Pratt.)

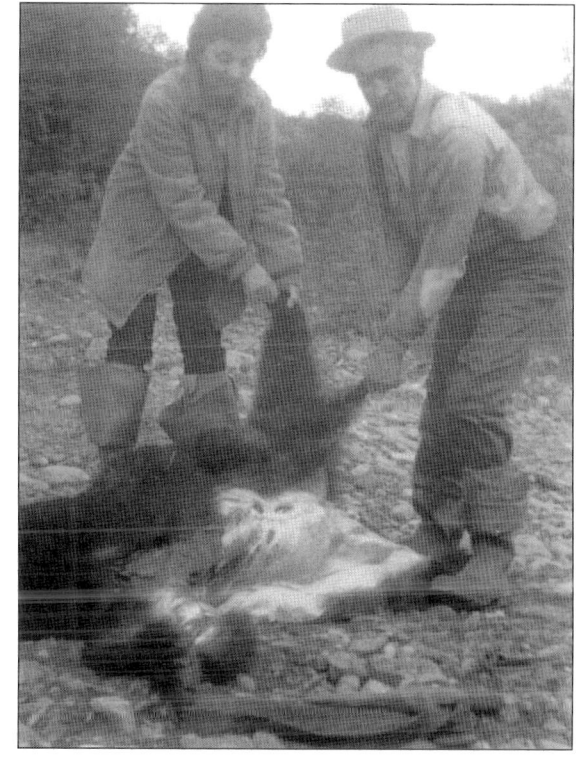

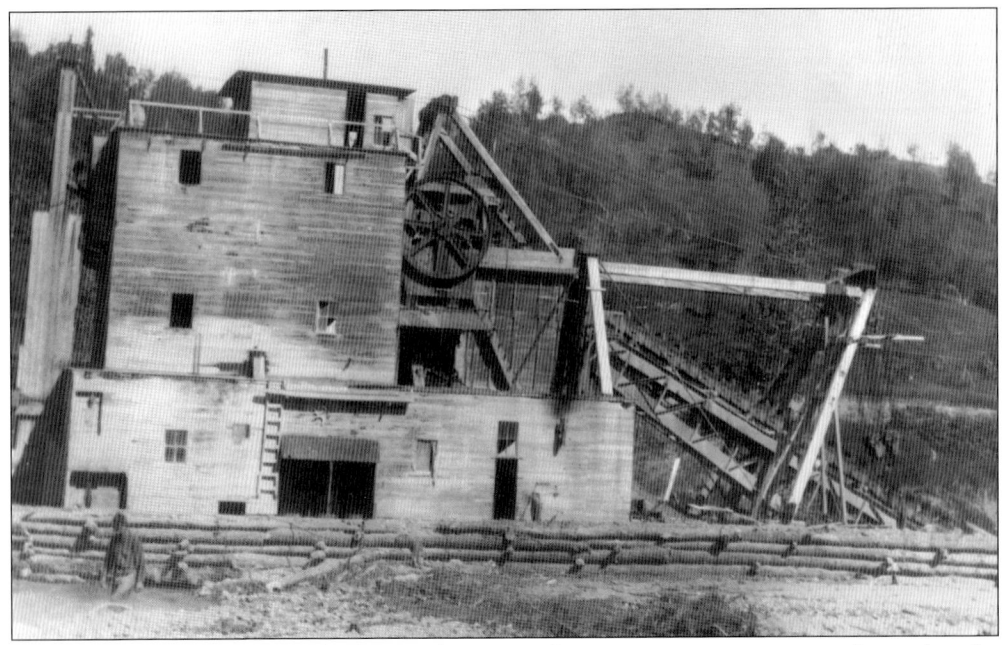

PELTON WHEEL. The Pelton wheel, seen above in a placer mining operation, was donated to the Talkeetna Historical Society and can now be seen near the museum's front entrance. Invented in the 1870s, a Pelton wheel is an impulse turbine, a very efficient type of water turbine. It extracts energy from the impulse, or momentum, of moving water, which in turn provides power to operate machinery. The newspaper articles below illustrate how the mining community in Moscow, Idaho, and the shipping community in Seattle were tracking the mining business and the machinery being shipped to Talkeetna and the remote mining areas beyond at Bird Creek, Peters Creek, and Cache Creek. Investors were anxious to have a quick, high return on their investment. (Above, courtesy THS; below, courtesy WSU-MASC.)

IDAHO PEOPLE SEEK MILLIONS

Investing $30,000 for Equipment of Peters Creek Placer Near Talkeetna, Alaska.

MOSCOW, Idaho, Nov. 23.—Thirty thousand dollars will be spent next spring in installing a complete hydraulic plant on the property of the Peters Creek Placer company, composed of Moscow, Troy and Lewiston investors, who control 30 claims, 250 miles from Seward, Alaska.

In the last season development has been carried on and backers are satisfied that the claims are rich in gold. Otis Ross, general manager and engineer, reports 750,000 cubic yards of gravel running from $1 to $1.50 in gold was prospected this season.

The property is estimated to include at least 5,000,000 yards only partly developed in the Cache creek district, for which Talkeetna is the trading center. The plant to be installed will handle about 100,000 yards during the five-month season next summer at an operating cost of about 30 cents a yard.

Mr. and Mrs. Frank Berger of Moscow recently returned from the prop-

ENLARGED PLANT TO TALKEETNA

Ship Carries Final Equipment for Alaska Continental.

The steamship Alaskan, scheduled to have sailed yesterday from Seattle, had aboard the last consignment new equipment and supplies for Alaska Continental Gold Mines, freight paid to Talkeetna, the point on the Alaska railroad nearest the company's properties on Bird and Peters creeks.

Arrival of this shipment at the mine, 40 miles from Talkeetna, will enable Superintendent Harry Howell to complete the enlargment of the hydraulic plant with which the property is equipped.

Sluicing with the present plant, according to latest advices from Mr. Howell, should begin within the next few days, while the greatly enlarged plant is confidently expected to be in full operation within the month, says William J. Porter, president.

Rock Creek Going Strong.

Four

Historic Talkeetna

By virtue of its location, nestled where three rivers meet 60 air miles from the base of Denali (Mount McKinley), Talkeetna has served as an important gathering place for centuries. It started with the Dena'ina and transitioned to a new phase when Talkeetna was named the Divisional Railroad Headquarters in 1916 for the Seward-Fairbanks railroad. Virtually overnight, hundreds descended upon the area, some as railroad laborers, some to trap or mine, and others, such as Isabella "Belle" Grindrod Lee McDonald, the Lee brothers, the Nagleys, and Ben Neumann, who were in the right place at the right time and were able to envision the business opportunities of filling a niche, providing much-needed supplies, lodging, meals, and the transportation of goods and people.

Early Talkeetna was located mainly along the river, which was vital for transportation. Due to the natural, meandering floodplains of the Talkeetna, Chulitna, and Susitna Rivers, severe erosion occurred over the decades. The location where much of the Talkeetna River's early activity and commerce took place has long since reverted back to its natural river state. Talkeetna's main thoroughfare was moved to its current location in 1949 after severe flooding and the erosion of nearly 12 acres of the townsite, including a considerable chunk of Main Street. Talkeetna's west and south townsite boundaries moved over time due to flooding.

Milepost 227 has served as the primary railroad stop in Talkeetna for nearly 100 years. In 1997, a new railroad station was built for passengers a short distance away from the original Talkeetna station, to meet the increasing demand of seasonal tourists exploring the land of the midnight sun and seeking to experience the historic rural village of Talkeetna. Similarly, the people who come to Talkeetna have changed. The following pages describe some of these historical players who represent the spirit of Talkeetna.

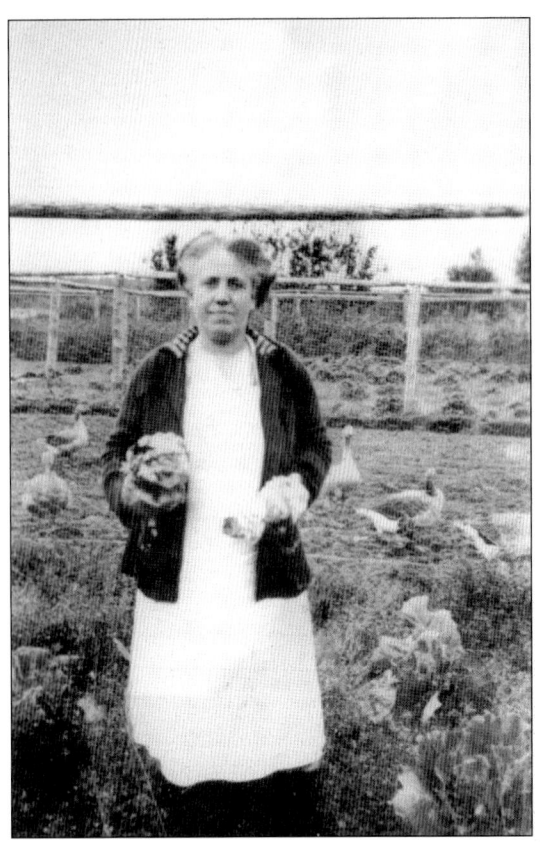

"Belle." Isabella "Belle" Grindrod Lee McDonald (left) was born on September 27, 1877, in Collingwood, Ontario, Canada. She arrived in Talkeetna in 1917, where she lived for more than 40 years, mostly at the Talkeetna Trading Post, and in the home below after her retirement. McDonald was Talkeetna's first businesswoman, operating the Talkeetna Trading Post: a freighting service, stable, blacksmith shop, and roadhouse. Local folklore indicates that Belle also operated the Bucket of Blood, a honky-tonk, and had a whiskey still to meet the needs of her clients. In 1918, she married Ed Lee, a guide, packer, and freighter moving supplies to Cache Creek with his team of horses. Sadly, just 10 years later, Lee committed suicide, likely due to a combination of alcoholism and a terminal case of throat cancer. Much later, Belle married J.M. "Mac" McDonald, a newcomer who supervised the Cache Creek Road improvement in 1934. (Both courtesy THS.)

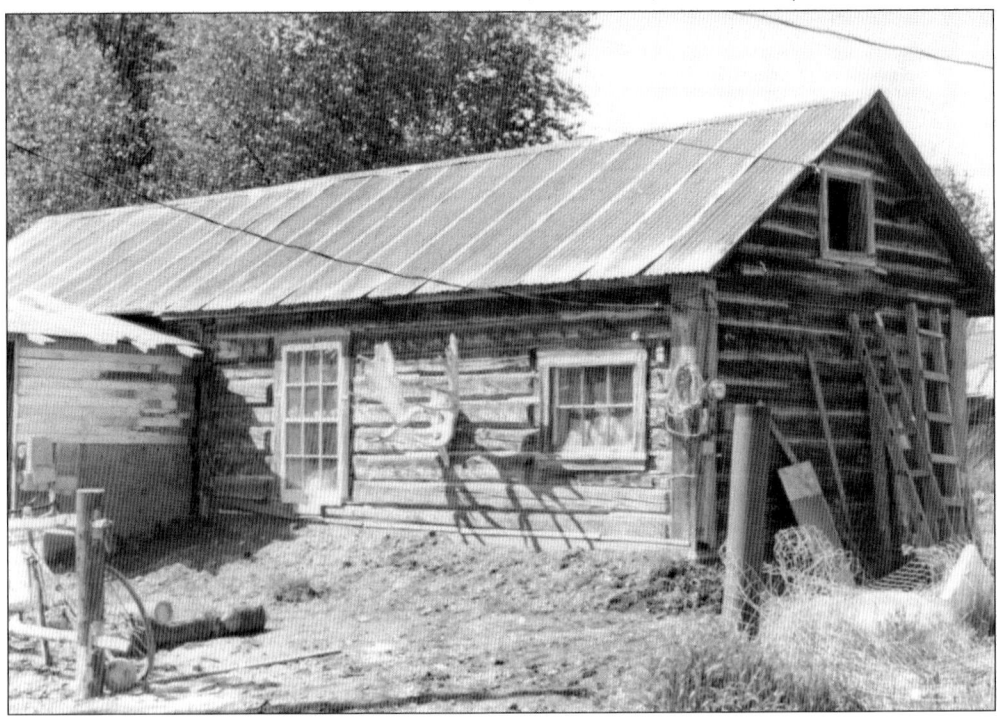

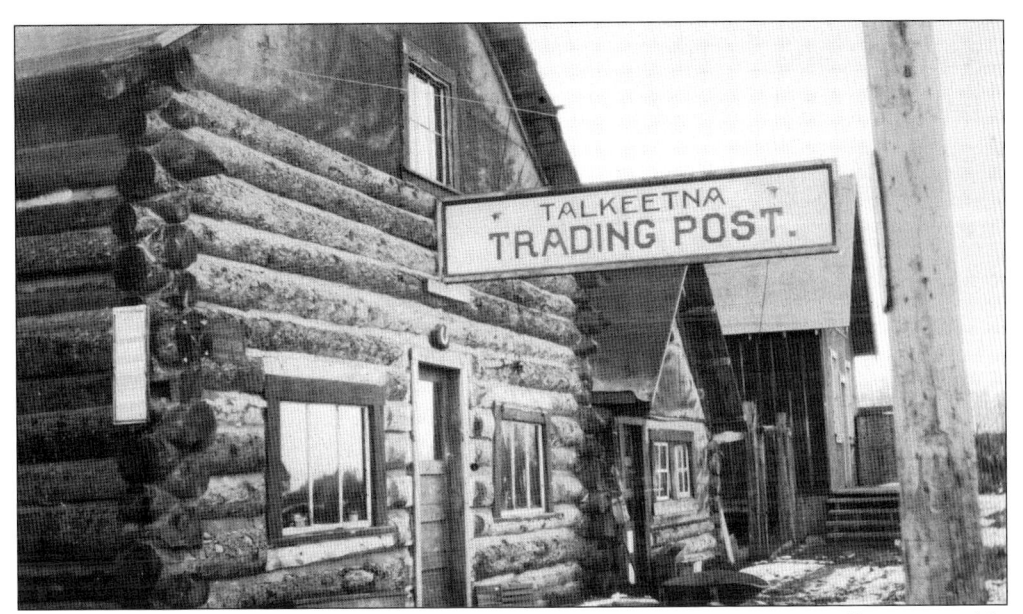

Talkeetna Trading Post and Aerial View. Nola Campbell wrote of Belle McDonald's Talkeetna Trading Post, "Belle's place was like home to many tired, weary and hungry men who came in from the hills. The walls were covered with hanging fur pelts of many kinds: mink, marten, weasel, lynx and wolf. Gold scales, beaver skins, blankets and kits were stacked in the corners, and traps and gear was piled around." Belle served two hardy meals a day, only deviating for freighters coming in late off the trail. She raised chickens and grew vegetables to supplement the wild game, fish, and fresh-baked bread she served at the roadhouse. Below is an aerial view of Talkeetna around 1940, showing the trading post buildings at lower right. (Above, courtesy UAF; below, courtesy BMS, THS.)

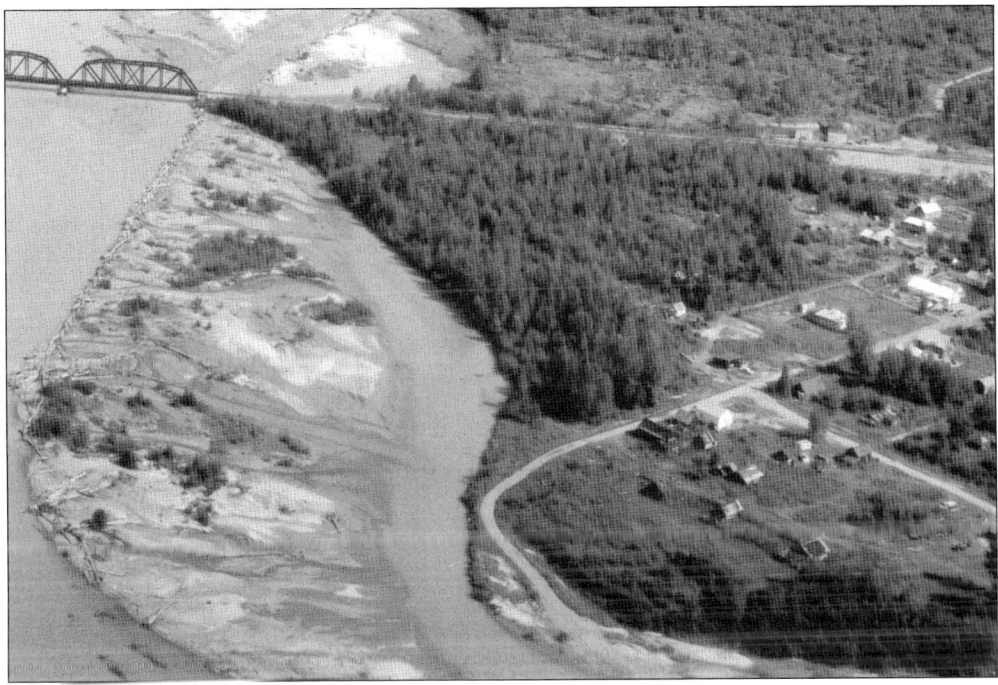

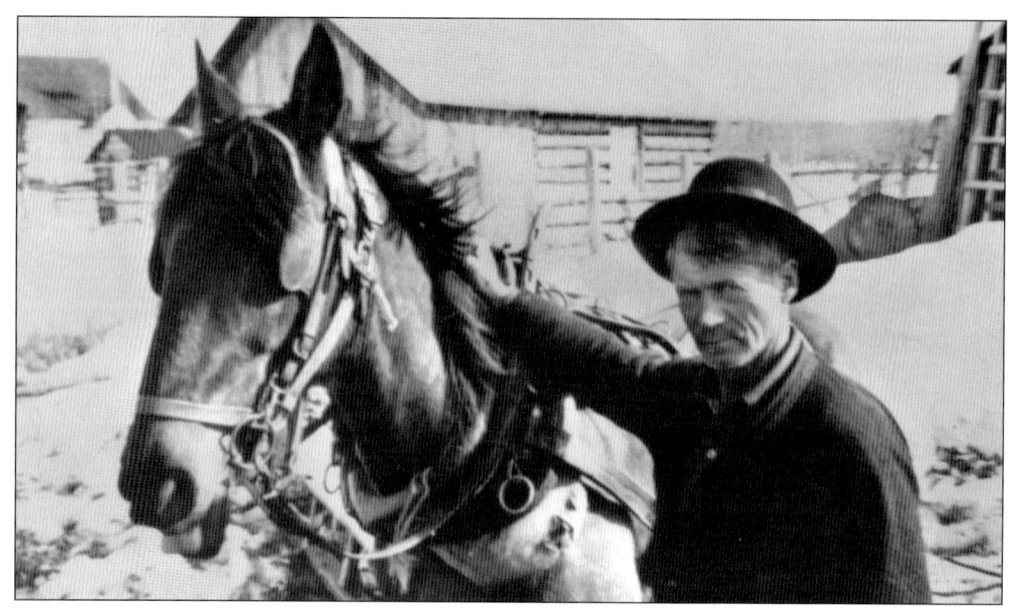

FREIGHTING SERVICE AND FORKS ROADHOUSE. Belle and Frank Lee's freighting service transported supplies from the Talkeetna Trading Post to remote mining and trapping areas. Frank Lee, Belle's brother-in-law, was the chief freighter for the Talkeetna Trading Post from 1917 to 1938. Above, Frank is pictured with his freight-horse, Bunny, named for her large ears, who is hitched to a sledge. The Lee brothers settled in Talkeetna from Michigan in 1916. Frank Lee hauled supplies year-round to the Cache Creek area, west of Talkeetna. In the winter, horse-drawn sleds were used. In the summer, wagons were used on crude trails. The horses were pastured across the Susitna River at the landing during the warmer months. Below, Shorty Bradley and his wife, Florence, are seen outside the Forks Roadhouse, 32 miles due west of Talkeetna, which they leased from Belle Gindrod Lee McDonald, serving customers in the Peter Creek area. Fully staffed during the warmer months, an honor system was in place during the winter, as the building was kept unlocked. The Bradleys' daughter Susie married pilot Cal Reeves. (Both courtesy THS.)

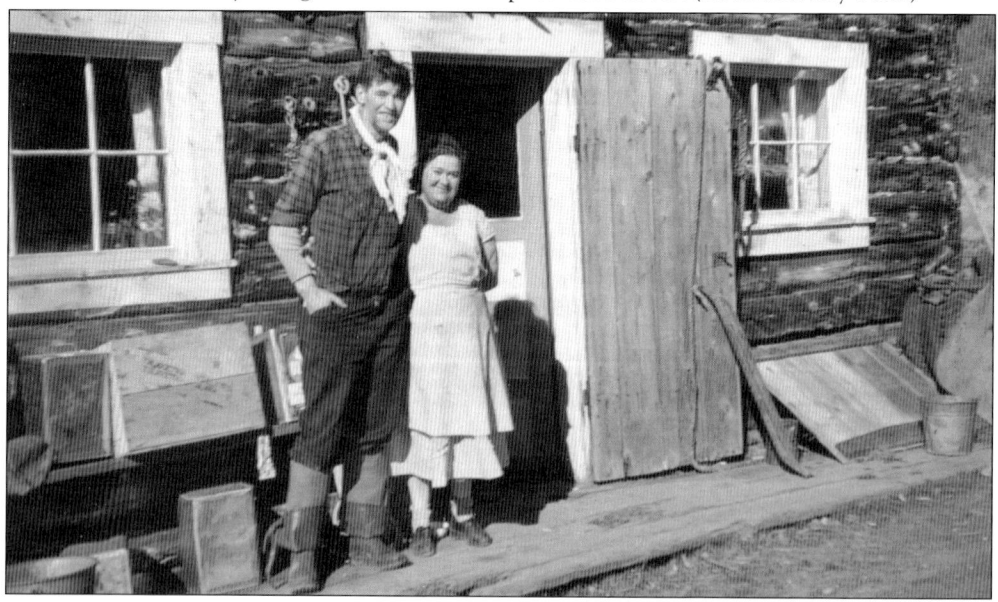

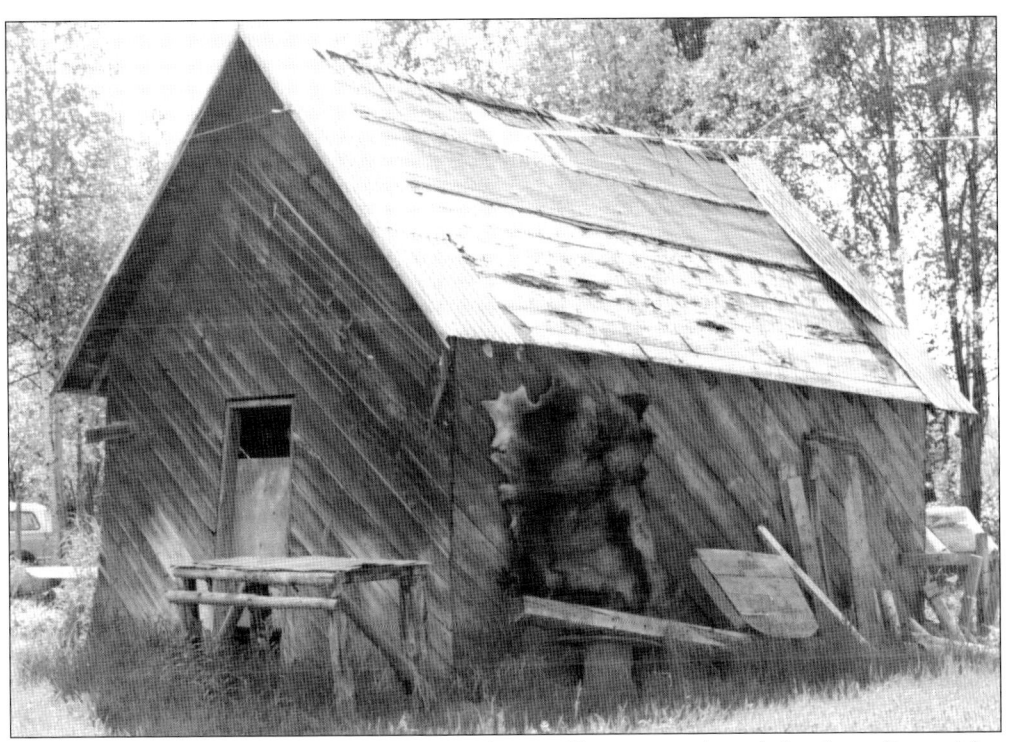

TRADING POST BARN. Horses were an integral part of business and needed to be well cared for. Despite the extremely cold temperatures and snowy conditions of Talkeetna winters, Frank Lee managed to take excellent care of his horses. This outbuilding most likely held feed, tack, and other equipment necessary for horse freighting. This barn eventually fell into disrepair and collapsed in the 1980s. (Courtesy THS.)

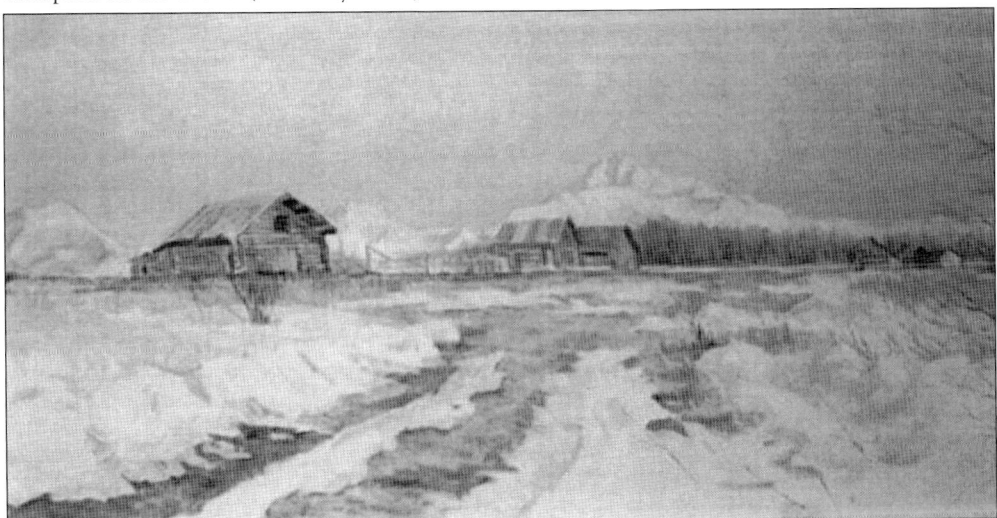

BUCKET OF BLOOD. Located on the corner of Main and B Streets, the Bucket of Blood (center) was a honky-tonk. Belle had a sister, known as "Talkeetna Daisy," who did not share the same hard-work ethic as Belle. Talkeetna Daisy is purported to have spent considerable time in the Bucket of Blood while visiting Talkeetna. Eleanor Trepte recalled, "Talkeetna Daisy's laughter could often be heard over the miners, music and noise of the Bucket of Blood." (Courtesy Curt Wagner, TCM.)

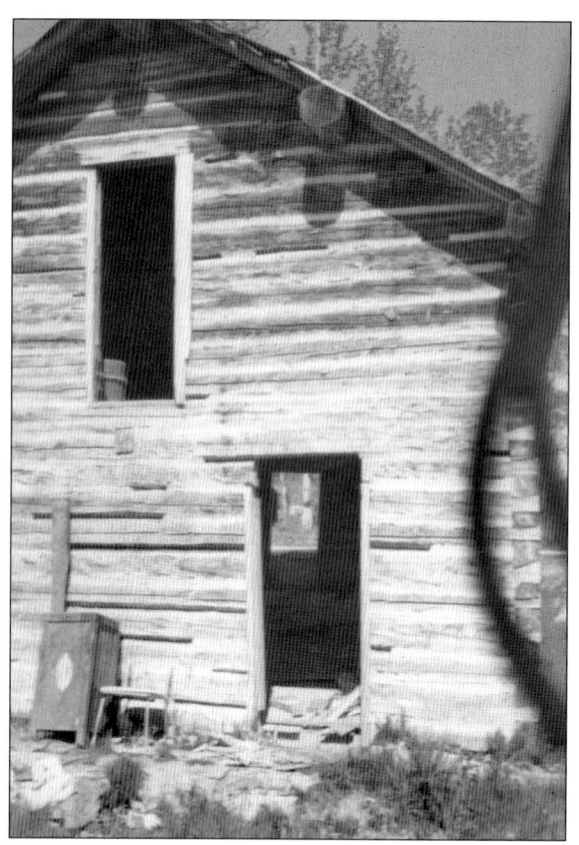

DEVAULT ROADHOUSE. Located east of the Talkeetna Trading Post, the Devault Roadhouse (left) played an active role in Talkeetna's early history. A trail between the two businesses was commonly used by trappers and miners looking to board their dog teams at the roadhouse while attending to business in Anchorage or elsewhere. At times, there could be upwards of 30 dogs to care for, generating a lot of work, mess, and noise. Although the roadhouse is now nearly forgotten from local memory, the 1974 image above shows the deterioration endured by many original Talkeetna structures. The building was scavenged for lumber, leaving no trace of the once-thriving roadhouse behind. Below, are from left to right, Freida DeVault, Gale Weatherell (little boy), Fritz (bear), Mrs. VanWinkle (Francis Weatherell's mother and Gale Weatherell's grandmother), and Jack Devault (kneeling). The Devaults became Eleanor Trepte's in-laws when she married at age 18. (Both courtesy Eleanor Trepte.)

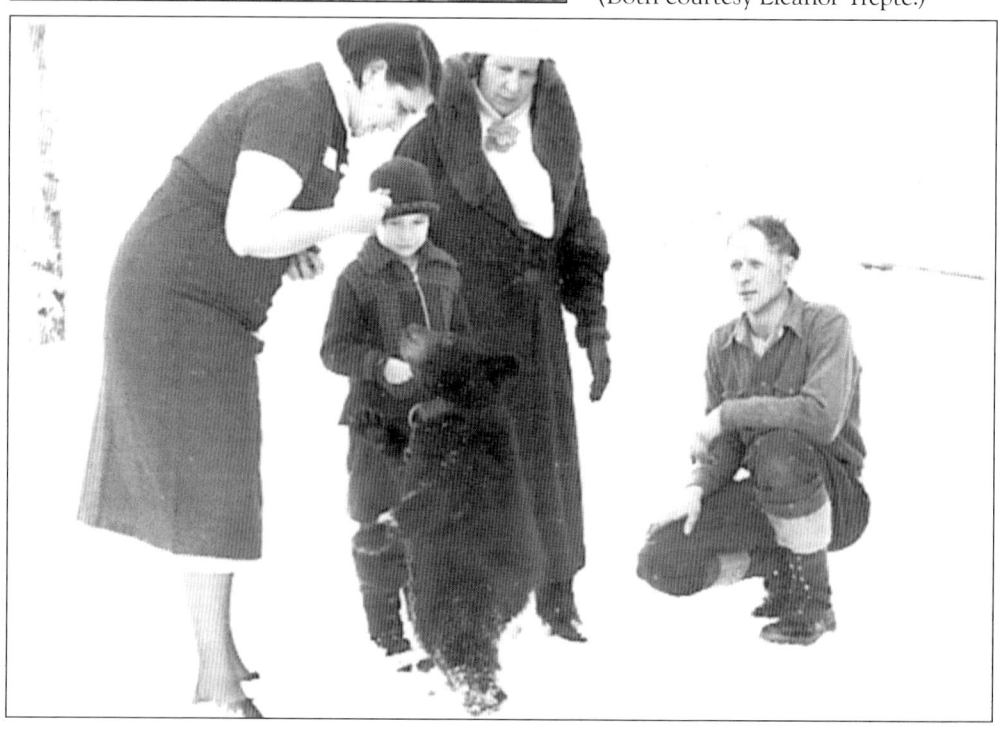

Three German Bachelors. Emigrants from Germany, the three German bachelors, made up of Tony and Henry Meise and an unidentified bachelor, are seen at right near their log cabin in downtown Talkeetna in 1934. The handsome bachelors were excellent builders, constructing their log home with common lap-notch corners. They mined and set their traplines in the Cache Creek area. The three German bachelors are seen below in the 1930s, standing outside of their traditional log cabin and petting dogs. An old whiskey barrel serves as a doghouse. Talkeetna was often a noisy village, with many barking dogs, day and night. (Both courtesy THS.)

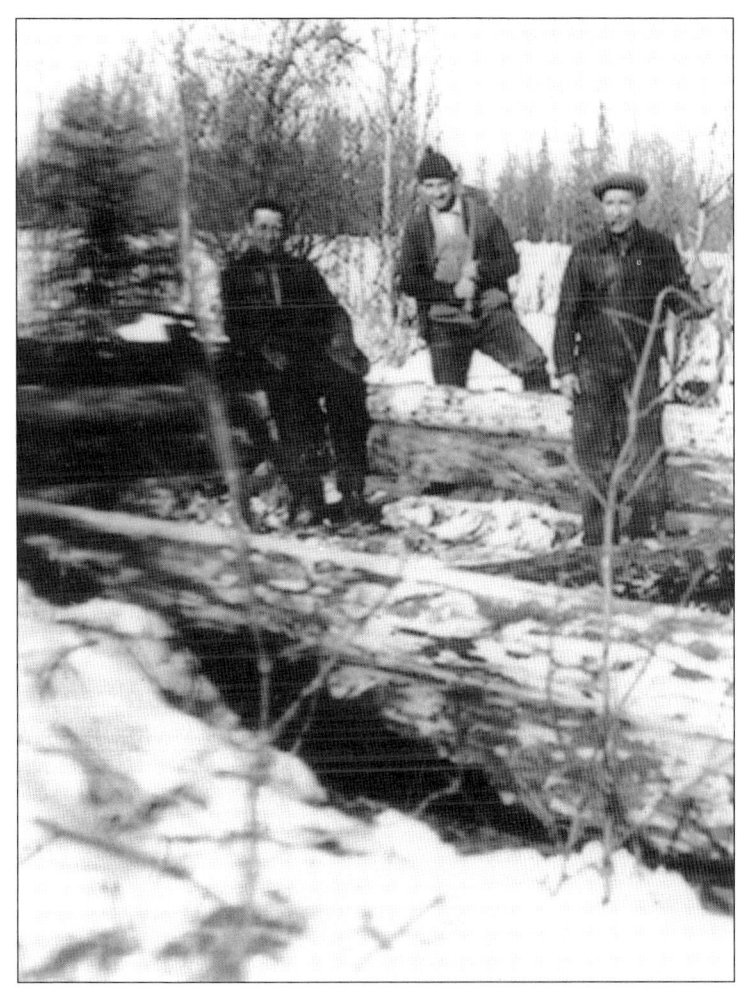

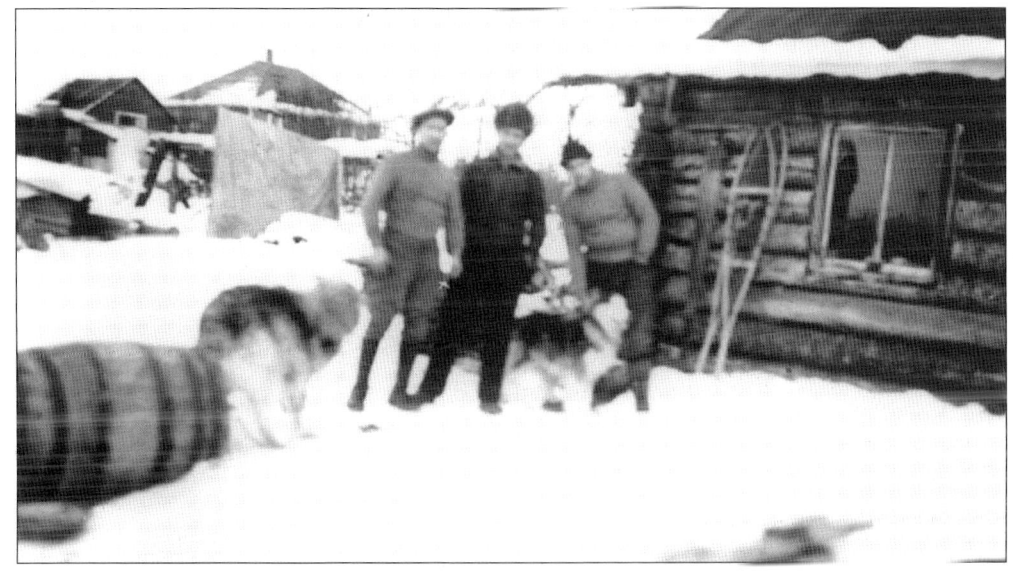

53

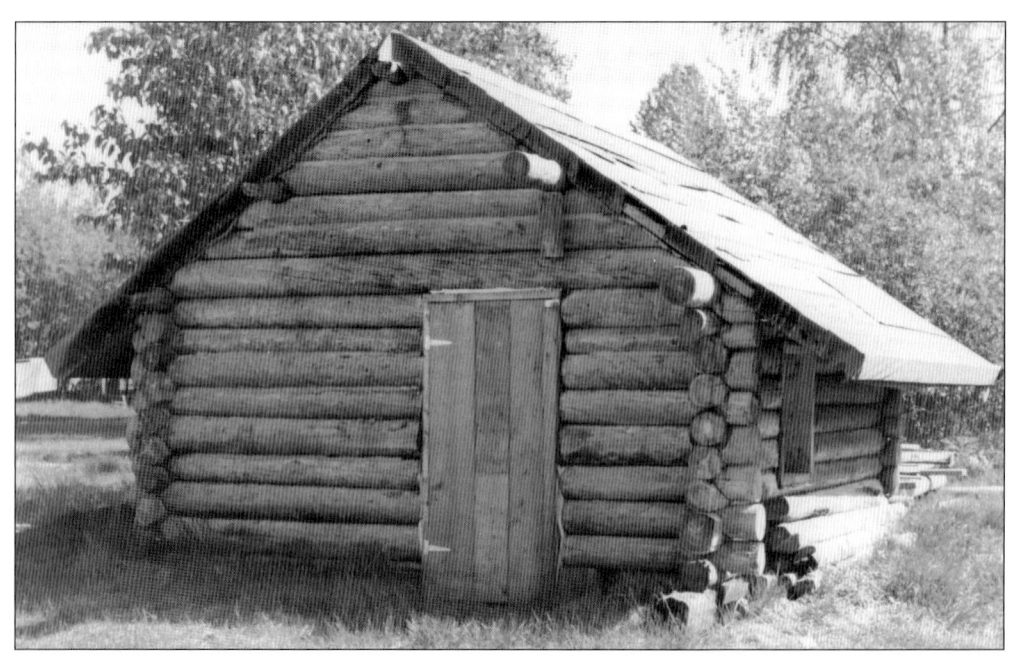

OLE DAHL. One of the very first settlers in Talkeetna was Ole Dahl (below), a Norwegian who arrived here in 1909. He trapped furs in the winter and spent his summers mining for gold in the Cache Creek area, above Nugget Creek. In 1916, Dahl became a surveyor for the railroad and married Annie Effim, a Dena'ina from Susitna Station. They built the one-and-a-half-story log cabin above with square-notched corners in 1920. The Dahls had five children, outgrew their small cabin, and moved to a larger one on Main Street. Both cabins survived and are listed in the National Register of Historic Places. Note the snowshoes, the cross-country skis, and the snow-covered train cars in the background. (Both courtesy THS.)

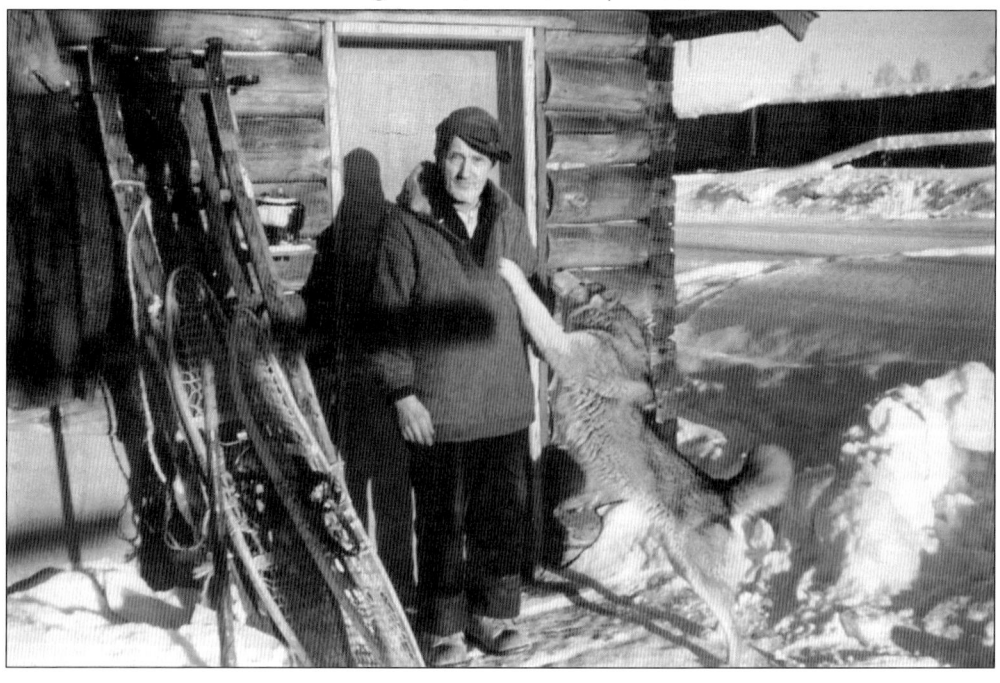

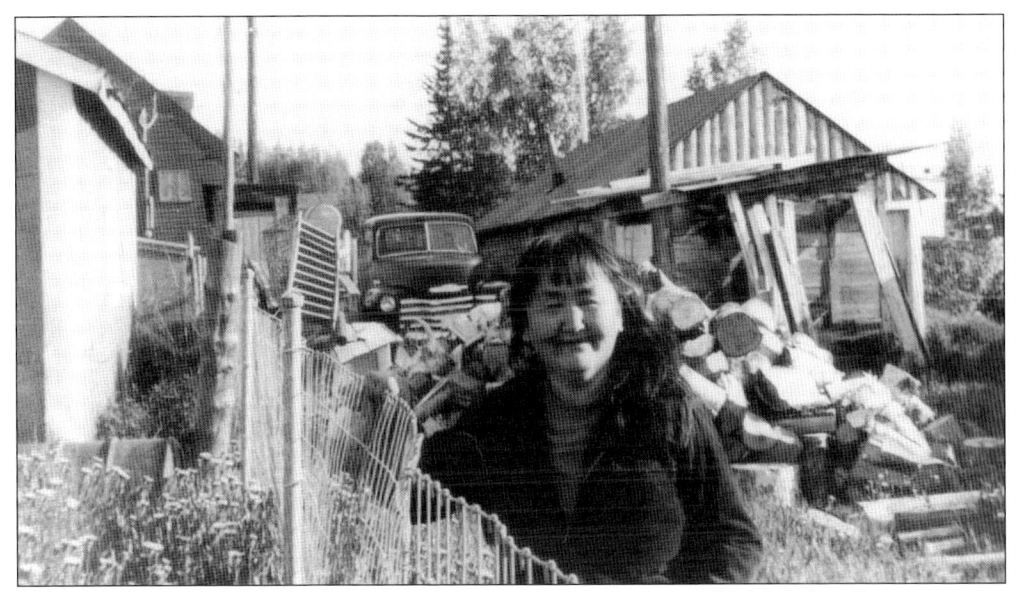

ANNIE DAHL. Born and raised at Susitna Station, Annie Effim Dahl (above), a Dena'ina, went to school in Eklutna. She met Ole Dahl at Susitna Station, and they were married in 1916. They eventually had five children: Bobby, Mary Anne, Ruby, Allan, and Ollie, who married Cliff Hudson and still lives in Talkeetna. In later years, Annie Dahl encouraged Ole to start a barbershop in their home. Local residents may recall sitting in the barber chair at Ole's place, shooting the breeze and watching the daily encounters at the Fairview, which was located kitty-corner from the barbershop. Above, behind Annie and to the left, is the corner of the one-room schoolhouse, which is now the Talkeetna Historical Museum. Below is an interior view of the Dahls' first log cabin, which was also donated to the Talkeetna Historical Museum. (Both courtesy THS, Roberta Sheldon.)

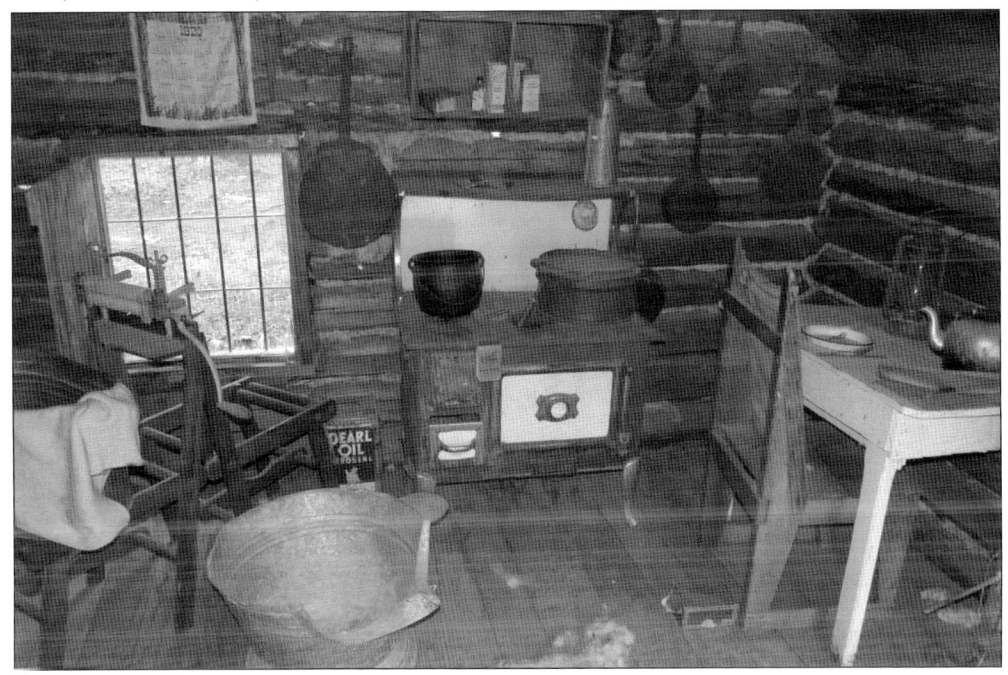

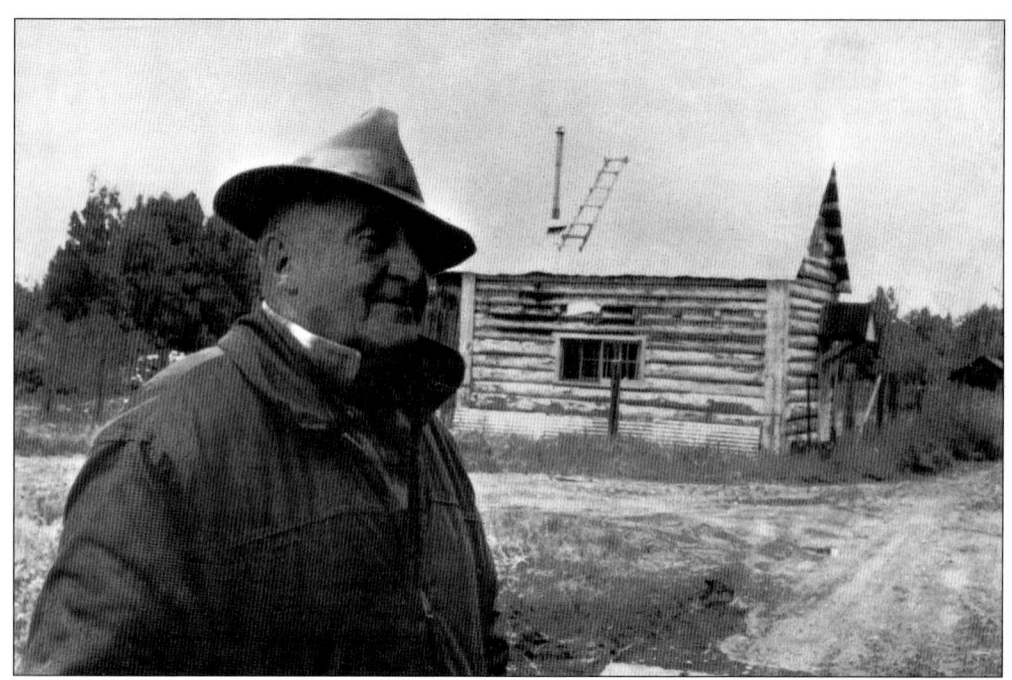

HARRY ROBB CABIN. Some people retire in warm places like Florida. But Yukon riverboat captain Harry Robb retired to Talkeetna and began a second career mining and trapping in the Cache Creek area. He bought this home in 1930 and lived here until he passed away in 1976. The log cabin was originally built in the 1920s by Dave St. Lawrence. It is listed in the National Register of Historic Places and is maintained by the Talkeetna Historical Society (THS). When Robb passed away in 1976, he left his log cabin and all of his belongings to the THS. The interior of the cabin has been left intact to remember Robb and to share with the many visitors who come to Talkeetna what the living conditions were like. (Courtesy THS, Sisul.)

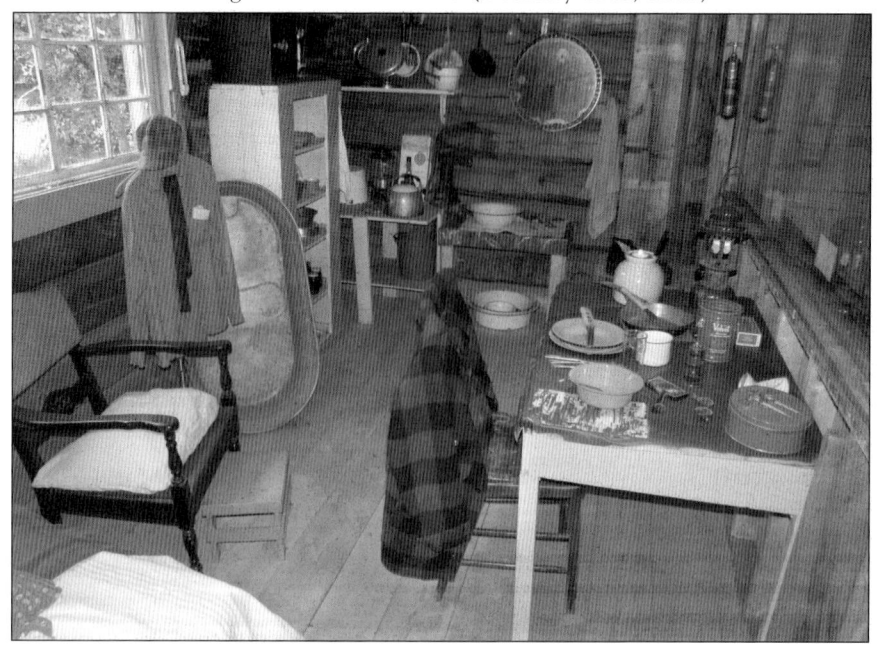

Fire! The Trepte family kept a cabin in Talkeetna. Sadly, after the neighbors had a wild, all-night party in 1936, Eleanor, who was 15 years old at the time, recalls hearing someone yelling "fire!" The neighbors' house had caught fire and in turn burned the Trepte's two-story log home, with everything in it. It was especially difficult since they were preparing for a long summer of prospecting/mining, and all their supplies were stored in the house. Fortunately, no one was injured. Trepte built a new home on the same site, seen below. This new home still stands in Talkeetna, and is known as "House of Seven Trees Bed and Breakfast." The packs the Treptes used for mining and trapping, seen on page 39, are on display inside. (Courtesy Eleanor Trepte.)

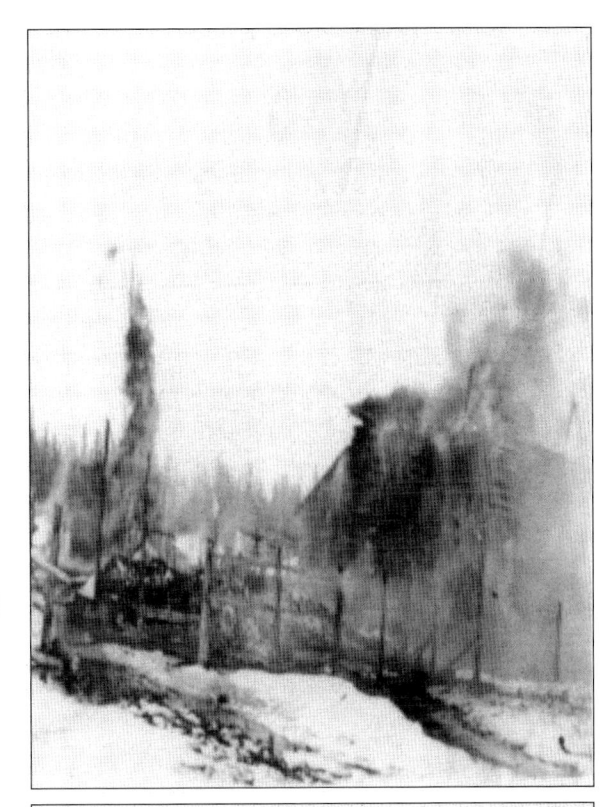

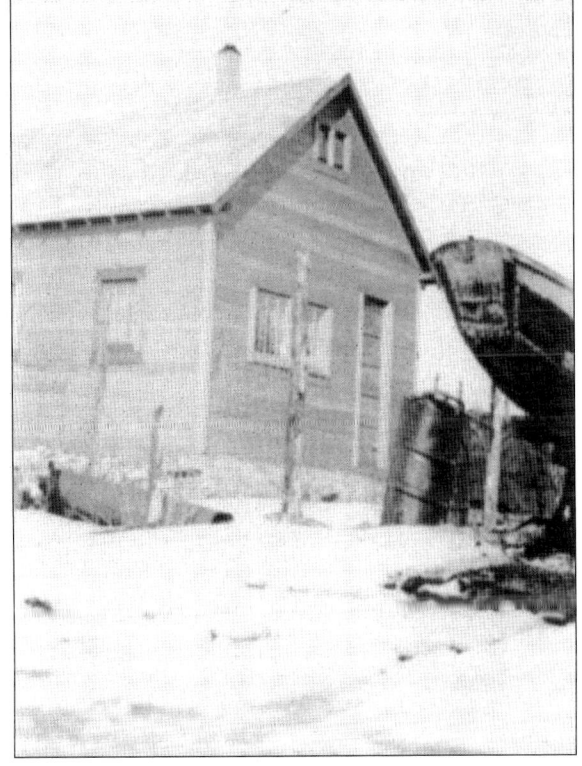

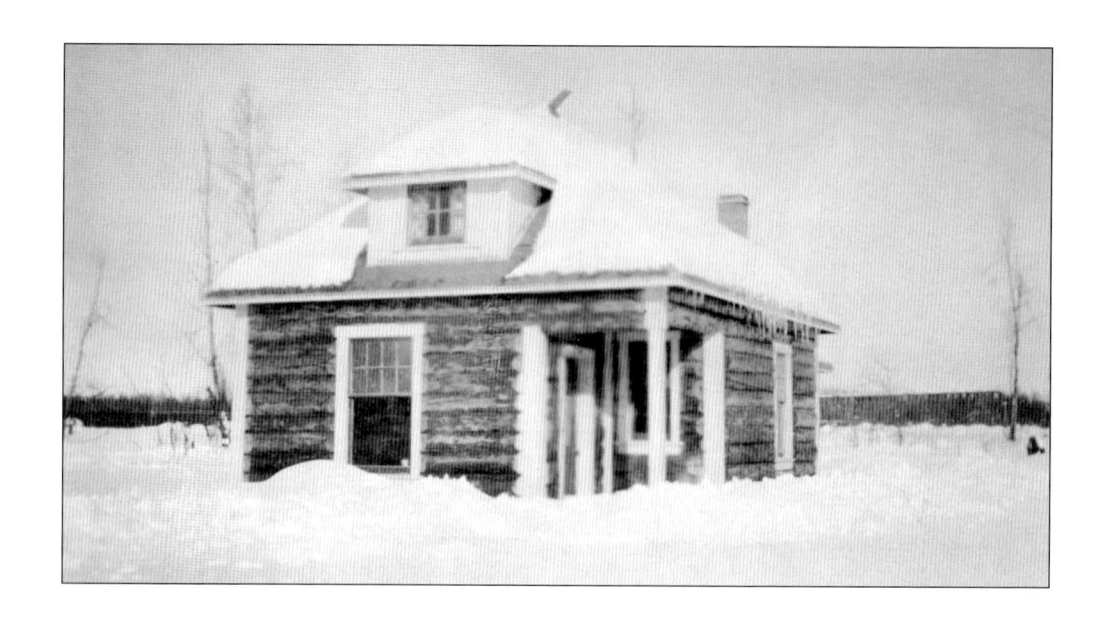

Tom Weatherell. The home above was built in 1940 for Tom Weatherell. The carpenter, Helmer Ronning, an immigrant from Norway, built the log home with dovetail-notched corners covered by boards. Weatherell did some prospecting in the Cache Creek area, but his primary activity was as a faithful, loyal clerk at Nagley's Store, where he worked for many years. Weatherell sold his cabin to Adolph J. "Missouri" Taraski, who lived here until he passed away in 1972. Below, Tom Weatherell (right) is seen on his front porch with Ed Anderson, another Talkeetna miner and trapper. (Both courtesy UAF.)

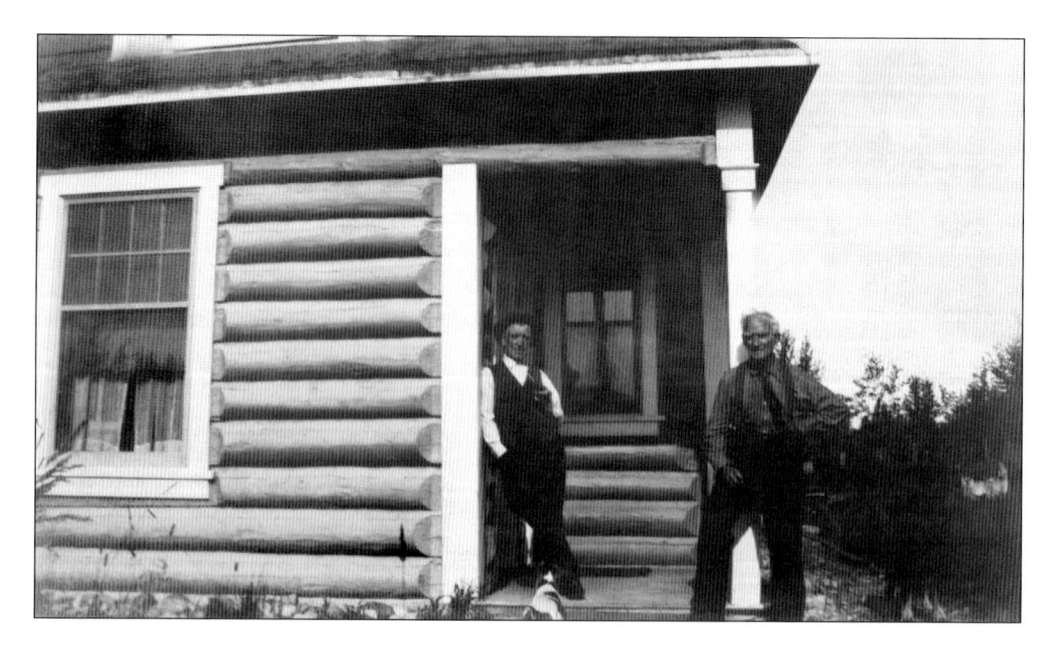

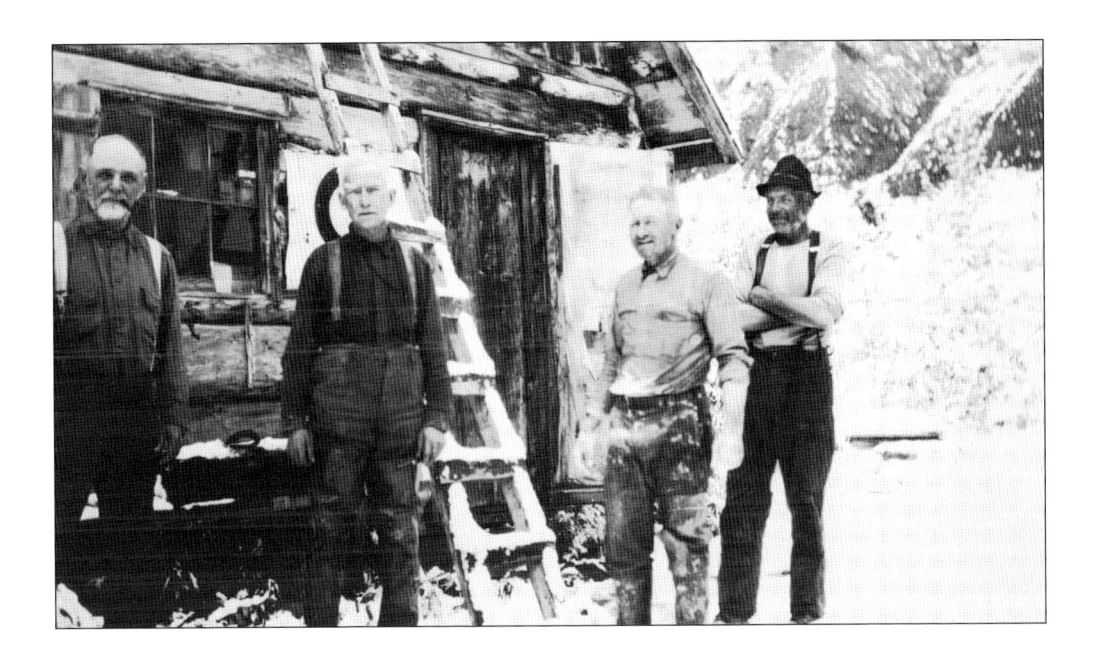

Tom Weatherell. Above, Tom Weatherell is second from left and Charles "Smitty" Smith is on the far right. The other two men are unidentified. Below, in a photograph likely taken around 1920 near Nagley's, Weatherell is second from left. Many in the group have mosquito nets pulled up on their hats, and with their packhorse and supplies, they appear to be heading out to do some prospecting. (Both courtesy UAF.)

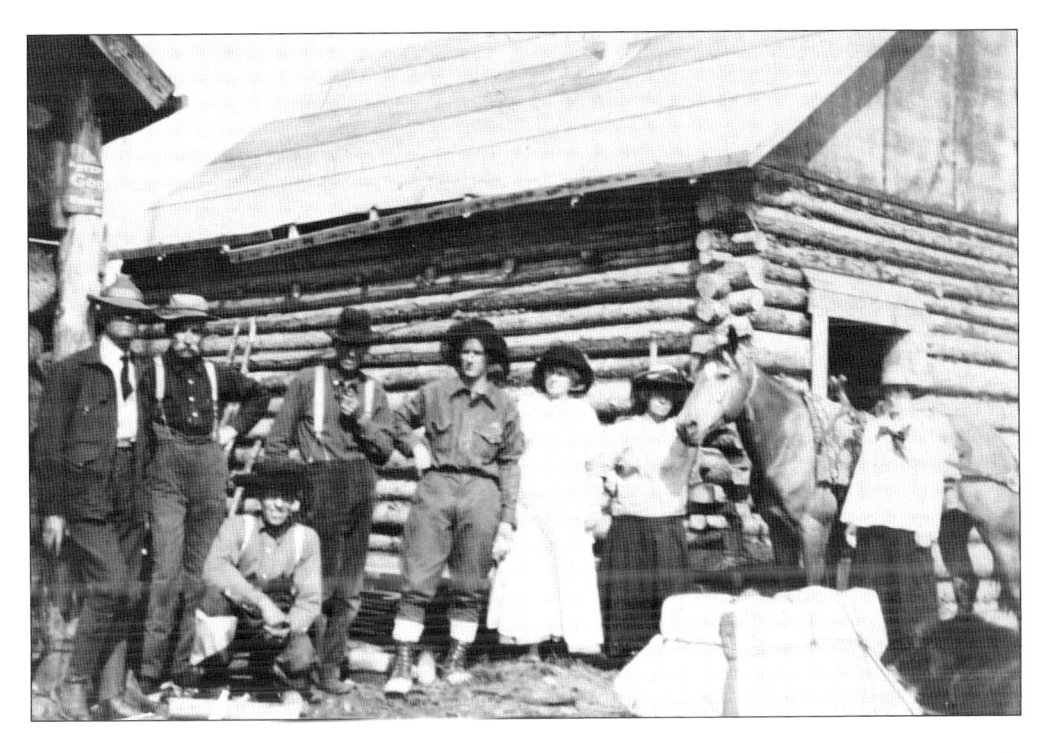

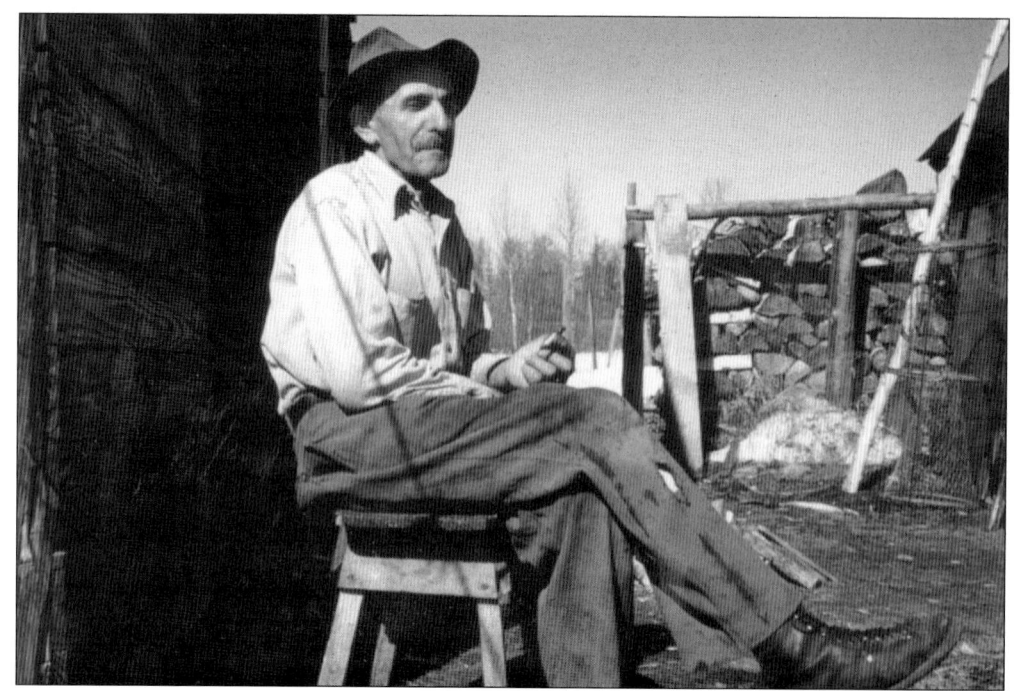

BLACK JOHN ZULICH. An immigrant from Czechoslovakia, Black John Zulich was a gold miner and trapper in the Cache Creek area. Black John built a one-and-a-half-story log cabin in 1934, behind the Fairview Inn near the Talkeetna Railroad Station. Many speculate the upper gable may have originally been used as a modified cache. Zulich often had a pan of beans and a pot of coffee heating on his woodstove. After he retired, Zulich tended a big vegetable garden, often wearing a red felt hat from the B&K Trading Post. Above, Zulich is sitting outside his cabin, wearing his red felt hat and smoking a cigarette in front of the ever-present woodpile. The cabin is seen below in the 1980s. It has since been purchased by Marlene Chilcoat and houses an espresso shop. (Above, courtesy THS; below, Marlene Chilcoat.)

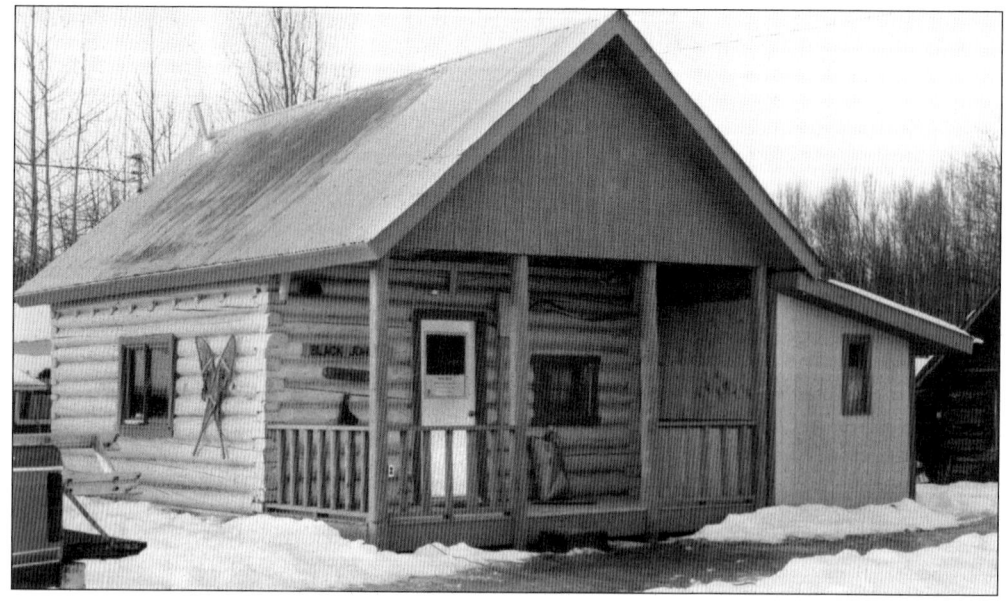

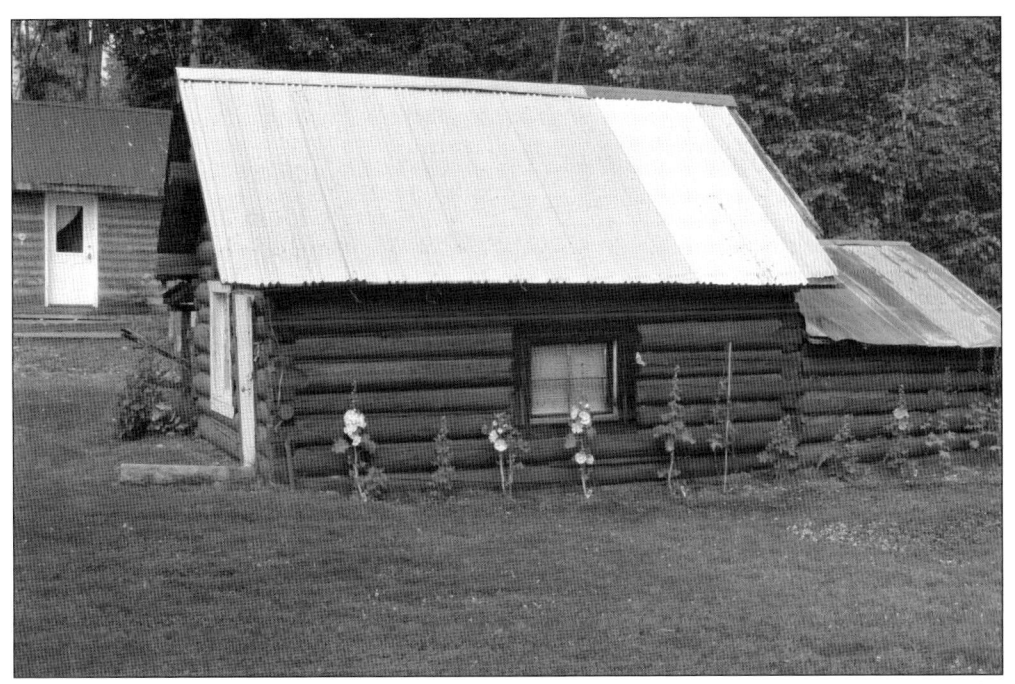

RED JOHN'S CABIN. Black John Zulich and Red John were longtime mining partners at Cache Creek. It is believed that both men acquired their nicknames as a result of their hair color. Red John went to check his trap lines one winter day and never returned. Zulich searched for him and found him dead, lying facedown in the snow, most likely having suffered a heart attack. (Courtesy Sisul.)

FRANK JENKINS CABIN. In 1939, Frank and Helen Jenkins were murdered at Cache Creek, along with Joy Brittell and Dick Francis. Author Roberta Sheldon reports in *Cache Creek Murder*, "Frank and Joy were pole-axed from behind with no sign of struggle . . . Mrs. Jenkins had been hit with a single blow to the back of the head and then beaten to a pulp . . . no person was ever arrested." It is likely that gold was a motivating factor. (Courtesy THS.)

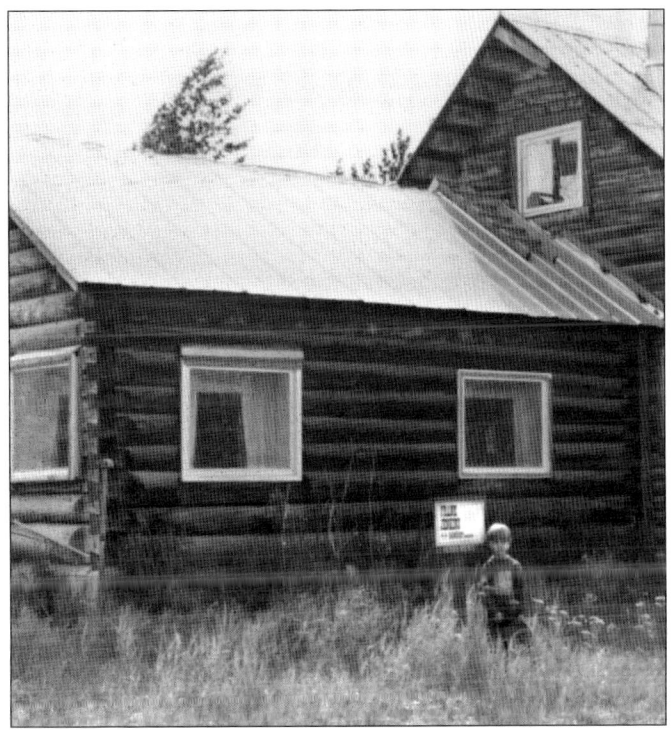

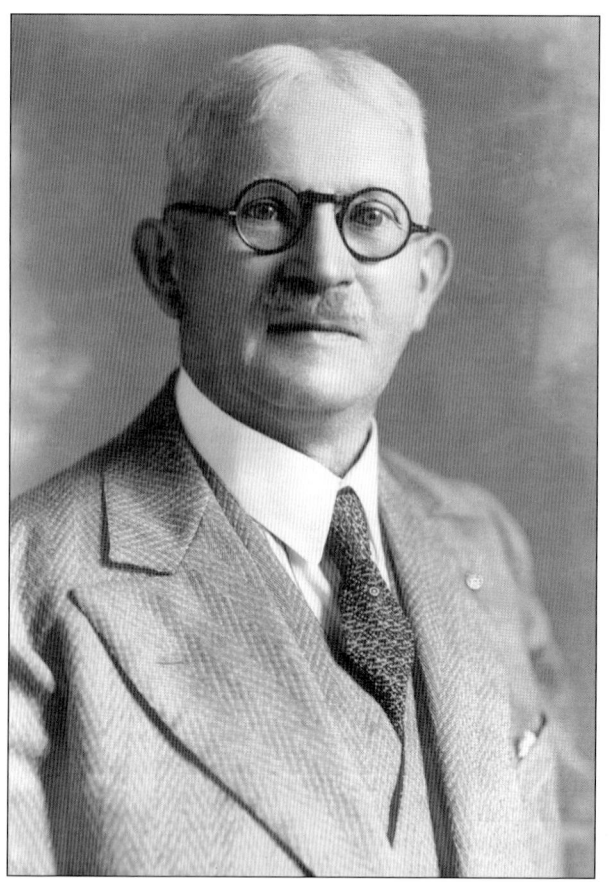

BEN NAUMAN AND FAIRVIEW HOTEL. Ben Nauman, a handsome, well dressed, and meticulous businessman from Anchorage, immediately saw the potential profit associated with a hotel at milepost 227, the logical overnight stop between Seward and Fairbanks. Construction began in 1921 and was completed in 1923. The Fairview Hotel became an important social center and gathering place almost immediately. It attracted people from all walks of life and became the primary informal meeting place for miners, trappers, and railroad workers, due to the fact there was no other place to meet or socialize. Originally, the Fairview Hotel had a bar and kitchen on the first floor, with seven rooms upstairs and a community bathroom. The Fairview made local history by having the first bathtub in town. It was listed in the National Register of Historic Places in 1982. Locals feel that the Fairview belongs to them. (Both courtesy THS.)

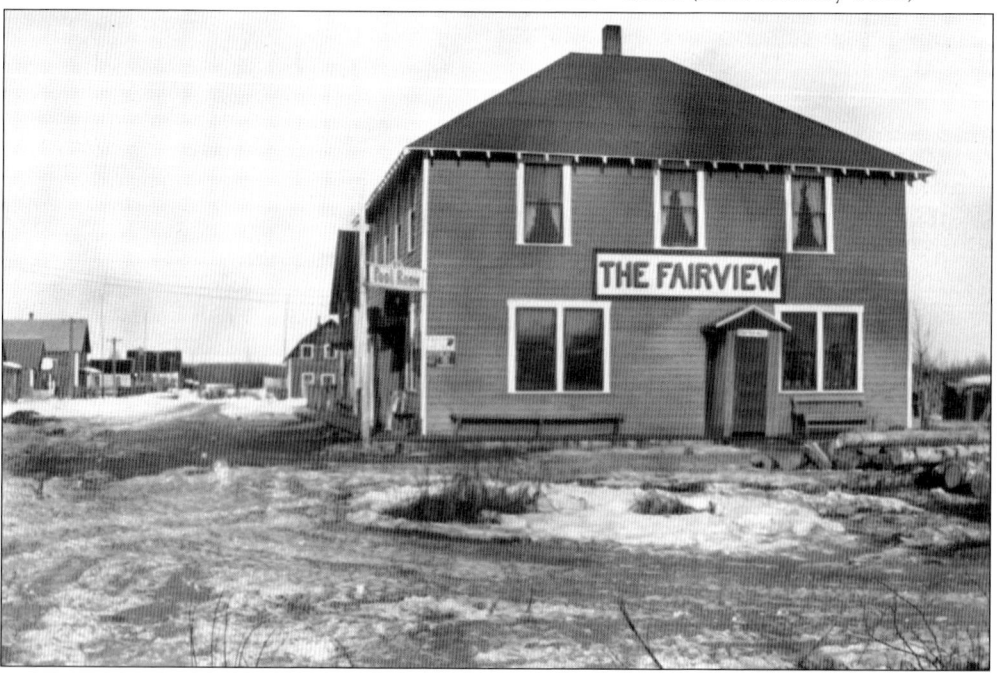

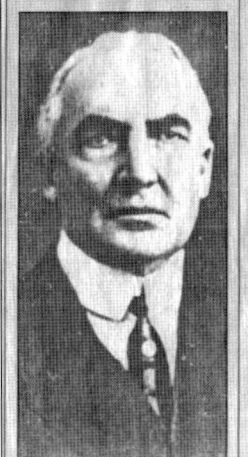

GOLDEN SPIKE. Pres. Warren Harding drove the golden spike to symbolize the completion of the Seward-Fairbanks railroad project on July 15, 1923. The *Anchorage Times* wrote, "The President took the train to Talkeetna as soon as the hammering was completed; had numerous drinks at the Fairview Inn and wound up dying three days later . . . For a long time Talkeetnans boasted that President Harding had been poisoned at the Fairview Inn . . . The consensus among many historians is that a heart attack brought on by stress resulting from the [Teapot Dome oil lease] scandal resulted in his death." (Courtesy AT.)

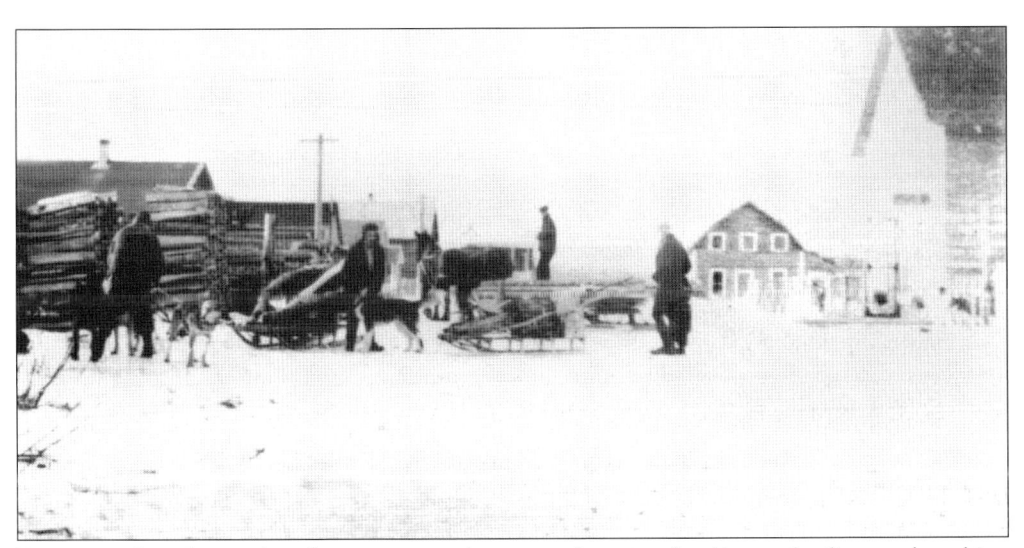

FIREWOOD. Locals were kept busy year-round cutting, chopping, hauling, unloading, and stacking wood for the Fairview Hotel. Wood was used for heating, cooking, and heating bathwater. (Courtesy THS.)

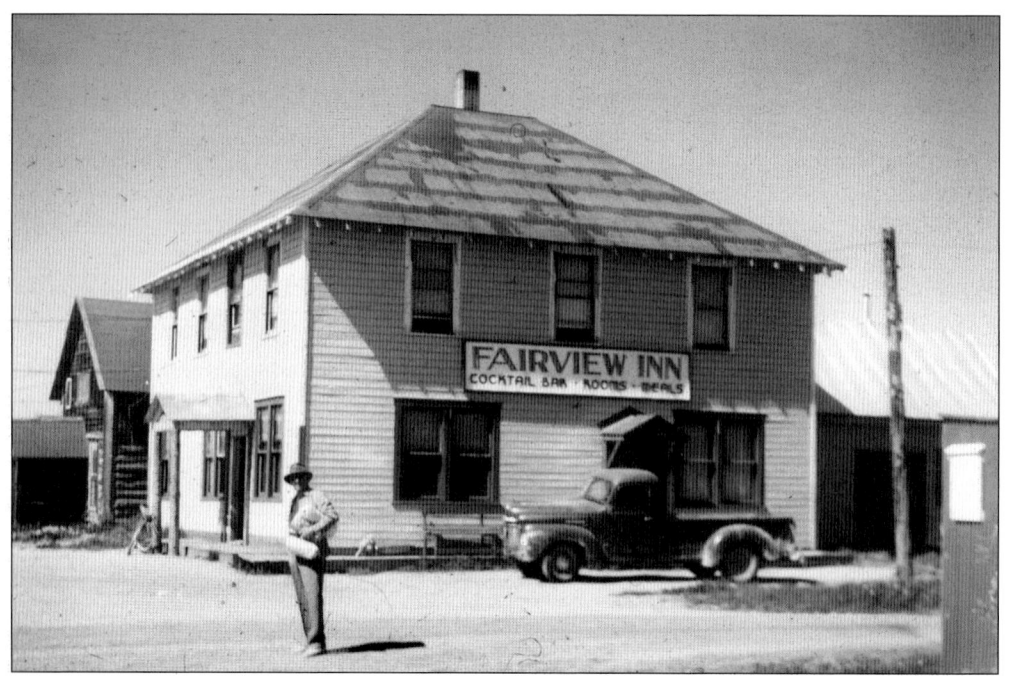

FAIRVIEW HOTEL, C. 1940S. Next door to the Fairview was the US commissioner's office and home. The US commissioner maintained vital records for Talkeetna and the surrounding area. For at least one of the US commissioners, the first stop after quitting time was the Fairview Inn. (Courtesy THS.)

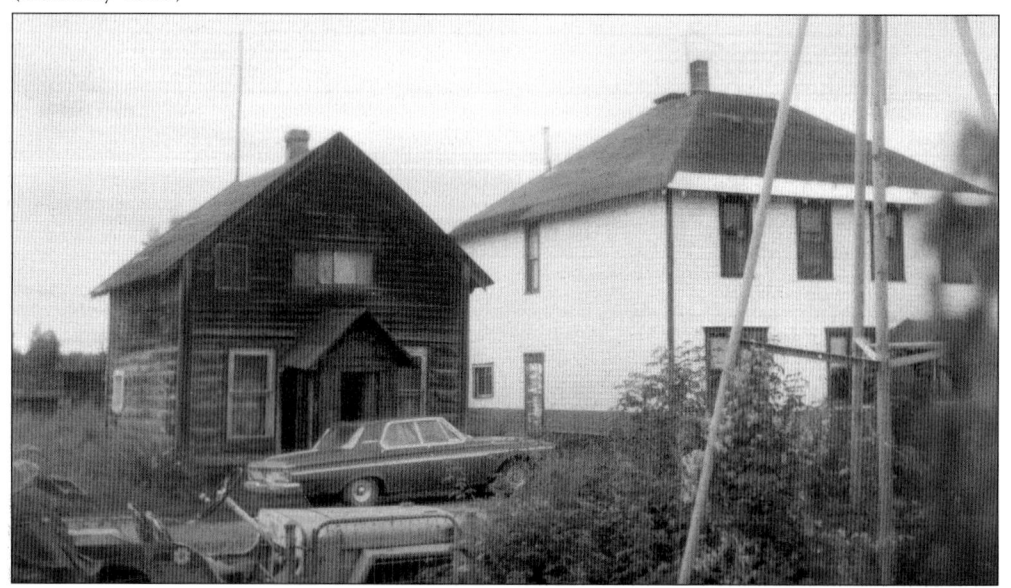

US COMMISSIONER. This 1964 photograph was taken by Roberta Sheldon from her yard, across the street from the US Commissioner Building, a key feature of Talkeetna since it was designated as the Alaska Railroad's divisional headquarters in 1916. The office was vacated in the 1950s and collapsed while being moved to another location in the 1960s. The US commissioner served as a magistrate of public records, recording mining claims, marriages, deaths, and births, among other duties. (Courtesy THS, Roberta Sheldon.)

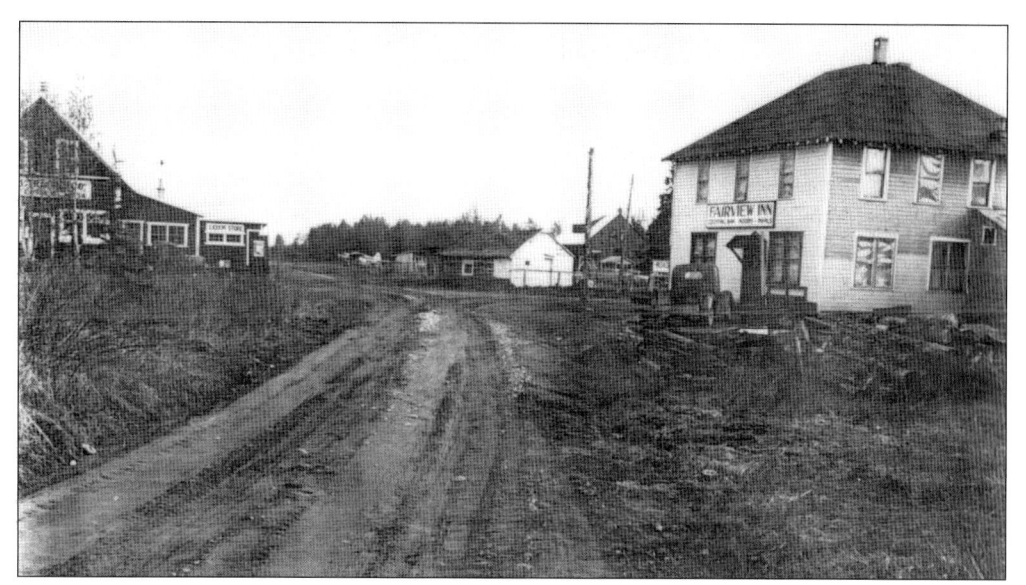

HEART OF TALKEETNA. Talkeetna has been a gathering place since the Dena'ina roamed here. The nucleus of this special place is seen here, with the Fairview Inn, Nagley's Trading Post, Talkeetna Air Service, the park, and the village airstrip, complete with one of Don Sheldon's planes. (Courtesy THS.)

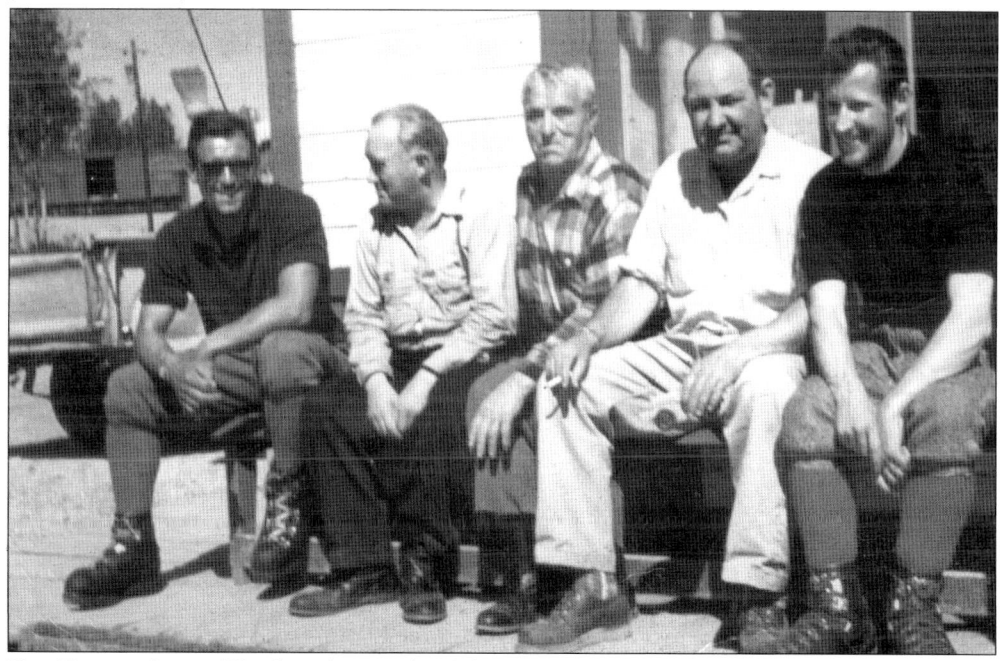

THE BENCH GANG. The bench outside of the Fairview welcomed people to gather, sit, talk, and share stories. This is one of the wonderful characteristics of Talkeetna, interesting people come here from all over the world. If they are lucky, they take away a new friendship or share a good story or laugh. This image from around 1960 is of two unidentified mountain climbers (far left and far right), wearing mountain-hiking boots, with local Talkeetnans (from left to right) Frank Moennikes, Joe Gliska, and Bill Price, an FAA employee, sandwiched in between them. (Courtesy THS.)

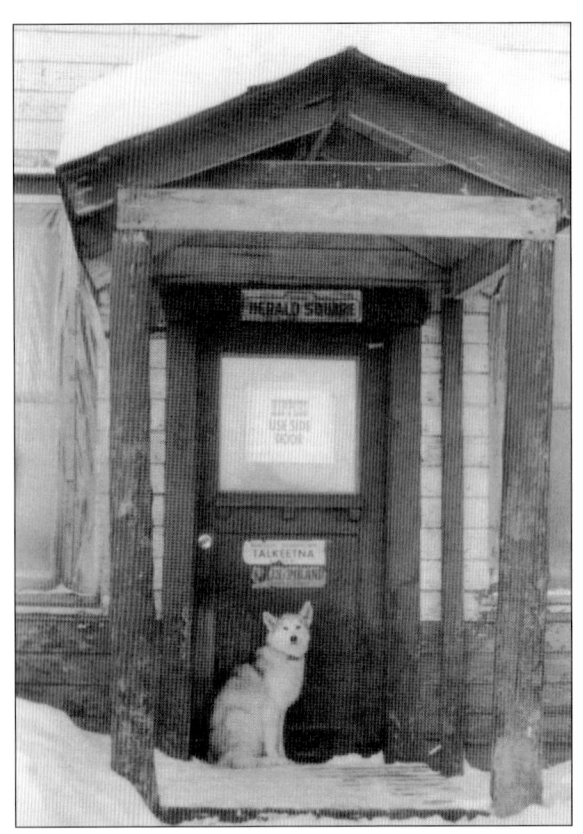

"HIPPIES USE SIDE DOOR." The 1970s brought turmoil to Talkeetna. Here, Wags, Lena Morrison's wolf dog, sits patiently at the Fairview Inn front door under the sign, "Hippies Use Side Door." The side door was kept locked and posted "closed." This tickled many of the locals, who were anything but pleased with the local impacts that the Alaska Department of Natural Resources' new homestead land program had on their village. (Courtesy THS.)

INSIDE THE FAIRVIEW. The interior of the Fairview Inn (below) remains almost unchanged: the bar, the mural of Denali painted by famous local artist Curt Wagner, the stories, the people, and perhaps most importantly, the camaraderie. The walls are decorated with images of the local cronies who spent many hours inside the Fairview. (Courtesy THS.)

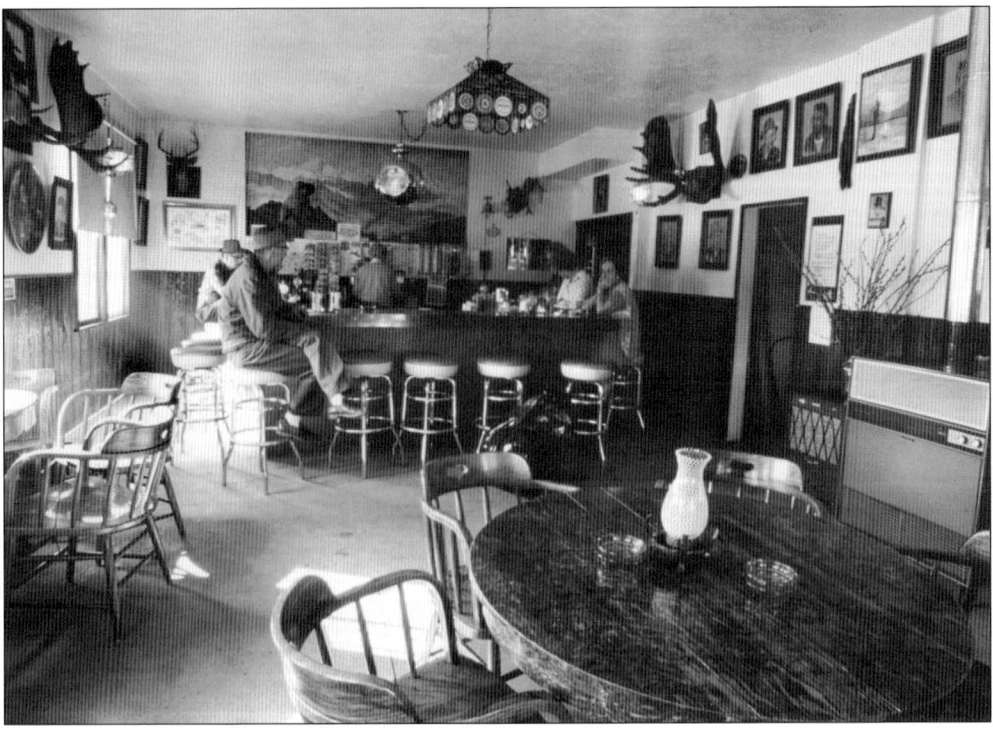

HOUSE RULES. Even in Talkeetna, there are rules. These are the Fairview Inn's house rules. In the land of the midnight sun, crowds are bigger and rowdier in the summertime. There are several weeks when it does not get dark, making it easy to lose track of time while enjoying good music, drink, and company. Last call is 3:30 a.m.—in June and July, it is still light out. (Courtesy Sisul.)

COLD, DARK, AND SNOWING. Each season in Talkeetna traditionally brings a shift of population and activities. In the long, cold, dark winters, the Fairview Inn beckons to locals and straggling visitors to gather inside. The opposite of summer, winter has just a few hours of daylight; on some stormy days in December, it barely even gets light. While the interior warmth beckons, it is also the season to view the spectacular Northern Lights. (Courtesy THS.)

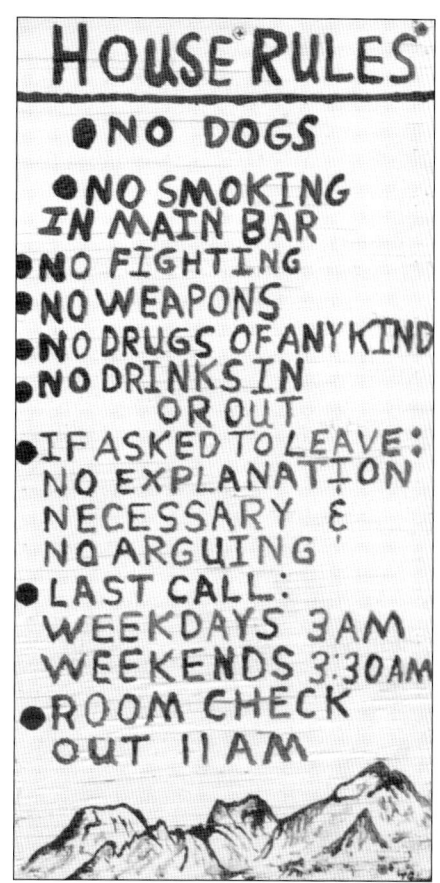

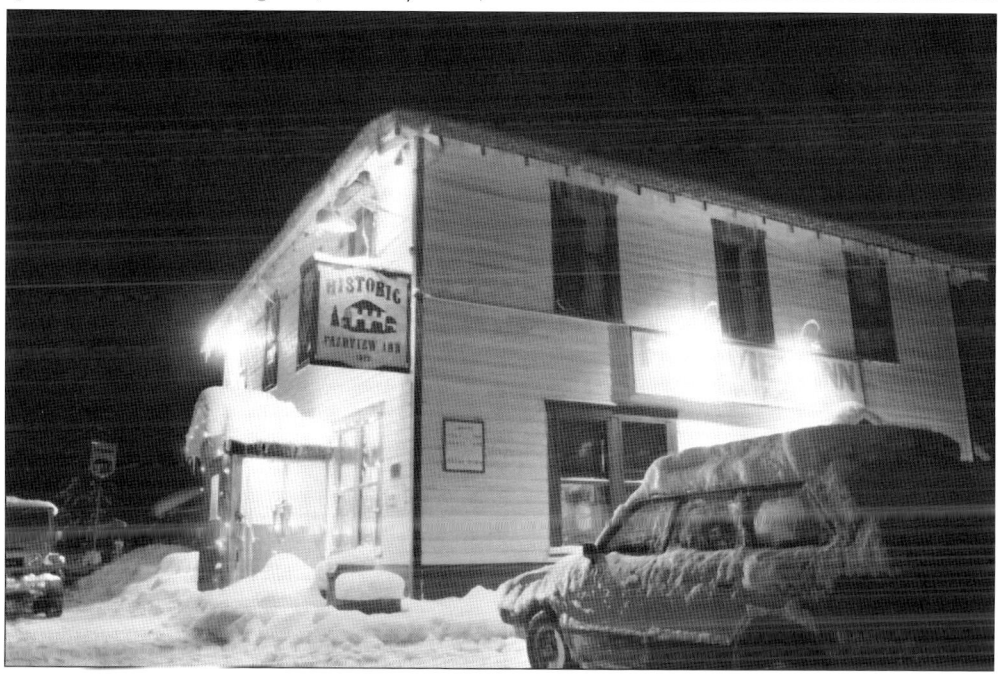

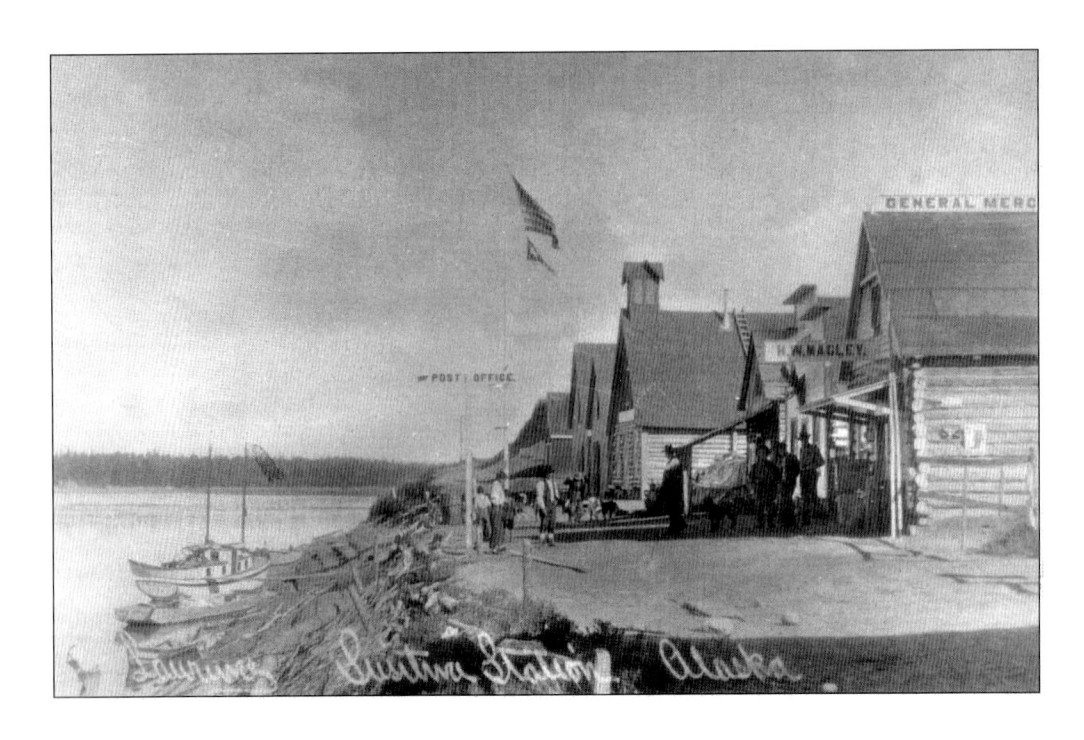

NAGLEY'S, SUSITNA STATION. Willard and Jessamine Nagley built the original log cabin–style Nagley's Trading Post at Susitna Station in 1917. Established before Anchorage, Sustina Station was located at the confluence of the Yentna and Susitna Rivers, 45 miles south of Talkeetna. A significant Susitna Valley Dena'ina village was located there, called Tsat'ukeg, or "Beneath the Big Boulder." Willard, originally from Washington, married Jessamine, a Purdue University graduate and schoolteacher, in 1912. The Nagleys had one son, Willard II. Goods were brought by boat from Anchorage along the Susitna River to Nagley's, and purchasers freighted their supplies by boat, packhorse, dog, or on foot in summer. In the winter, sleds were loaded with supplies and pulled by dogs or horses. Below, a loaded sled is hitched to 10 husky dogs. The Nagleys outfitted miners and trappers in the area. (Both courtesy Nagley's.)

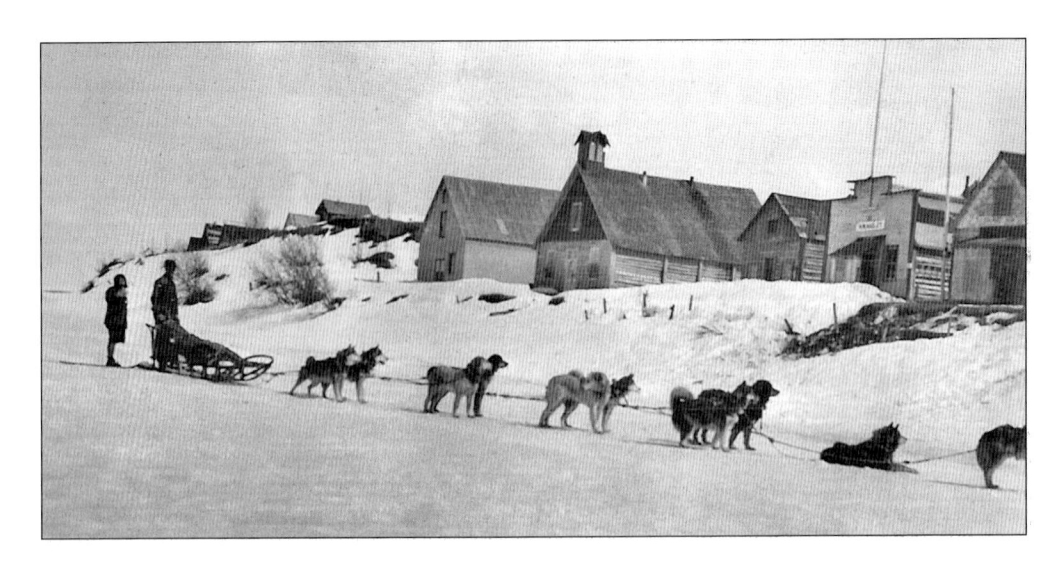

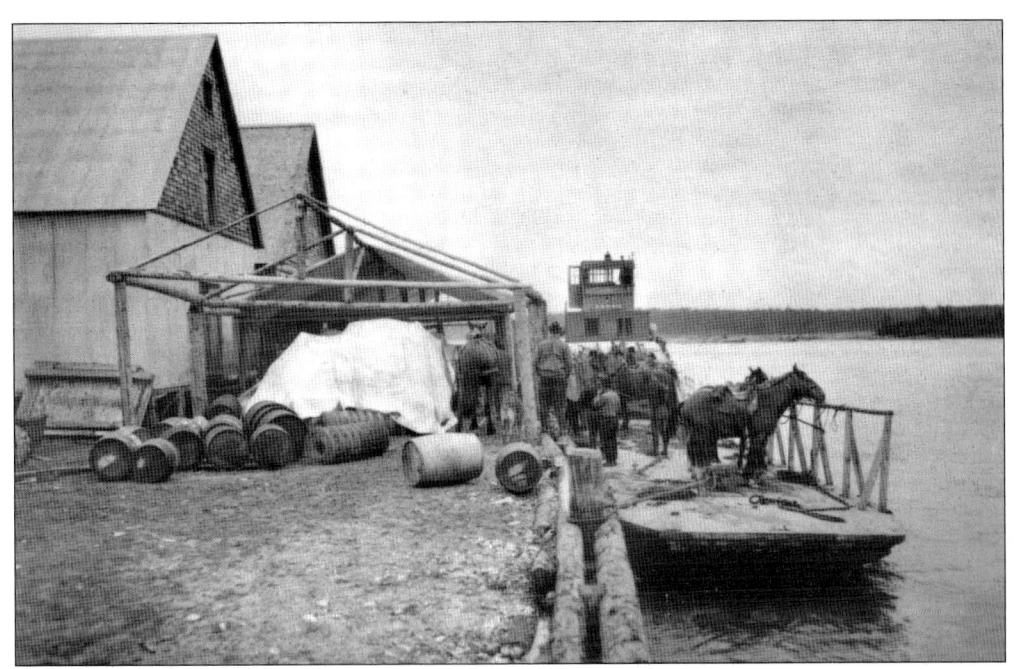

Nagley's, Talkeetna River. When Talkeetna was established as the railroad construction camp and supply point, Willard Nagley foresaw the demise of Susitna Station. He may have used the warehouses above to temporarily store his goods. In 1922, Nagley built a trading post in Talkeetna at the corner of Main and B Streets. This new location proved to be quite successful. Below, tourists from the Curry Hotel pose with some local native Alaskans in front of Nagley's in 1923. Note the distinctive windows, which are a signature feature of Nagley's. Also, note that the bark is still on the logs and that the notched corners have been covered by boards. Soon, Susitna Station was only a memory. (Above, courtesy AMHA; below, courtesy THS.)

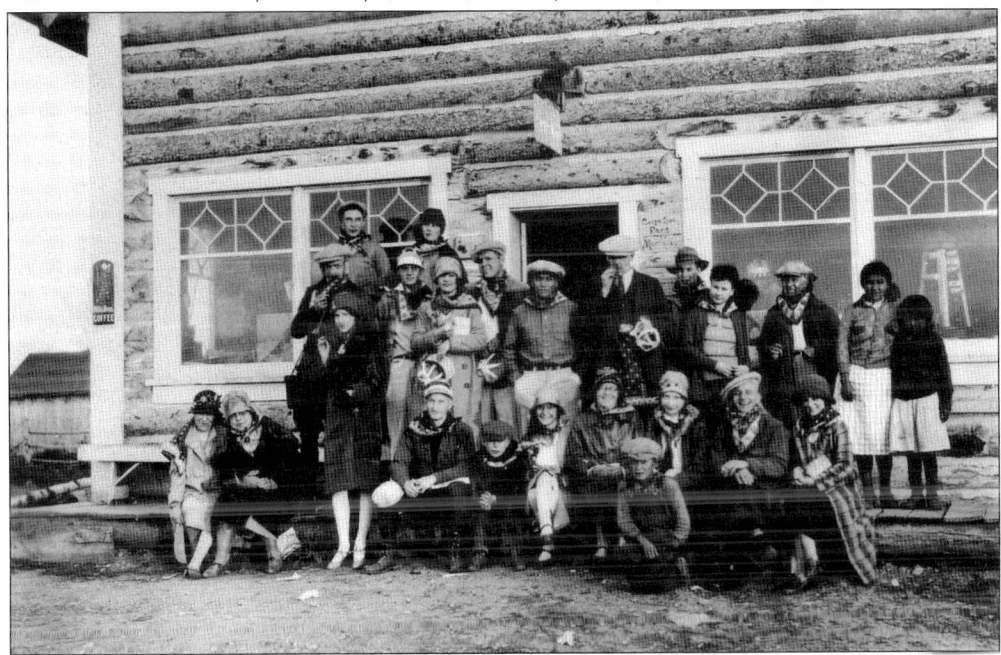

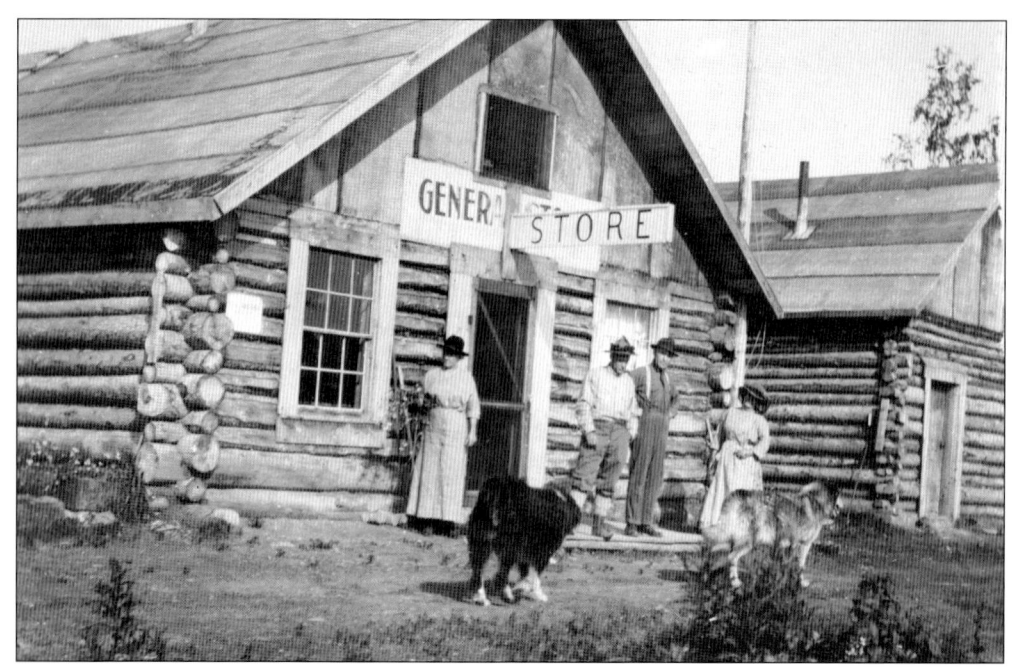

NAGLEY'S IN & OUT, 1920s. Willard and Jessamine Nagley managed their store in this log cabin, initially located near the river. The front wooden porch has long been a gathering place for locals. Above, Tom Weatherell (first male on right) is seen with other unidentified miners and women. All have mosquito netting on their hats to ward off the swarms of the vicious critters. The large dogs were used to pack supplies in the summer and to pull sleds in the winter. Below is a very early interior view of Nagley's. The counter, shelving, and front door look similar to Nagley's today. A potbelly stove, fueled by an endless supply of wood to keep the occupants warm, is also seen. (Both, courtesy UAF.)

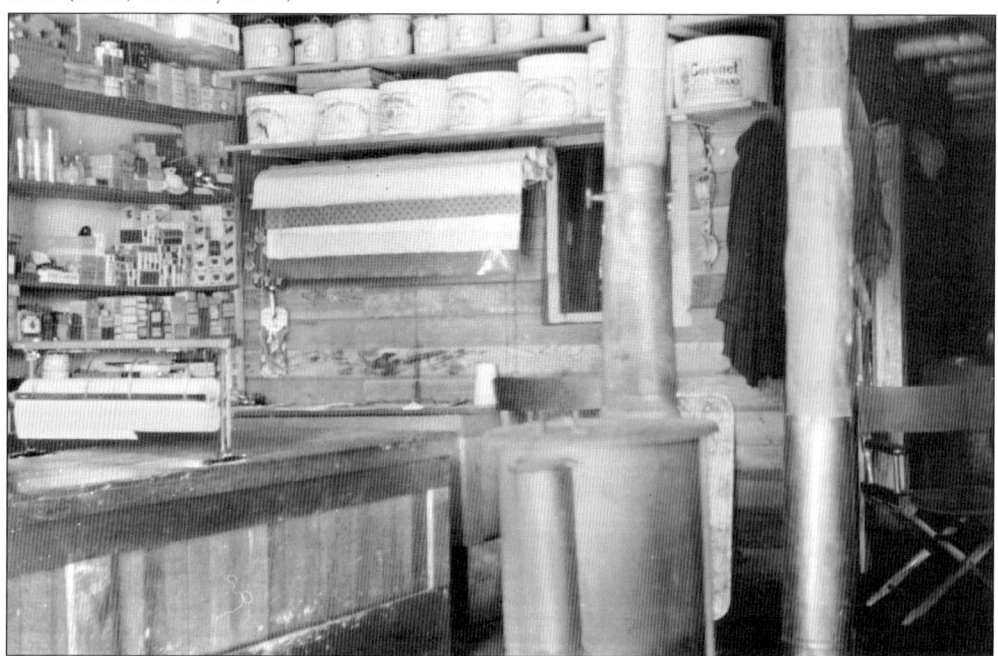

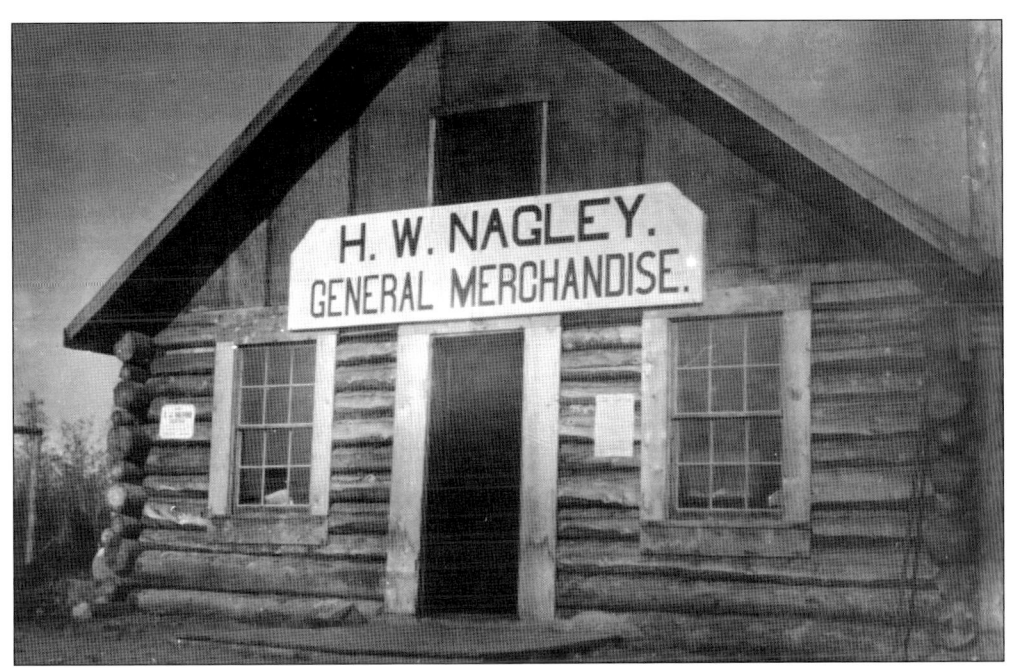

NAGLEY'S AND B&K, 1940s. As time marched on, minor changes were made to the exterior of Nagley's, while the interior remained relatively unchanged. Through the years, Nagley's outfitted a large number of trappers and miners, and often, payment was made in furs or gold dust. The image below shows Jim Beaver (left) and Don Barrett inside the building after it had been sold to Barrett & Kennedy (B&K), examining a wolf pelt in the 1940s. The shelves are stocked with a wide variety of groceries and supplies, and look much the same as they do today. Visitors to the store today notice a sign posted on the wall behind the ice cream counter that reads, "If We Ain't Got It, You Don't Need It!" (Both courtesy THS.)

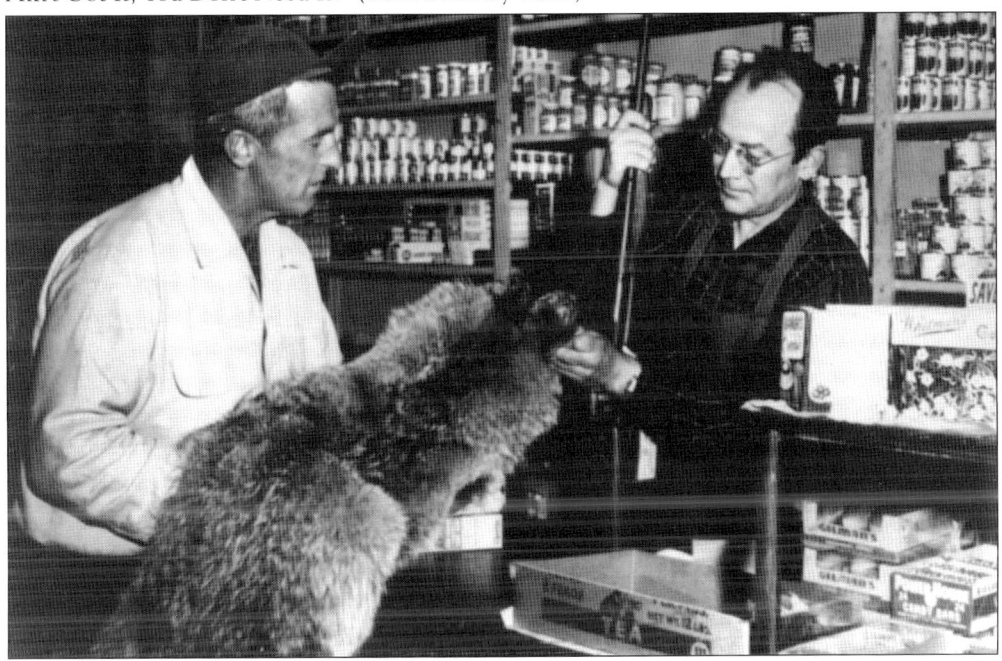

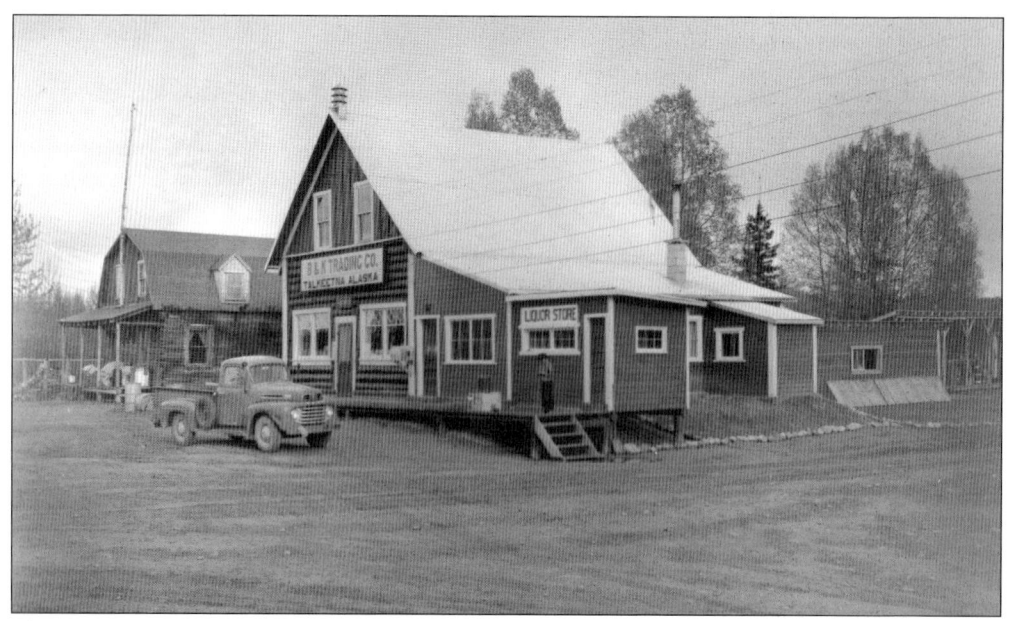

NAGLEY'S, MAIN STREET. Bank erosion and flooding along the Talkeetna River prompted Nagley to relocate his trading post in 1945. It took several days for George Weatherell and his tractor to inch the building three blocks east. The store was reportedly open for business throughout the journey. That year, Nagley sold his business to Barrett & Kennedy, who renamed the business B&K Trading Co. Beside the store is the home of pilot Glenn Hudson, the brother of Cliff Hudson, which burned in 1960. Below, Adele Shaff, a one-time owner of B&K, is seen behind the counter in the 1970s. The name of the trading post was changed back to Nagley's in 1994. A fire damaged much of the original building in 1997, but no one was injured and the original interior logs, plank floor, and overhead beam were salvaged and restored. (Both courtesy AMHA.)

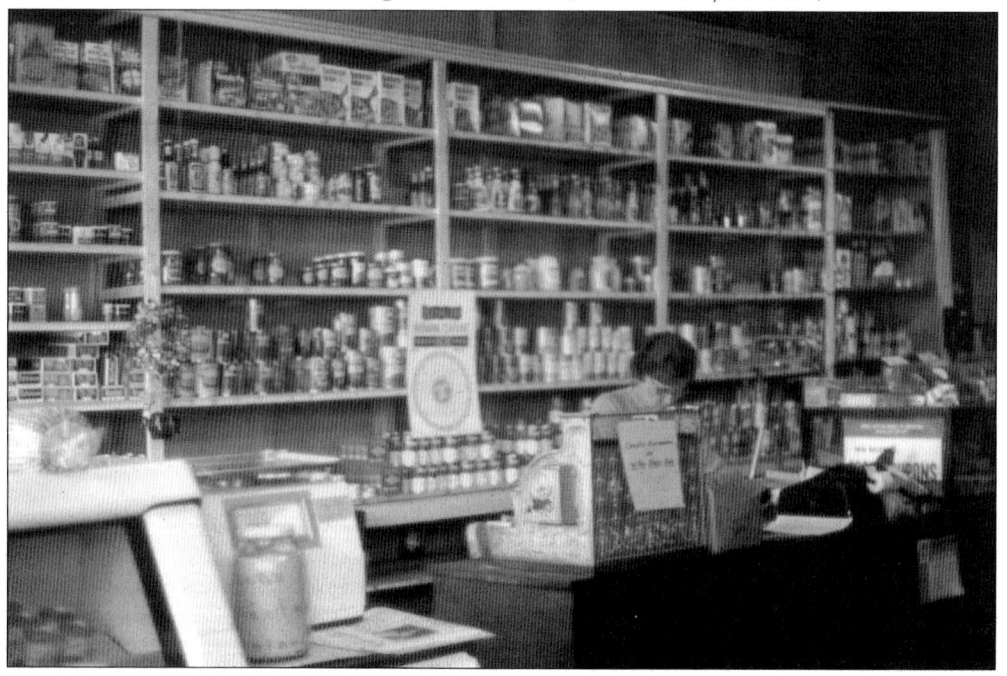

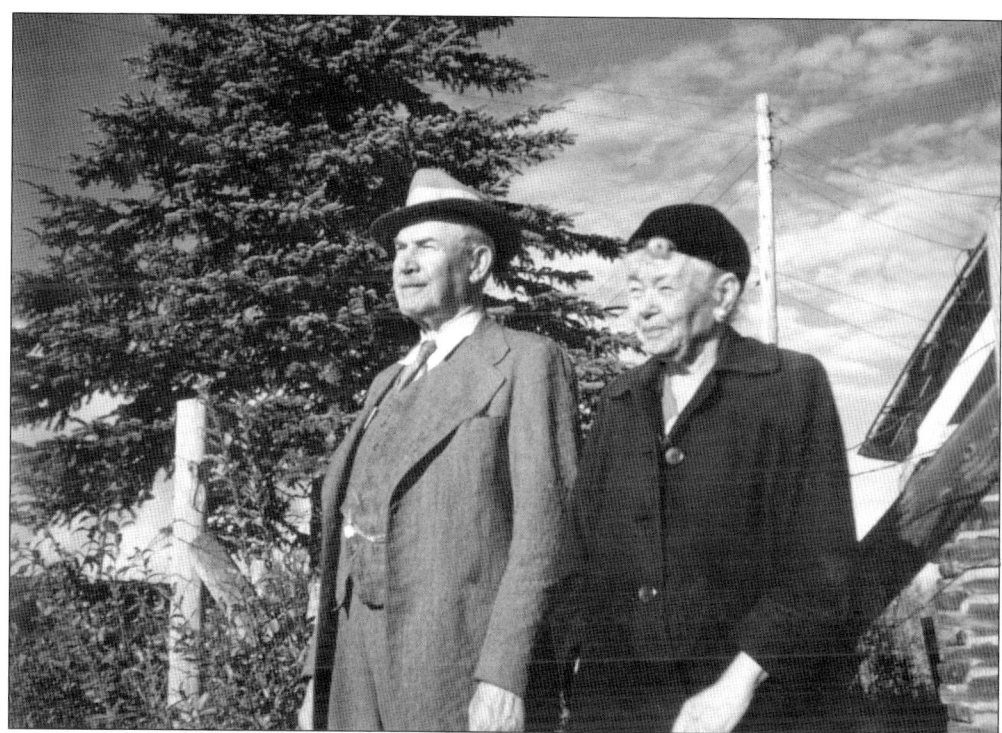

NAGLEY'S AND MAYOR STUBBS. Willard and Jessamine Nagley played a very important role in Talkeetna history. It is a tribute to their hard work and efforts that their Trading Post was the first in Talkeetna and remains the oldest operating mercantile in the village. Many people have been in and out of the trading post doors and survived in lean times because of the Nagleys. Wouldn't Willard and Jessamine be surprised to learn that Nagley's is now the host of "Mayor Stubbs" (right), who is befriended on Facebook by thousands of people around the world who follow his antics as he roams and "rules" over Talkeetna? Instant communications and the Internet are far from the remote, cold Alaska the Nagleys knew when they first opened Nagley's Trading Post in 1917. (Above, courtesy THS; right, courtesy Nagley's.)

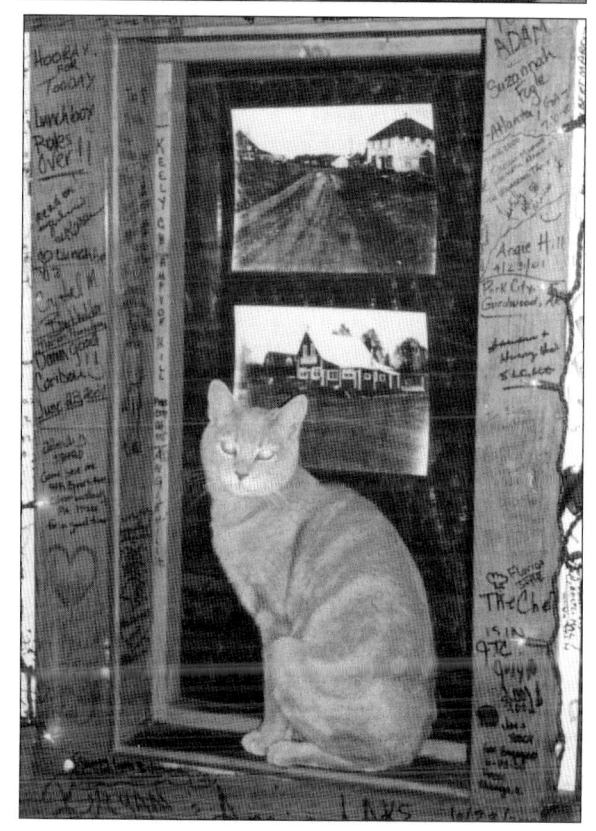

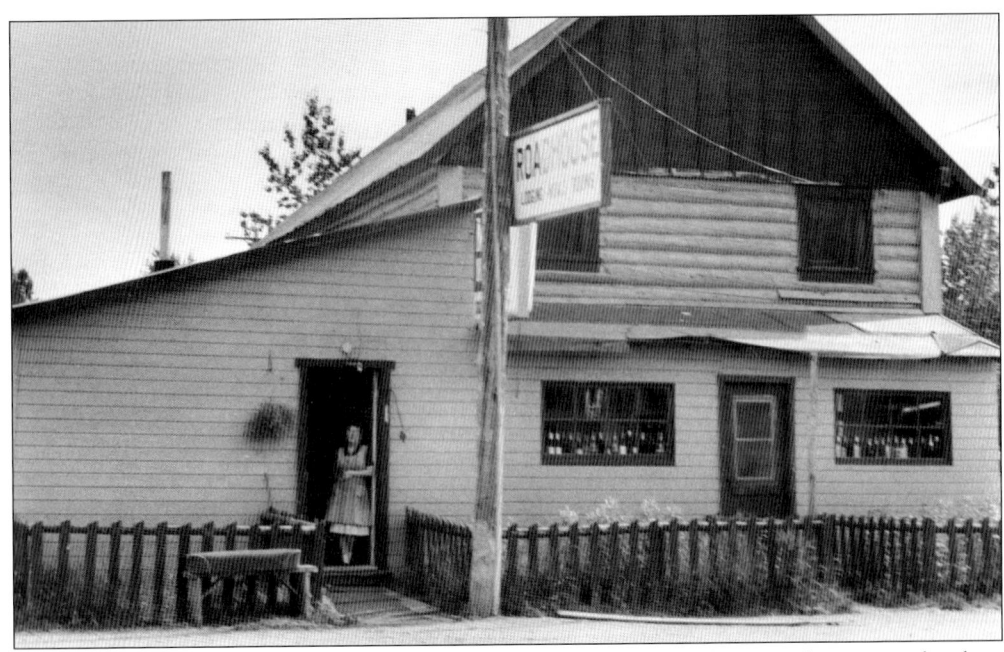

TALKEETNA ROADHOUSE. This two-and-a-half-story log building was built in 1919 by teamster brothers Frank and Ed Lee to be their private residence. It was converted into the Talkeetna Roadhouse in 1944. Carroll and Verna Close added the frame addition in 1951. (Courtesy UAA.)

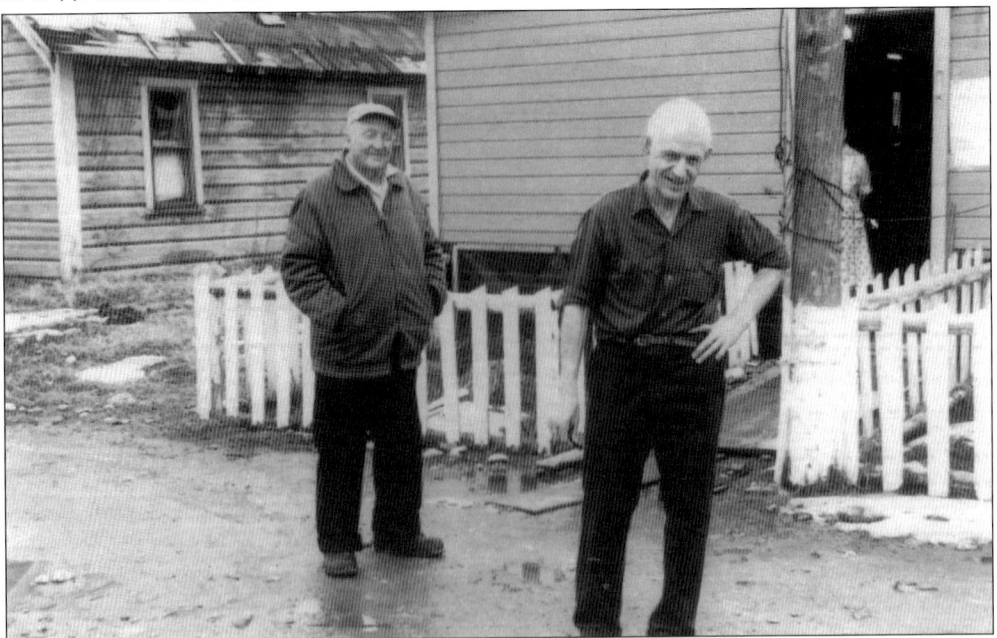

CARROLL CLOSE. Close (right), the owner of the Talkeetna Roadhouse from 1951 to 1978, and Harry Robb, a retired Yukon riverboat captain, are seen here near the front entrance of the roadhouse. Ron Garret wrote of the Closes, "Some would say Carroll and Verna Close ran a tight ship at the Roadhouse . . . Over the years they developed quite a structured manner in their operation and they generally found little reason to deviate from their normal method of operation." (Courtesy THS, Roberta Sheldon.)

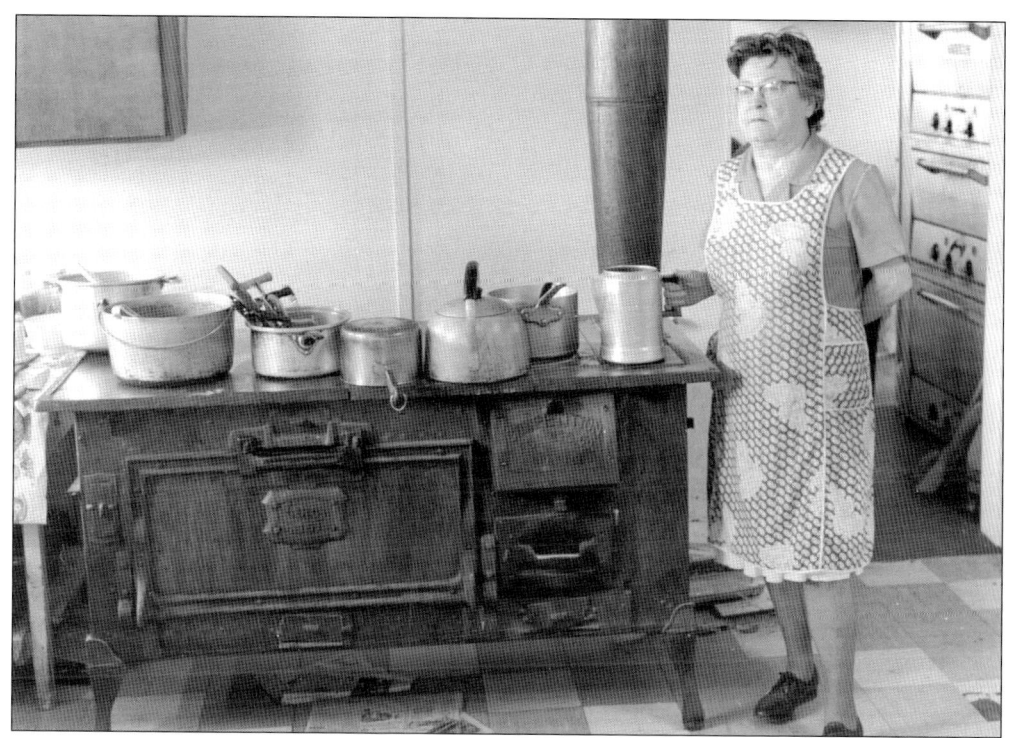

VERNA CLOSE. This signature wood-fired, cast-iron stove baked fresh bread and pies, and cooked moose stew, potatoes, and many other delicious, hearty home-cooked meals in generous servings for nearly three decades. Verna, originally from Oregon, met and married Carroll Close in Anchorage in 1946. The roadhouse served two meals a day, with dinner family-style at a long table and lunch served at the counter. (Courtesy THS.)

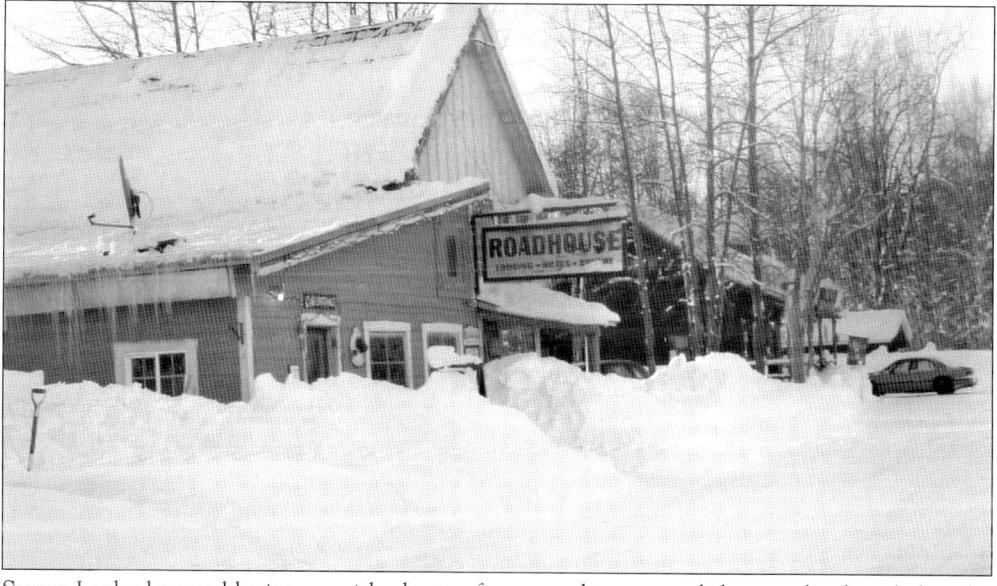

SNOW. In the long cold winters, with plenty of snow and ice, tunnels have to be shoveled to the front door for access. Plenty of wood is needed to keep the wood-burning stoves going in the frigid weather—often 30 degrees below zero— of Talkeetna's long winter months. (Courtesy Sisul.)

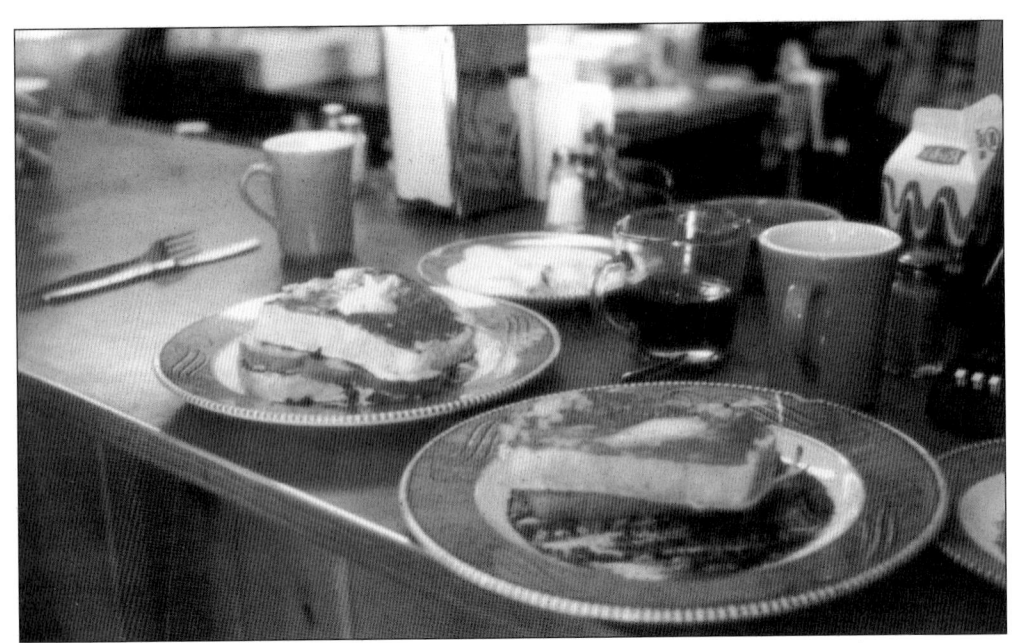

GOOD FOOD. If someone was not a guest at the roadhouse, they were required to make reservations for dinner. Carroll Close required this so that he knew how much food to prepare. Guests were told what time dinner was served, and if they were late, they would miss dinner. The roadhouse has always been well known for serving generous servings of delicious home-cooked food. In the 1970s, French toast and scrambled eggs were popular; more recently, sourdough pancakes and omelets are favorites. Today, guests order their meals like in a regular restaurant, with choices of half or full portions—a full portion omelet has six eggs. Meals are still served at long tables, which encourage strangers to interact. Meeting people from around the world is part of the fun of eating at the roadhouse in the summertime. (Both courtesy THS.)

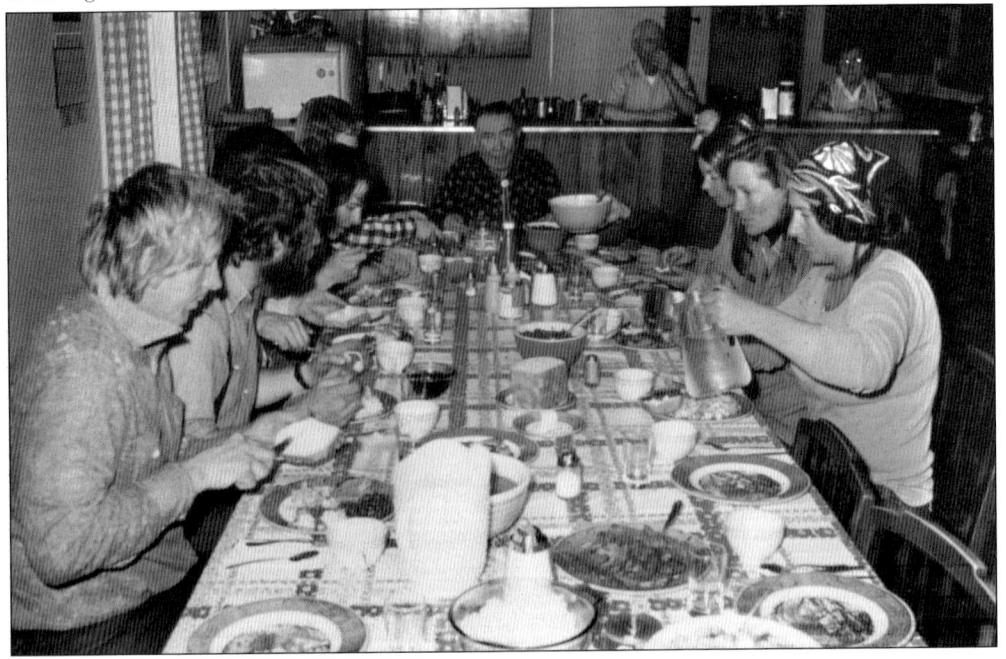

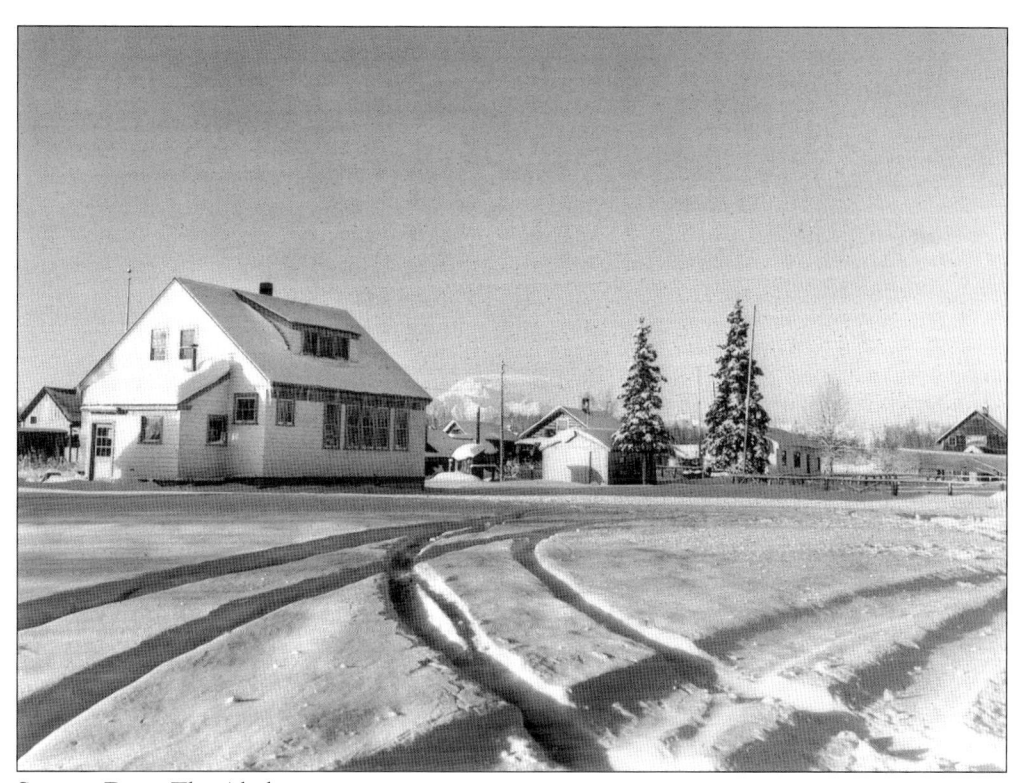

SCHOOL DAYS. The Alaska Railroad Commission reserved a school site in 1919, but Talkeetna did not have a teacher and one-room schoolhouse until the 1936–1937 school year. Prior to that, children were homeschooled, attended classes at the roadhouse, went to boarding school, or did not go to school. Above, the original white schoolhouse sits in a beautiful snow-covered landscape with Denali (Mount McKinley) in the background. The first kindergarten through eighth-grade class, at right, had 12 students: From left to right are (first row) Johnny Sherward, Georgia Poggas, and Betty Mayfield; (second row) Happy Nicoli, Turpi Nicoli, Jimmy Poggas, and Daisy Sherward; (third row) Eleanor Trepte, Lillian Sherward, Mable Sherward, and Nellie Martin. Their teacher was Ben Morian. (Both courtesy THS.)

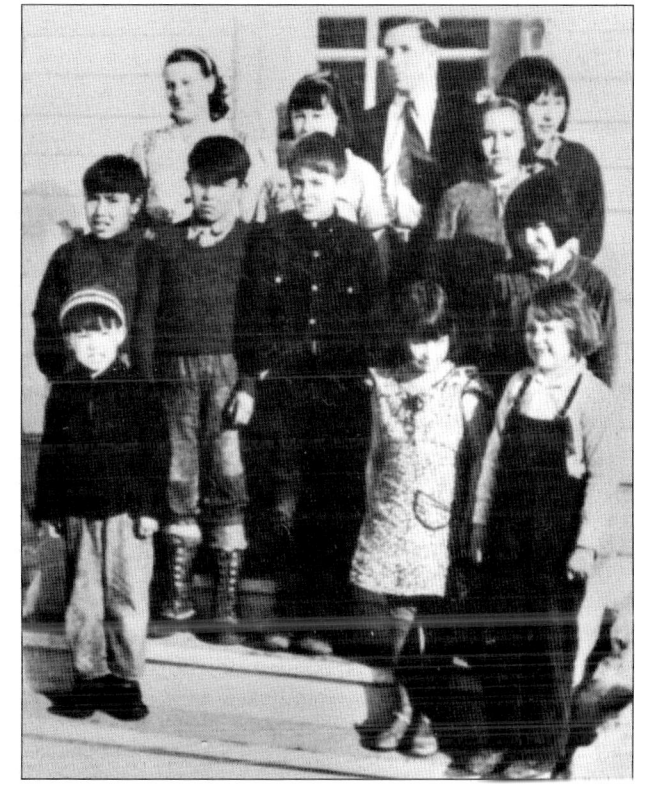

77

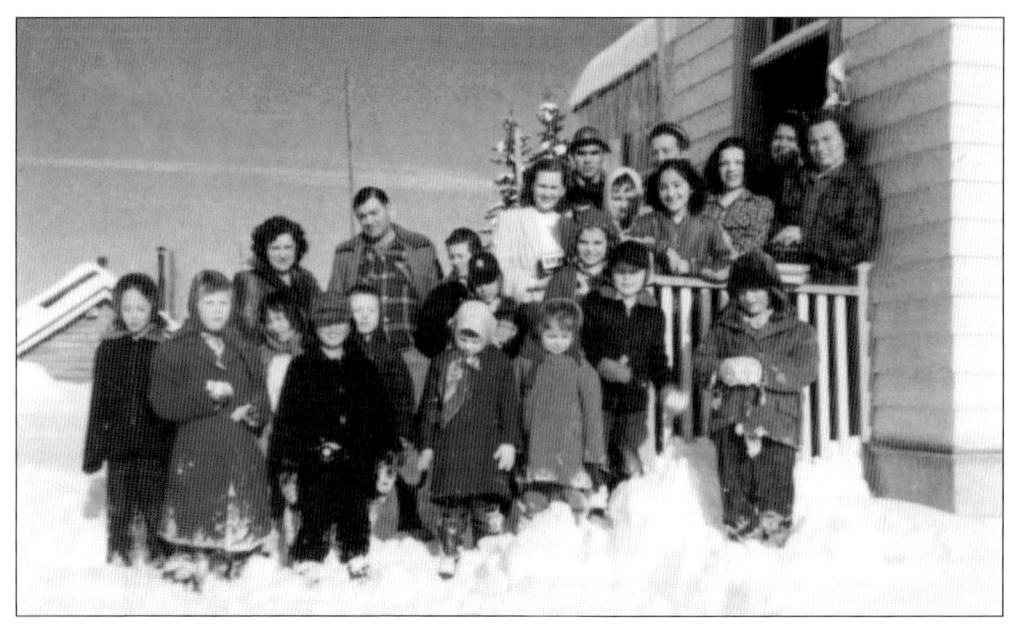

INSIDE AND OUT. Above, the students standing at the side-door amidst several feet of snow include, in no particular order, Sally ?, Neil Glenn, Ricky Heigh, Alan Beyer, Arthur Slaloah, Yvonne Cutler, Bettie Cutlee, Rhoda Beyer, Wanda Beyer, Gerald Nickoli, Karen Cutlee, Gary Beyer, Mark Hamblin, Mary Ann Dahl, Bryson ?, and Ferne ? The photograph was taken the week of May 4, 1953. Below is the layout of the standard one-room schoolhouse common across the United States. A potbellied stove provided heat to the classroom, study room, and cloakroom, and there was an outhouse nearby. The teacher lived upstairs in an apartment. (Both courtesy THS.)

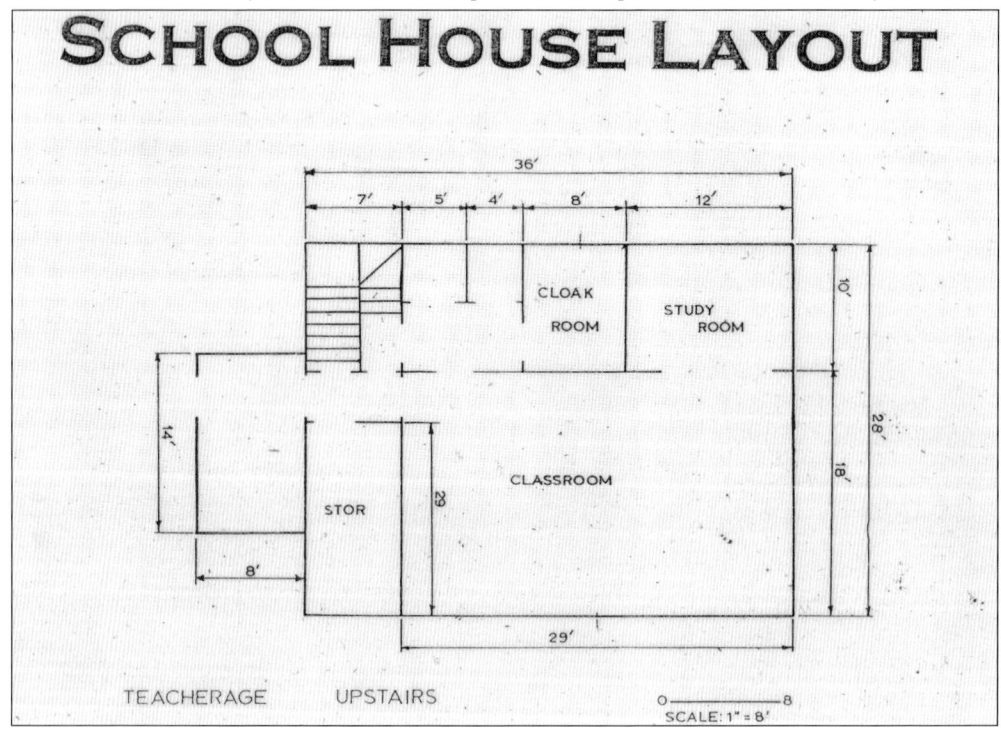

MAKING THE GRADE. The dreaded report card had its presence in Talkeetna. Seen above is the report card of Pat Beaver when she was a first-grader at Charles Lucier's one-room schoolhouse in the 1954–1955 school year. Beaver passed into second grade for the next school year; however, her first-grade year ended abruptly when the schoolmaster left his post, citing safety concerns. Pilots often warmed up their planes in the schoolyard, offering students little protection from whirling propellers. The one-room schoolhouse below closed in 1971, when a new elementary school opened in Talkeetna. This schoolhouse became the Talkeetna Historical Society in 1974. The Pelton wheel from Cache Creek is seen on the left. (Both courtesy THS.)

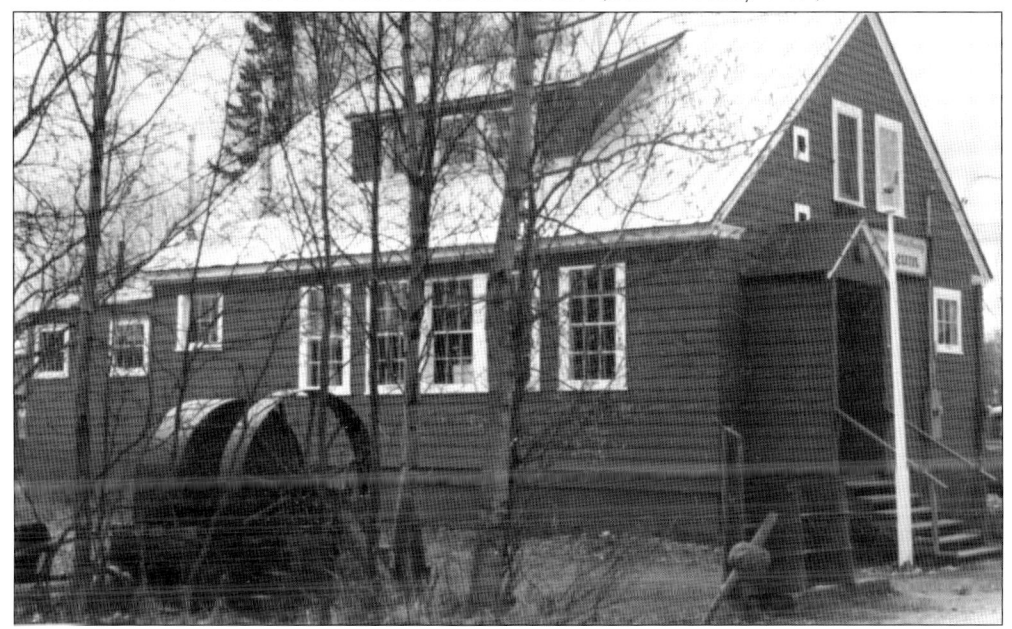

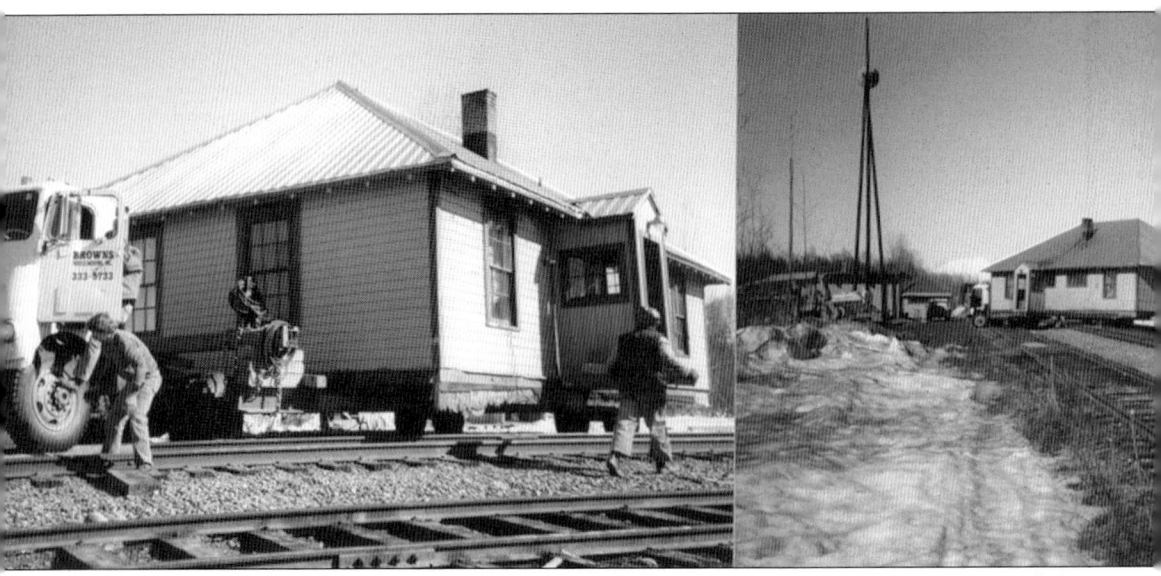

ON THE MOVE. In 1987, the Talkeetna Historical Society saved both the freight depot and the section house, or crew bunkhouse, from demolition. The buildings were moved from their original 1923 location via a moving trailer, which slowly worked its way through town and placed the

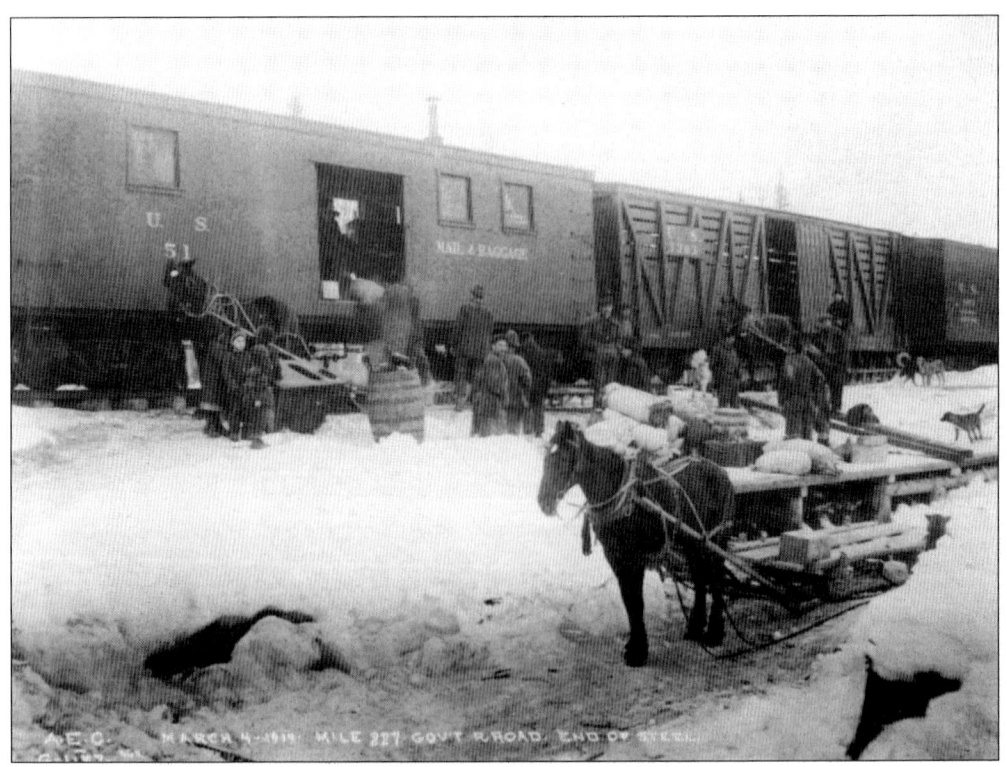

MILEPOST 227. The Alaska Railroad served as a lifeline to Talkeetna, located at milepost 227 of the 450-mile Seward-to-Fairbanks railroad system. Food, supplies, equipment, people, and news were all transported on this flag line. Supplies were moved from the train to the various trading posts in town via horse or dog sleds in the winter and wagons in the summer. (Courtesy THS.)

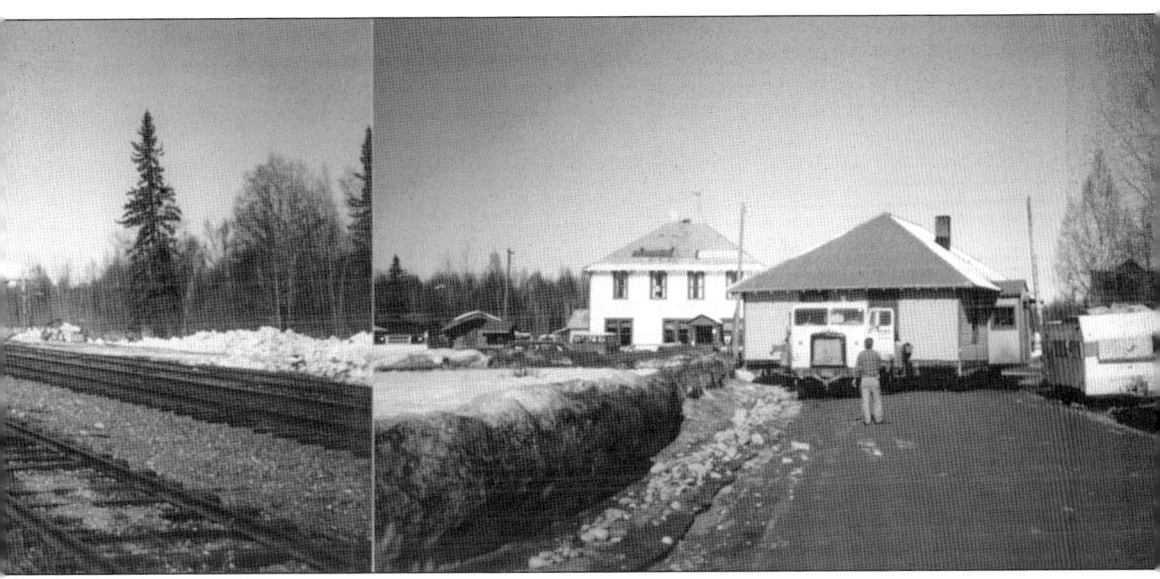

building behind the old Talkeetna one-room schoolhouse. These buildings now house the historical society's mountaineering, mining, and railroad exhibits. (Courtesy THS.)

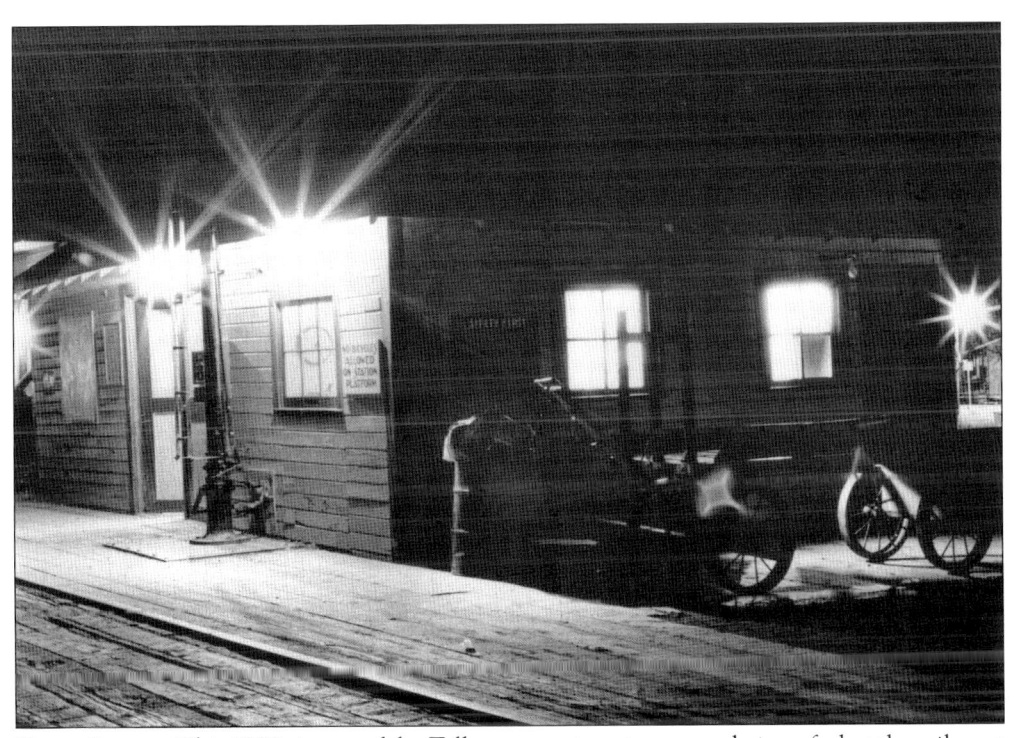

NIGHT LIGHTS. This 1980s image of the Talkeetna station gives a good view of what the milepost 227 railroad station looked like, with its wooden platform. In the dead of winter, darkness descends early on Talkeetna. (Courtesy THS.)

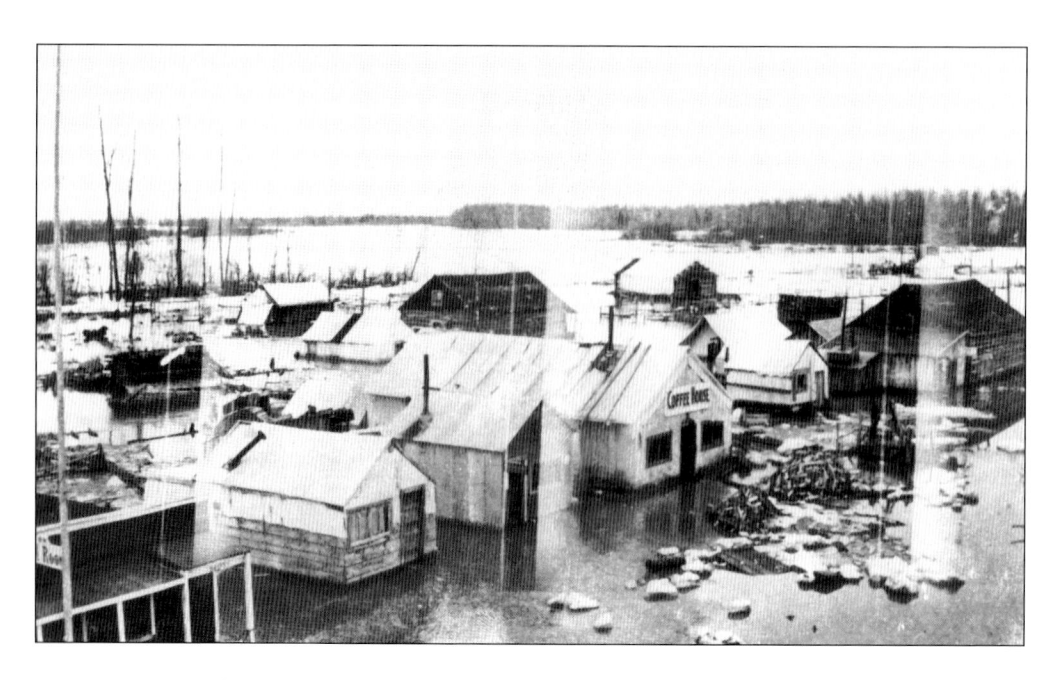

1949 Flood. Each spring, the breakup of the frozen river signals the joy of a new season and the threat of flooding. Significant flooding is not unusual, as the wild Talkeetna and Chulitna Rivers merge and meander as the Susitna River to the sea. The flood of 1949 was the result of an exceptionally wild year. More than 12 acres of the village along the Talkeetna River were washed away. The entire village flooded—a lot. A significant portion of the original Main Street was lost in the flood. The Alaskan Engineering Commission investigated and recommended that the river be allowed to revert to its normal meandering floodplain condition. Several buildings located near the river, including Nagley's, were moved farther inland as a result of this flood. Fortunately, there were no fatalities. (Both courtesy THS.)

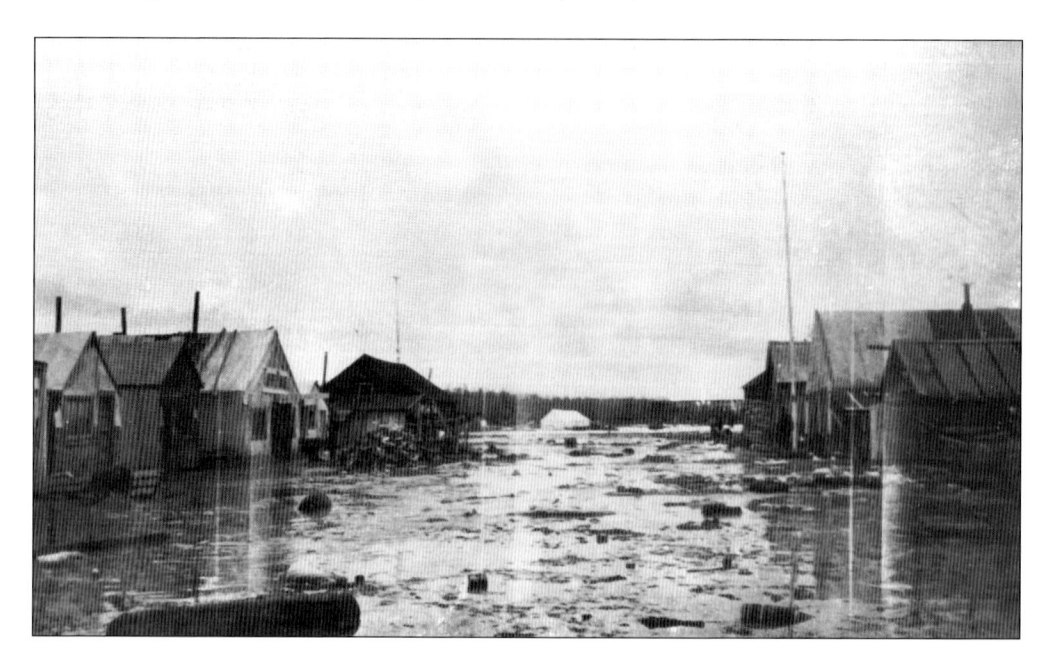

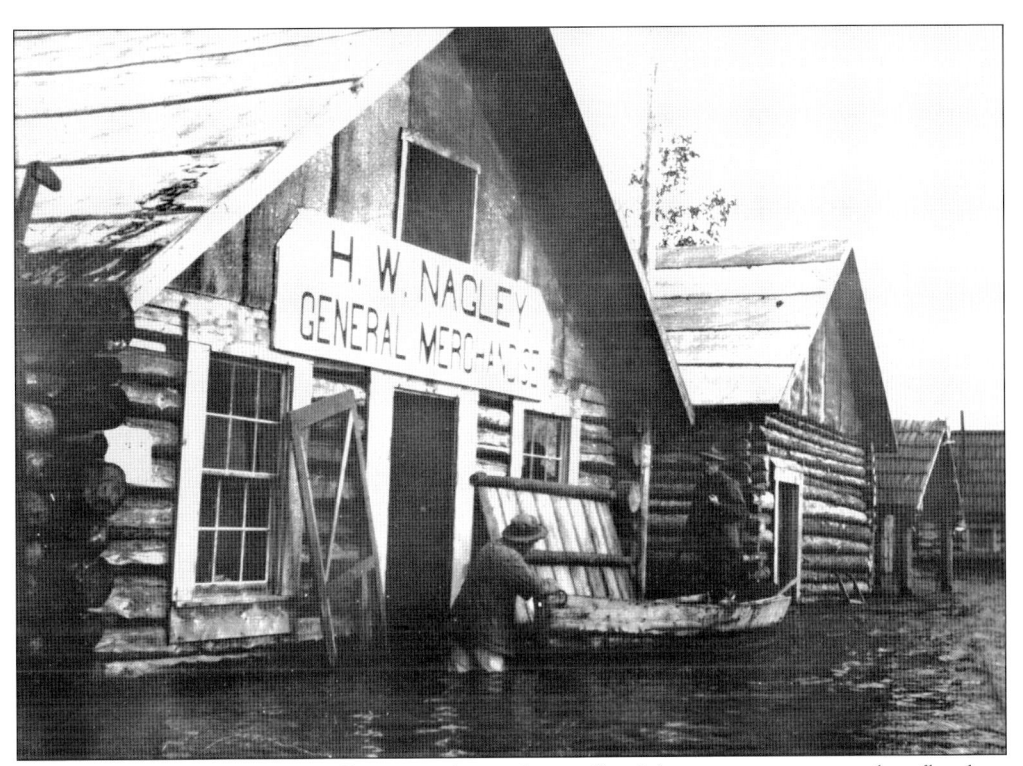

Canoeing in Floodwater. Talkeetna is located on a floodplain, so it is expected to flood on occasion. Above, the water was thigh-high in front of Nagley's in 1930. Eventually, the water from that flood receded. Flooding has occurred in recent years, but not as severely as in earlier years. The image below from around 2000, showing Mike Fisher in his canoe, illustrates the ongoing threat of flooding, especially when heavy rains combine with spring breakup. (Above, courtesy UAF; below, courtesy Pat Beaver Pratt.)

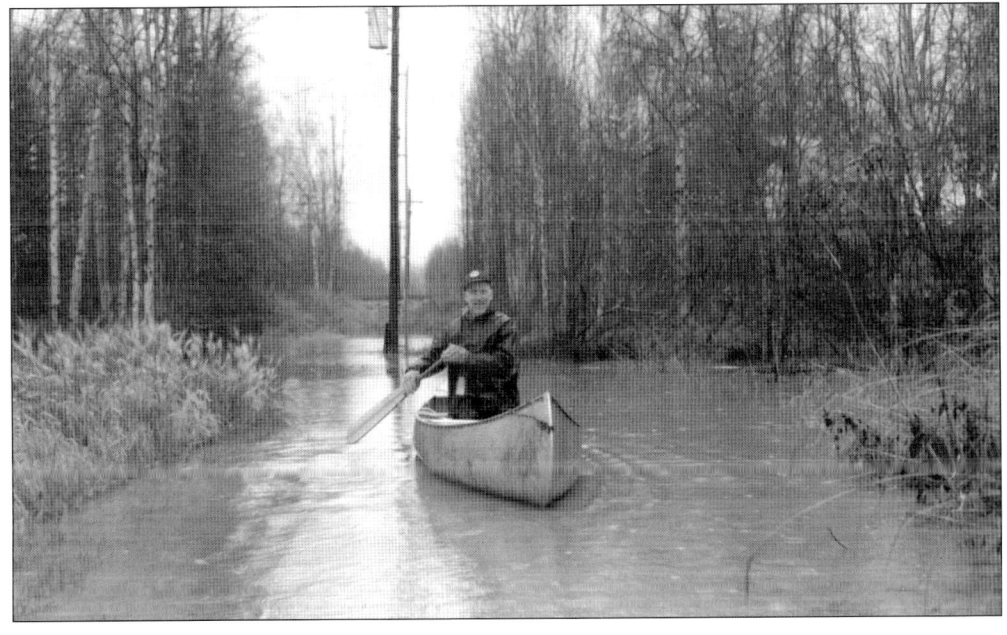

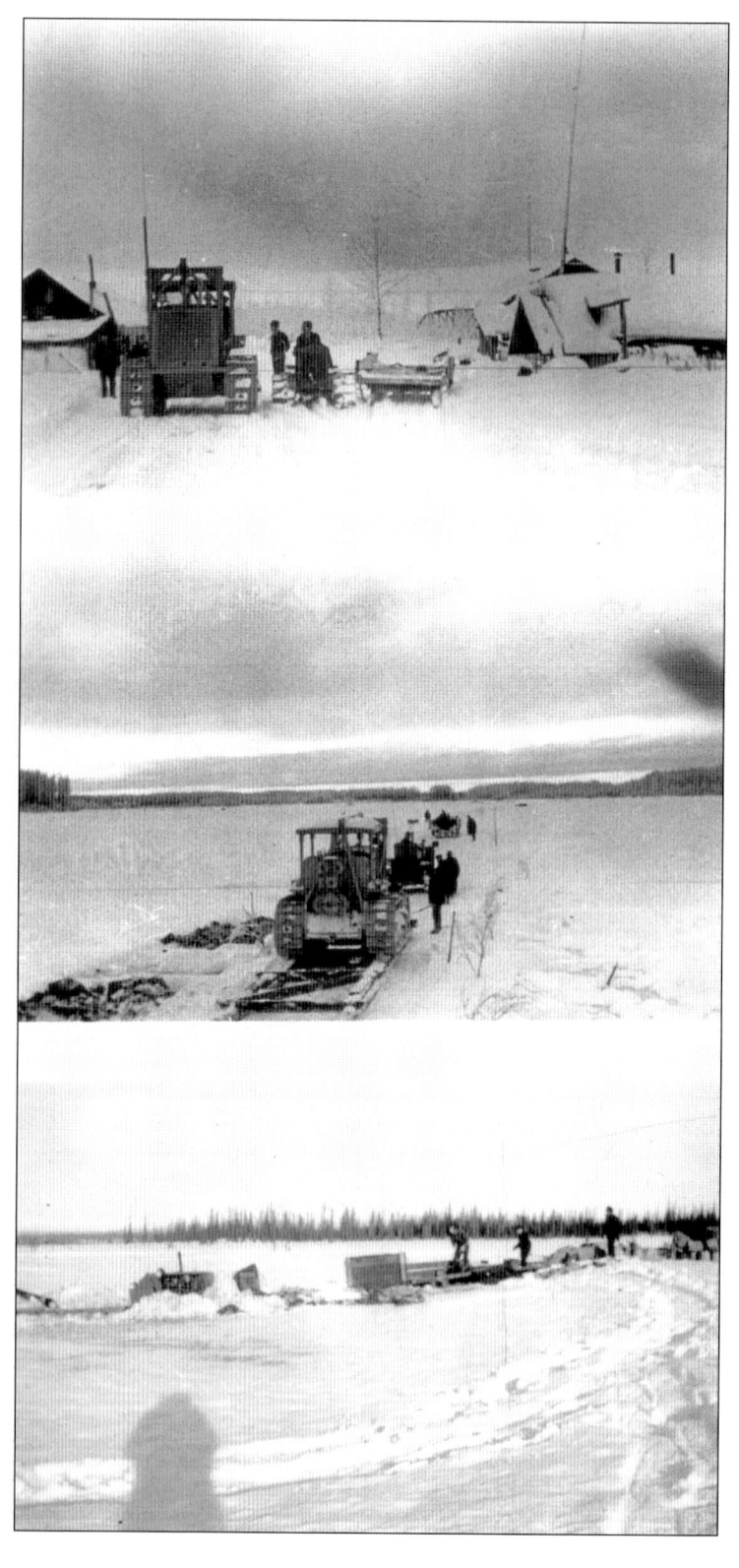

GOING, GOING, GONE. Freighting supplies from Talkeetna to the remote wilderness where miners and trappers needed them has always been difficult, challenging, and expensive. These images, taken by Tom Weatherell around 1940, show the shift from horse or dog sledges to the mechanical cat. The cat moved through Talkeetna's Main Street, heading toward the frozen Talkeetna River. Unfortunately, the weight of this cat and the supplies proved too much for the ice conditions, and the whole thing broke through the ice and plunged into the frigid waters below. The lowest image shows Talkeetnans salvaging the supplies from the icy fingers of the Talkeetna River. (Courtesy UAF.)

Five

BUSH PILOTS

The introduction of airplanes and Alaskan bush pilots is probably one of the most significant events that shaped Talkeetna, especially after the 1940s. Prior to that time, rivers, railroads, and trails were the primary mode of transportation over the very rugged terrain, as there were no roads from Anchorage to Talkeetna until the mid-1960s. During World War II, bush pilots provided a critical link to the outside world for Talkeetna. Bush pilots provided air transportation to remote areas of Alaska that were not easily accessible. Bush pilots in the Talkeetna area also helped pioneer and shape the emerging bush aviation industry after World War II.

Bush pilots opened up the landscape by immensely improving the transport of people, mail, and supplies. Cliff Hudson's slogan was "Fly an Hour or Walk a Week." Walking through bear-filled and mosquito-infested tundra and forests, across rivers and mountains, was no easy task.

Perhaps the most important innovation for the Talkeetna bush pilots was the introduction of glacial landings: airplanes outfitted with skis to enable landings and takeoffs on the glaciers of the Alaska Range. Ski-landing gear was experimented with in the 1930s by the famous Bob Reeve in Valdez. Talkeetna's legendary Don Sheldon pioneered glacial landings, initially with stationary skis and later with retractable ski-landing gear. Sheldon and Bradford Washburn, of *National Geographic* and Boston's Museum of Science, partnered together over a 10-year period to produce the first topographic maps of Denali, which are still used today by many climbers planning their ascent of North America's tallest peak. A scale version of their topographic map is on display in the mountaineering exhibit at the Talkeetna Historical Society, which is maintained by the Talkeetna National Park Service.

Today, bush pilots still play the same vital role for recreation, transportation, and rescue. Each year, the National Park Service awards contracts to qualified air services stationed in Talkeetna, who provide air-taxi services for thousands of climbers and tourists to flight-see or make glacial landings at base camp in the Denali National Park and Preserve.

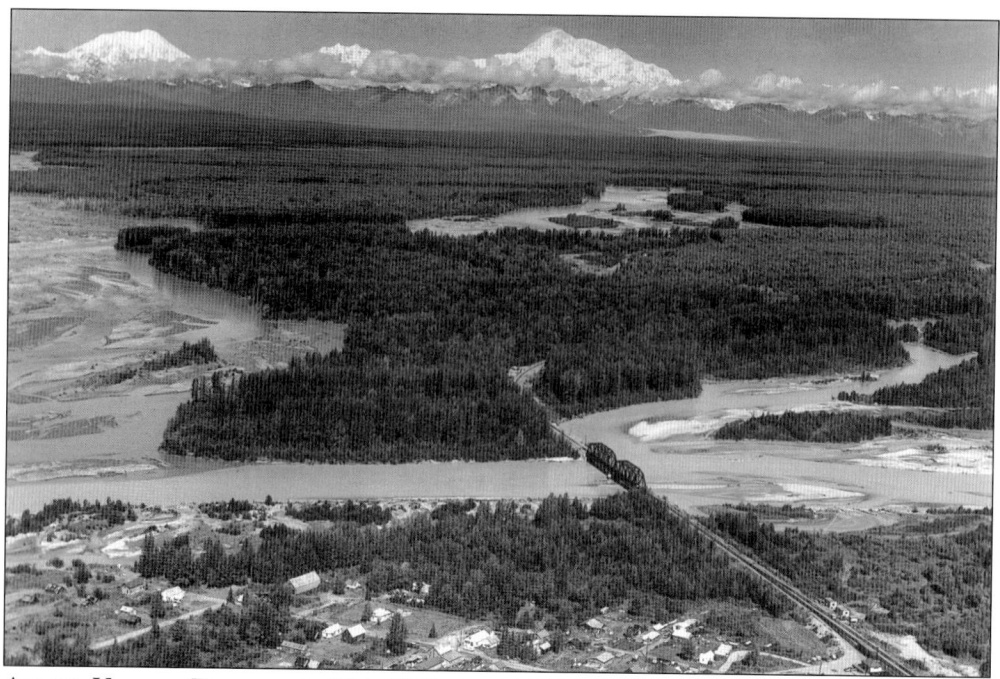

AERIAL VIEW OF TALKEETNA. This 1960s aerial photograph provides a snapshot in time of Talkeetna, showing the village airstrip (lower center), the Alaska Railroad Bridge, the confluence of the Susitna, and Talkeetna Rivers, and the ever-present Denali 60 air miles away. (Courtesy THS, BMS.)

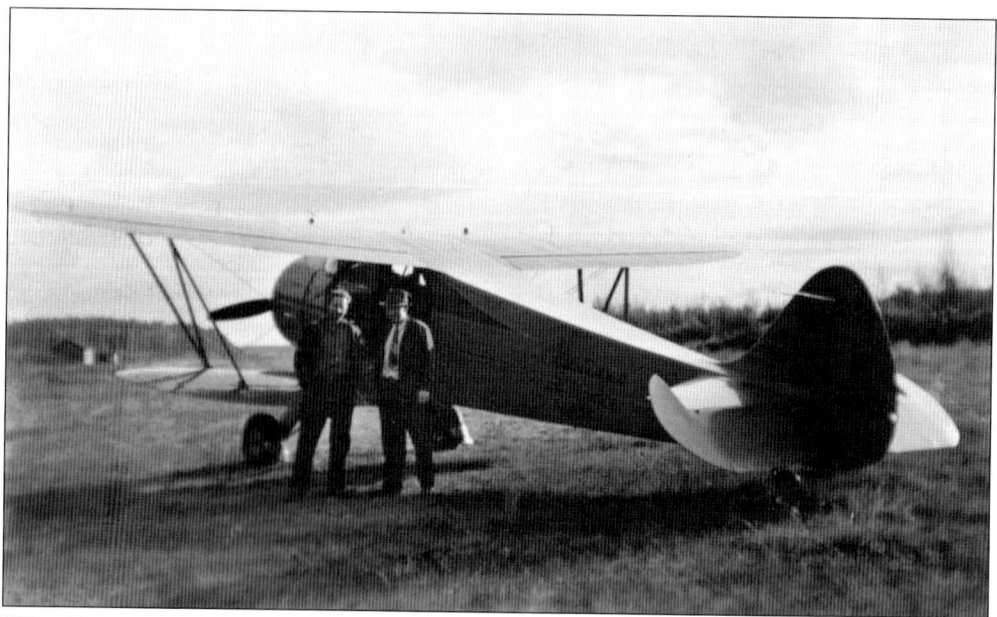

"THE FLYING DANE." Haakon "Chris" Christenson, born in Denmark in 1902, immigrated to America and pioneered air service to miners outside the Talkeetna area. He flew a bright-red Grumman Widgeon and a Waco aircraft. He was one of the first pilots to make glacier landings and bring supplies to miners. Sadly, he was killed in a plane crash in a snowstorm while en route from Seattle to Cordova in 1956. (Courtesy Eleanor Trepte.)

FLY AN HOUR OR WALK A WEEK serving Kantishna mining district

FLY AN HOUR. This 1940s slogan coined by an unknown pilot in the Kantishna mining area sums up the value of traveling by airplane. Originally developed to serve miners and trappers, bush piloting soon expanded to include fishing, hunting, and mountaineering trips. For many bush pilots, when not flying, fishing was a favorite pastime. Below, pilot Cliff Hudson poses with a trout at one of the local rivers around 1940. Hudson married Ollie Dahl, the daughter of Ole and Annie Dahl. Annie was a Dena'ina descendant. Ollie Hudson and her children still live in the area. (Courtesy THS.)

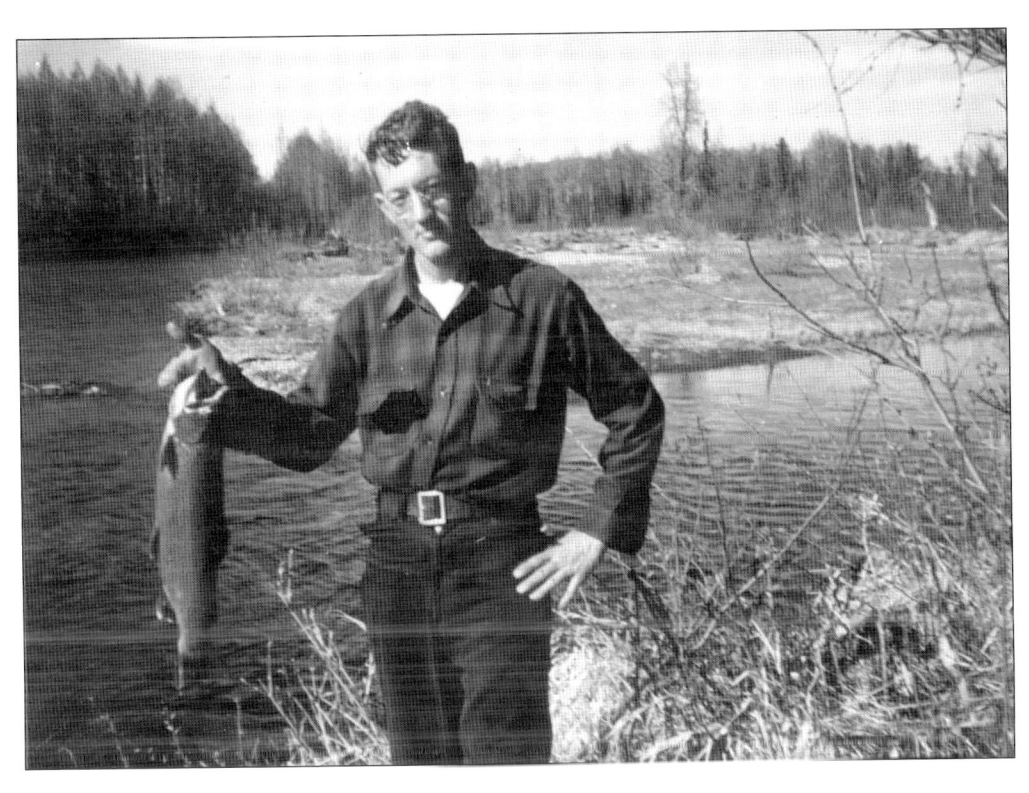

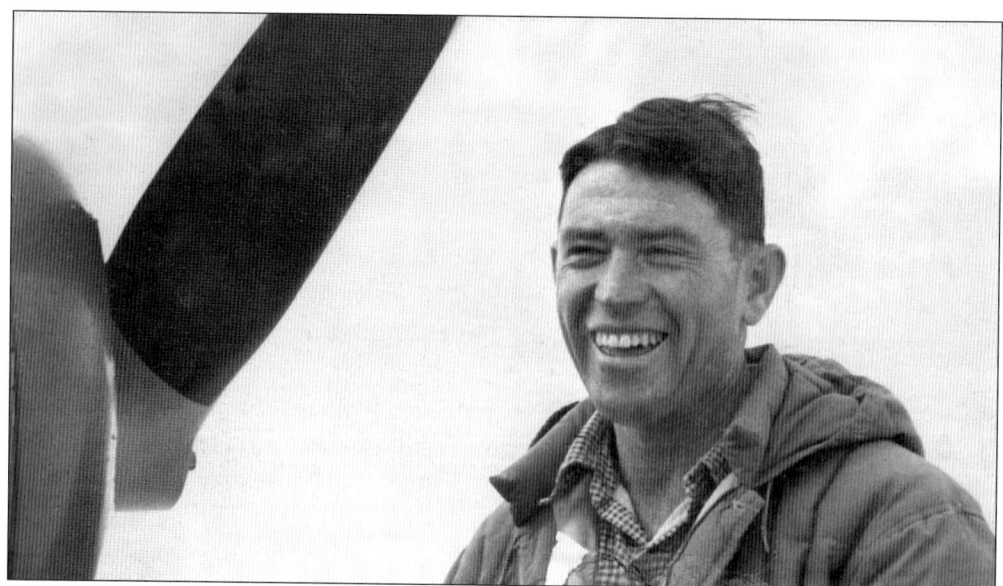

DON SHELDON AND "STUB" MORRISON. Don Sheldon (above) symbolizes the legend of bush pilots and glacier landings. His skills, compassion, and heroic risk-taking delivered hundreds of people safely to their destinations, provided a communication link to remote miners and trappers, and saved lives. Sheldon reinvented mountain transportation to Denali by pioneering glacial landings with both fixed and retractable ski-landing gear. Sheldon (below, right) became business partners with Robert "Stub" Morrison (below, left) in 1948, and together, they began building Talkeetna Air Service. Sheldon taught Morrison to fly, while Morrison provided much of the initial financial investment needed for the costly startup. Sadly, Morrision was killed at a young age in an airplane crash in 1951 in "radiation fog conditions" between Talkeetna and Anchorage. Sheldon also left the world too soon, succumbing to cancer in January 1975 at the age of 53. (Above, courtesy THS; below, courtesy Roberta Sheldon.)

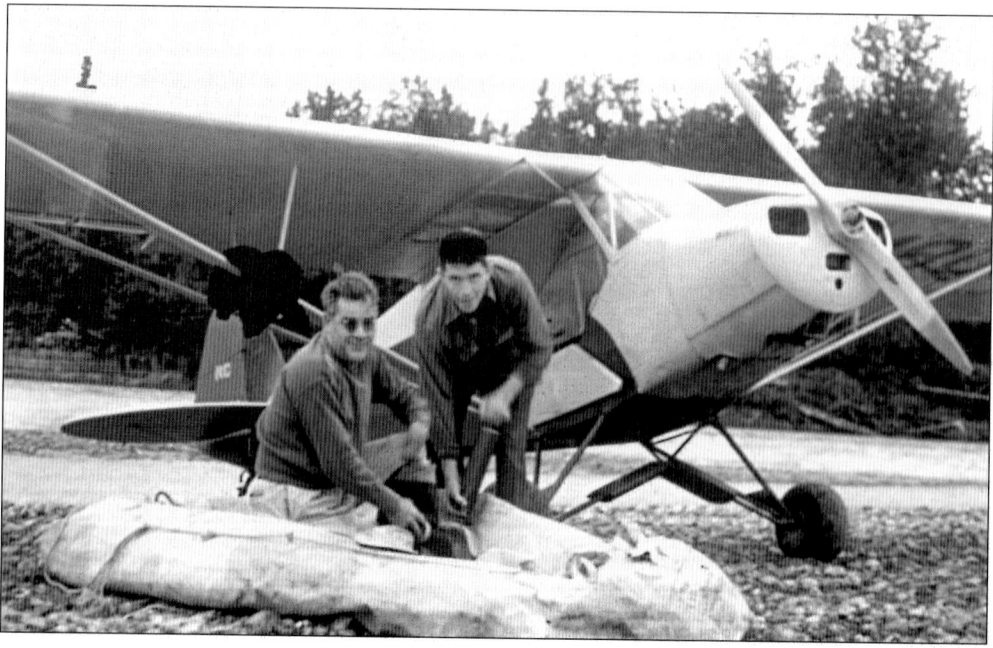

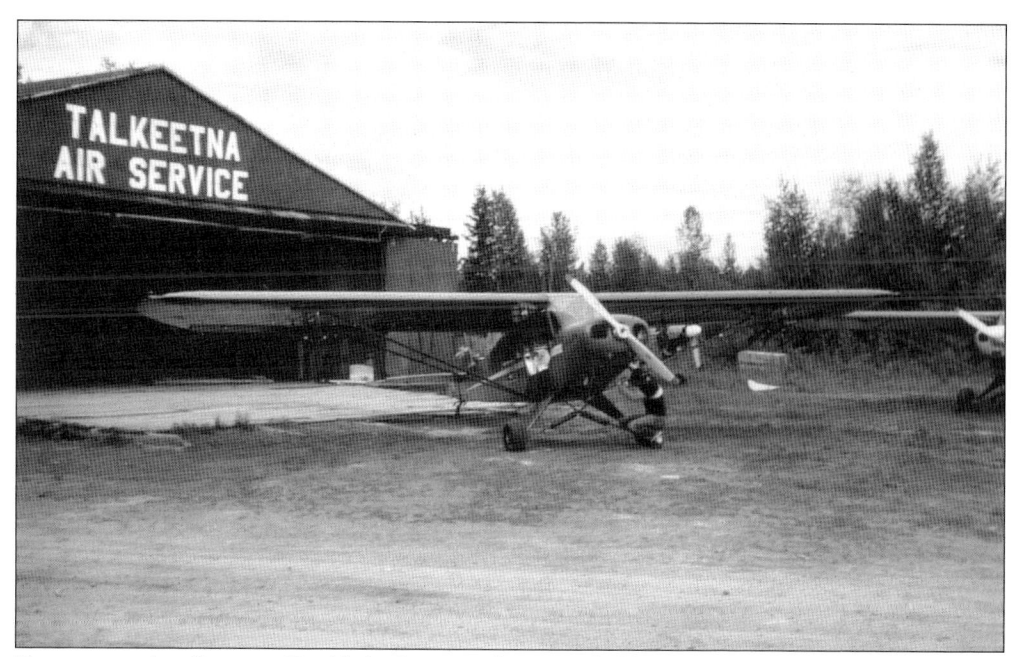

TALKEETNA AIR SERVICE. Established in 1948 by Don Sheldon, Talkeetna Air Service provided air service to remote areas for mining, fishing, and hunting. With the advent of glacier landings in the late 1950s and 1960s, Talkeetna Air Service became the primary staging area for climbers, who arrived by train, storing their supplies and sleeping in the hangar until the weather allowed for takeoff. (Courtesy THS.)

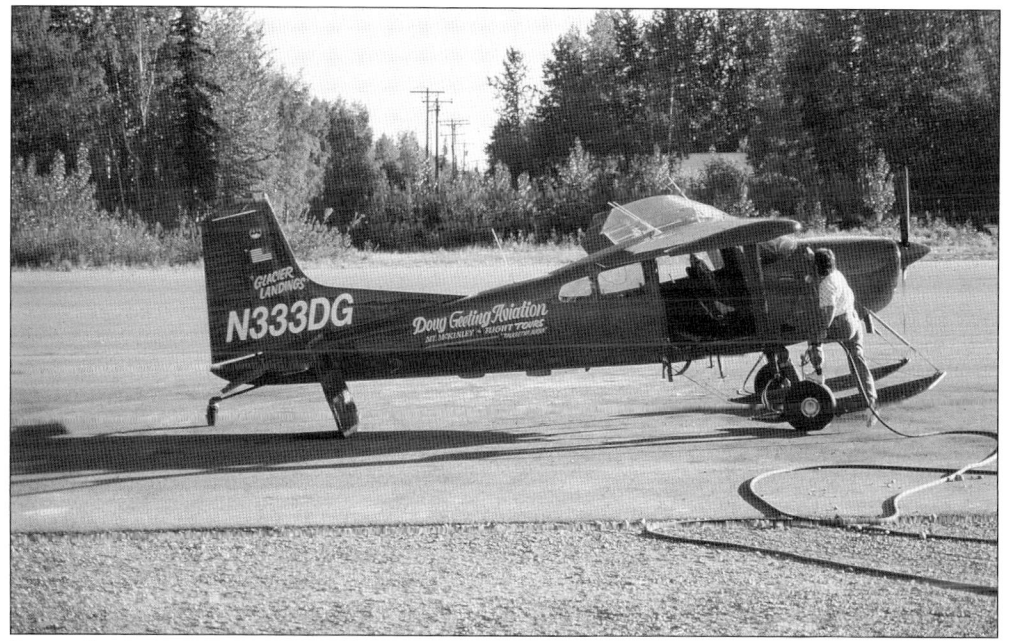

DOUG GEETING AVIATION. Established in the late 1970s, Doug Geeting Aviation specialized in landing on glaciers, lakes, and rivers, delivering clients to remote areas for outdoor recreation. Geeting Aviation was sold to K2 Air Service in 2006. Geeting is also a singer and guitarist who has recorded several albums, including one titled *The Alaskan Mile*. (Courtesy Sisul.)

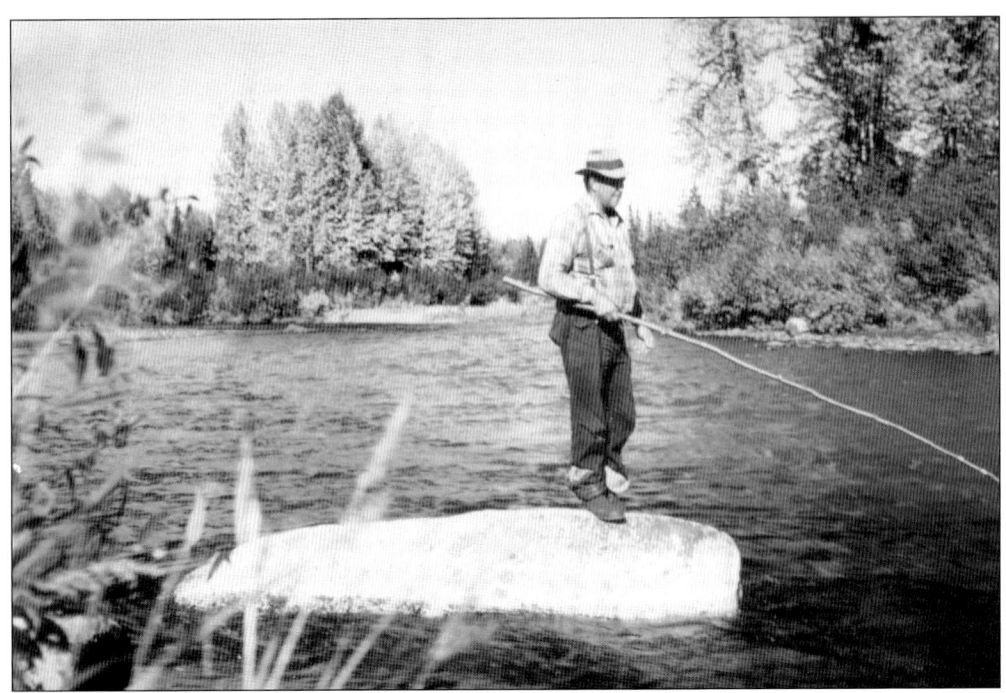

"I'D RATHER BE FISHING." Many bush pilots entered their vocation because they enjoyed the outdoors. They soon realized that they could combine their love for flying and fishing and make a living at it. Pilot Cal Reeves is seen here fishing in one of his favorite fishing holes. Below, Reeves once crashed his plane on the village airstrip. No one was hurt, but Reeves was covered with flour, which was part of the cargo he carried. Reeves would certainly have preferred to be fishing that day. (Courtesy THS, Eleanor Trepte.)

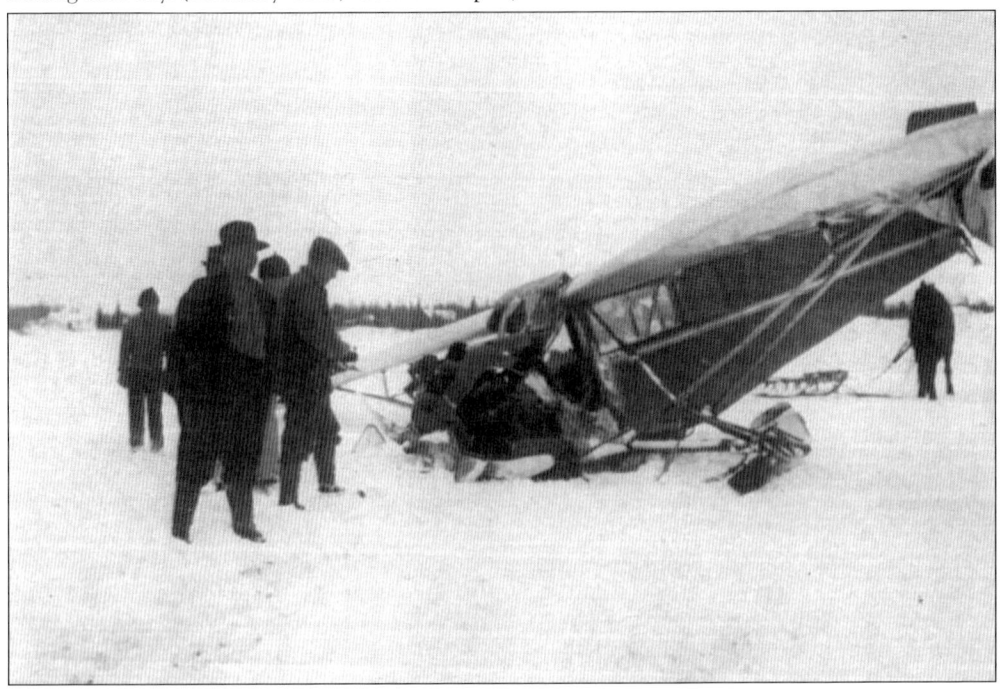

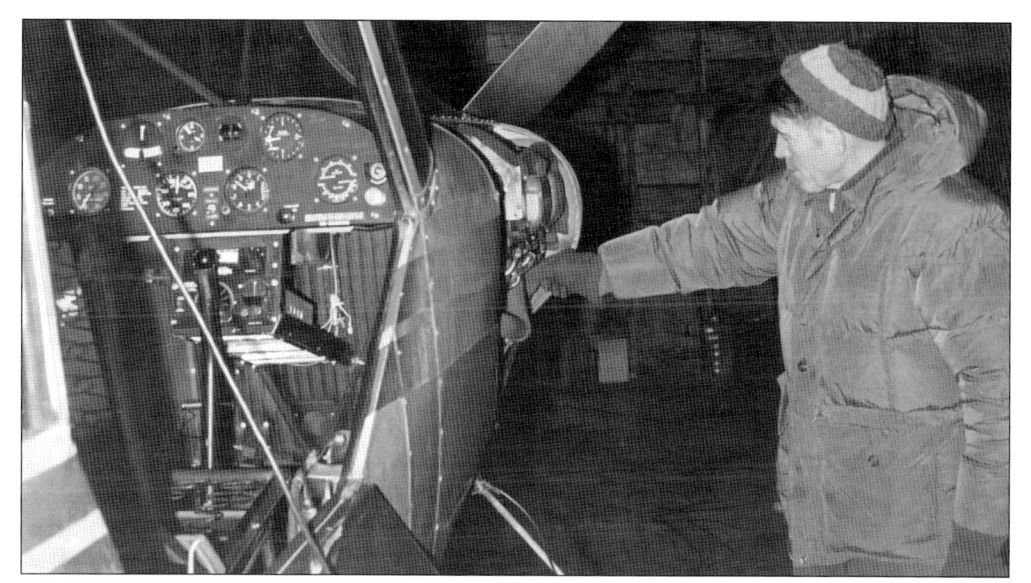

CONTROL PANEL. Don Sheldon checks the engine on his Cessna 180 inside the Talkeetna Air Service hangar in the 1960s. Bush pilots need to be excellent pilots, know their geography, able to read and predict weather patterns, have good judgment, and be good mechanics—there is no AAA service in the Alaskan bush. (Courtesy THS.)

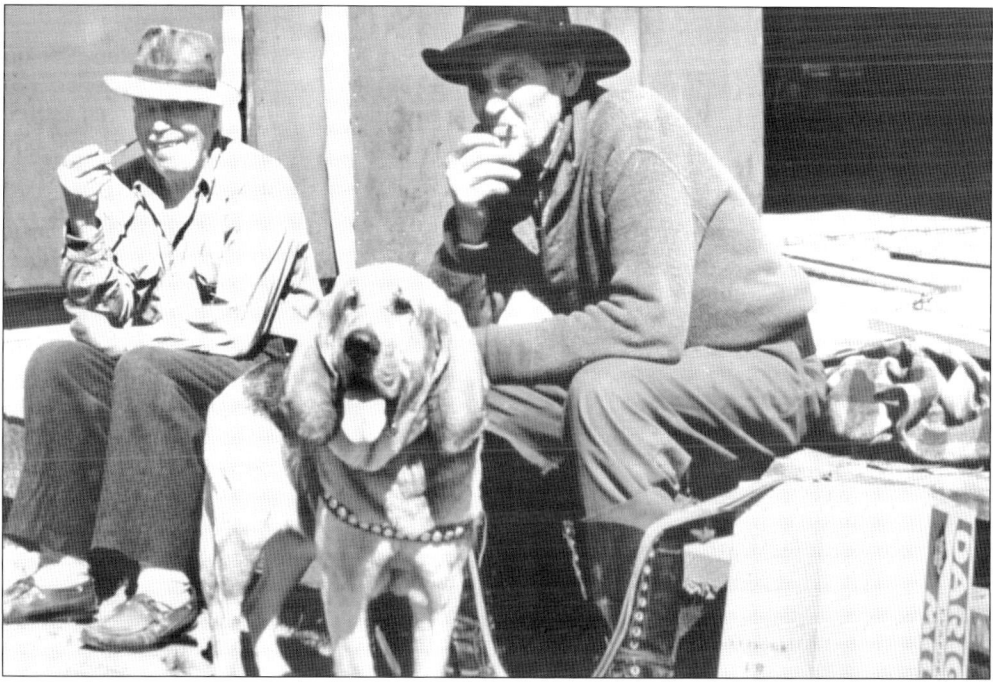

ON A SEARCH. Adolph J. "Missouri" Taraski (left), Delilah the bloodhound, and "Shorty" Bradley are seen here on the Talkeetna Air Service ramp in 1961. Shorty, who was very tall, and his wife, Florence, ran the Forks Roadhouse and raised bloodhounds. When Don Sheldon got a call for help, he occasionally got Bradley and Delilah to assist with the search. On this particular search, they were not able to locate a missing man. Luckily, he was discovered 11 weeks later, nearly starved to death but alive. (Courtesy THS.)

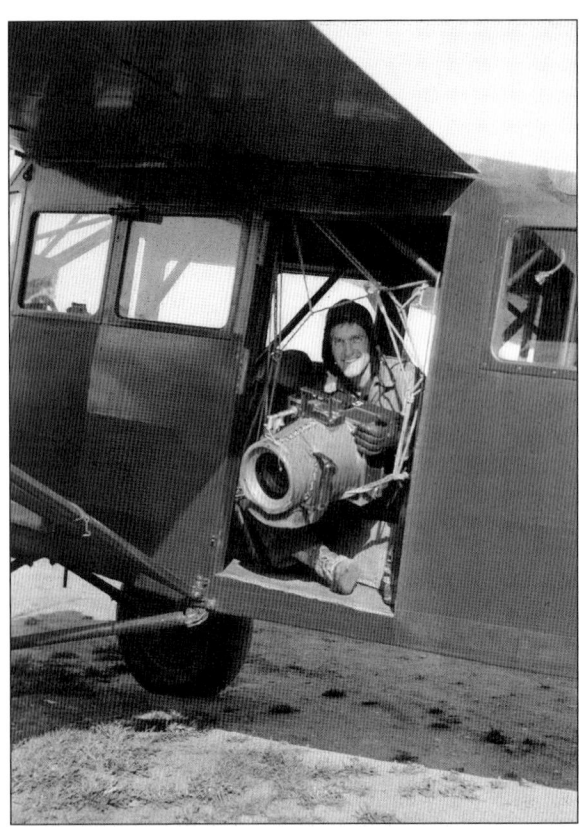

Dr. Brad Washburn. Mountaineer and Boston Museum of Science director Dr. Brad Washburn is roped into an aircraft in Talkeenta in 1957 in order to take aerial photographs through an open plane door while in the air. Talkeetna's Don Sheldon began piloting for Dr. Washburn in 1951, assisting on topographic work on Denali's Kahiltna Glacier. Washburn and Sheldon worked together for over a decade to complete the first detailed topographic maps and routes to the top of Denali. (Courtesy Bradford Washburn, Decaneas Archive, Revere, MA.)

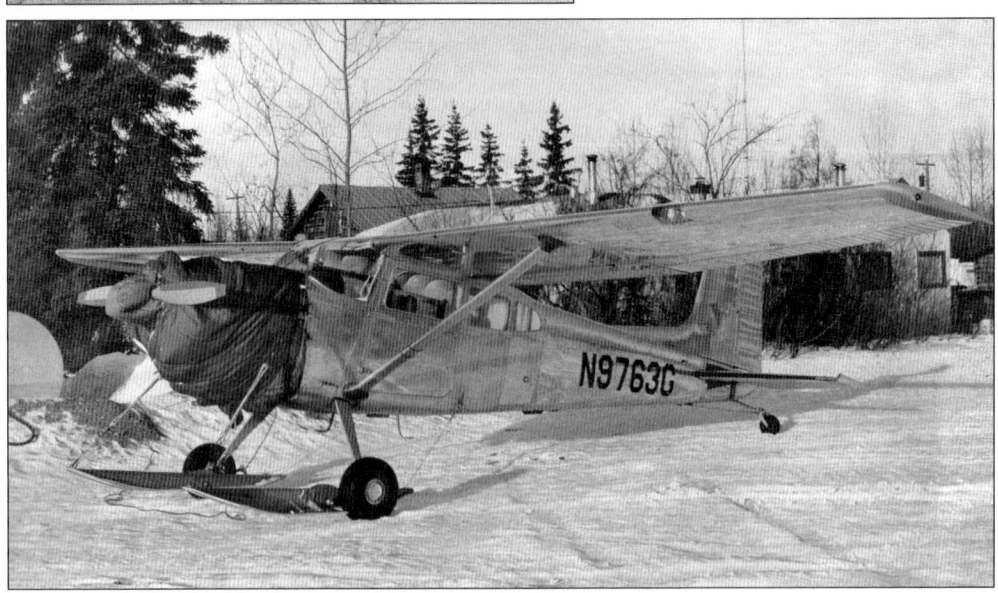

Glacier Landings. The invention of retractable ski-landing gear was a key element in the evolution of glacier landings. Without retractable gear, it was not feasible to take off or land from a non-snow-covered runway, and the gear was too limiting to be practical. One of Don Sheldon's Cessna 180s with retractable skis is seen here in the winter of 1968–1969. The engine was covered for winter travel. (Courtesy THS.)

Six

DENALI

The Dena'ina people call Mount McKinley Denali, or "The Great One." Denali is the highest point on the North American continent and the third highest of the Seven Summits, the highest mountains on each of the seven continents. Denali stands 20,320 feet (6,194 meters) above sea level and is considered one of the coldest mountains in the world. It has five major glaciers covering over one million acres: Ruth, Muldrow, Kahiltna, Eldridge, and Tokositna.

Walter Harper, Harry Karstens, Robert Tatum, and Hudson Stuck were the first to successfully summit Denali's South Peak in 1913. Since then, more than 38,500 people from around the world have attempted to summit Denali. Approximately 50 percent of them have been successful. It takes an average of 19 days to climb the mountain. Annual climbing permits are limited to 1,500. The record number of registered climbers occurred in 2005, when 1,340 people attempted to ascend Denali. Training, planning, good judgment, and luck are needed for a successful summit.

Until the 1950s, most climbers began their summit from the Fairbanks side of Denali and took months, using horses or dogsleds to pack in their supplies prior to their summit attempt. Talkeetna's Don Sheldon pioneered glacier airplane landings, using skis for landing gear and transporting mountain climbers to base camp, located at 7,200 feet of elevation on the Kahiltna Glacier, saving months from climbers' schedules. Today, this is the most common route used to scale Denali. Talkeetna is 60 miles "as the raven flies" to Denali and is the last stop before base camp. Every climber is required to register at the Talkeetna ranger station. Prime climbing season is from May to July.

Climbers have hailed from up to 60 different nations. The largest percentages of climbers come from the United States, Canada, the United Kingdom, Poland, Japan, Korea, Germany, Spain, and Norway. While there are climbers from many states, Alaska, Washington, Colorado, and California are most frequently represented. The average age of climbers is 38 years old, and 10 percent of them are women. The busiest month on record was June 2005, which had 358 summits. June 15, 2005, was the busiest summit day on record, with 101 climbers reaching the top

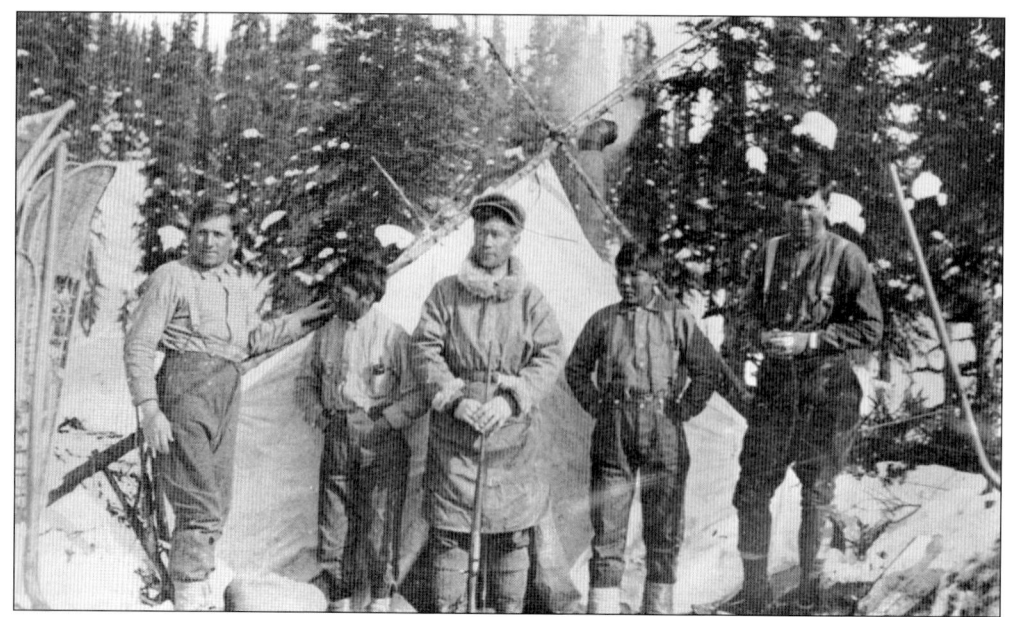

First Successful Summit. Walter Harper, a Dena'ina Athabascan native, was the first to set foot on the highest point in North America. On June 7, 1913, climbers Robert Tatum (left), Harry Karstens (center), Walter Harper (right), and Hudson Stuck became the first to summit Denali's South Peak, at an elevation of 20,320 feet. They are seen here at the Clearwater camp in 1913. Prior to their summit, attempts by other climbing teams were unsuccessful. (Courtesy THS.)

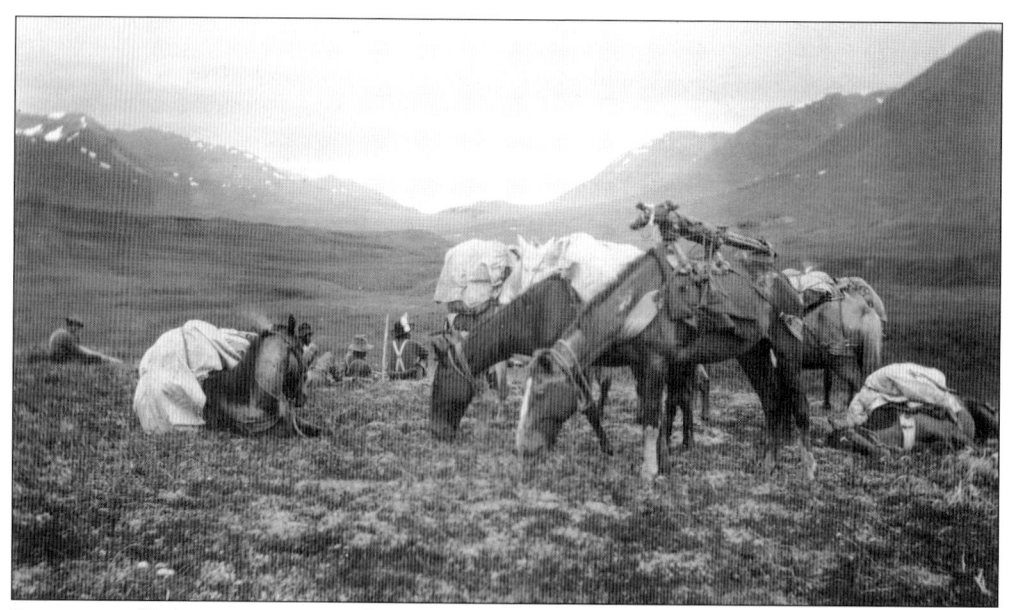

Packhorses. Early summit attempts began in the lowlands, as hikers made their way across mosquito-infested tundra, forests, and rivers before beginning their ascent, with packhorses hauling their thousands of pounds of supplies. This photograph shows the 1912 Belmore Browne expedition. Browne hailed from Tacoma, Washington. Packhorses and members of the expedition team take a break on their long journey to attempt Denali, which ultimately failed. (Courtesy DCL.)

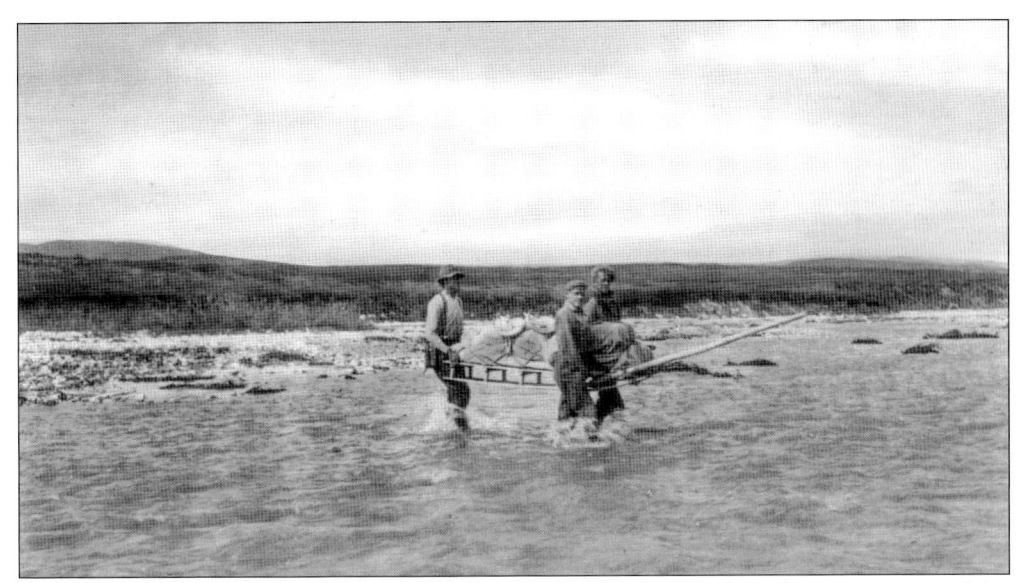

FORDING ICY RIVER. Part of the 1912 Browne expedition is seen here beginning one of the thousands of river crossings they made just to reach the toe of the glacier, where they began their summit attempt. It took the team many weeks to hike across the wilderness and to ford dangerous, icy rivers, all the while packing food, equipment, and supplies weighing hundreds of pounds per climber for the long overland trek to the glacier. (Courtesy DCL.)

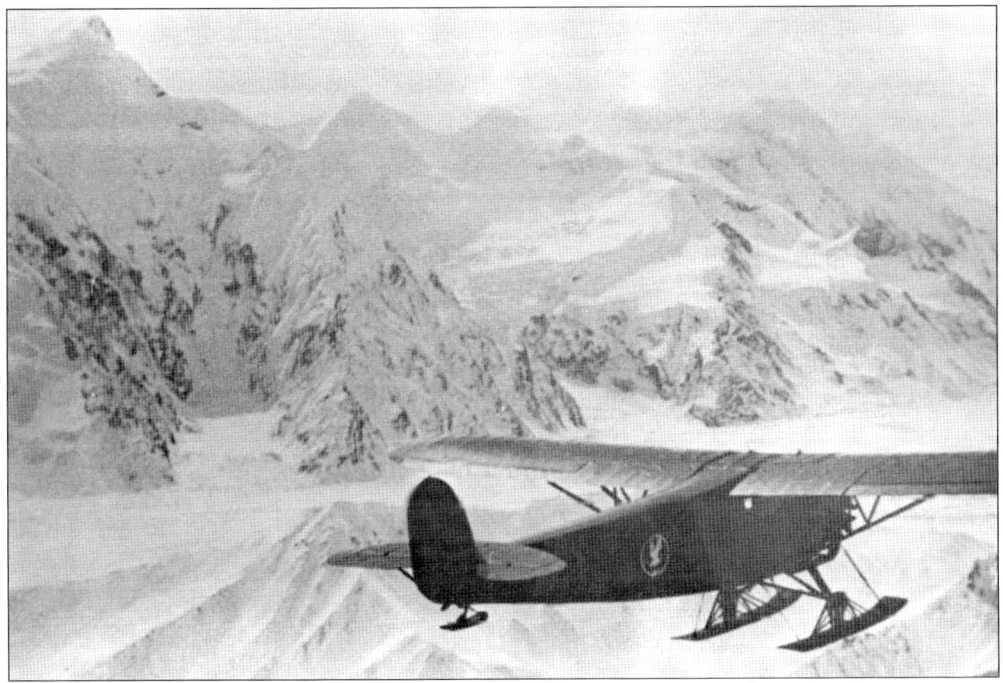

GLACIAL LANDINGS. It takes approximately 45 minutes to fly climbers and supplies the 60 air miles from Talkeetna to the 7,200-foot-elevation base camp on the Kahiltna Glacier. Dr. Brad Washburn surveyed and mapped the mountain over a 10-year period in the 1950s, with Don Sheldon as his trusted pilot. Dr. Washburn pioneered several new routes to the South and North Peaks, with his West Buttress Route used by many climbers summiting the South Peak. (Courtesy NPS.)

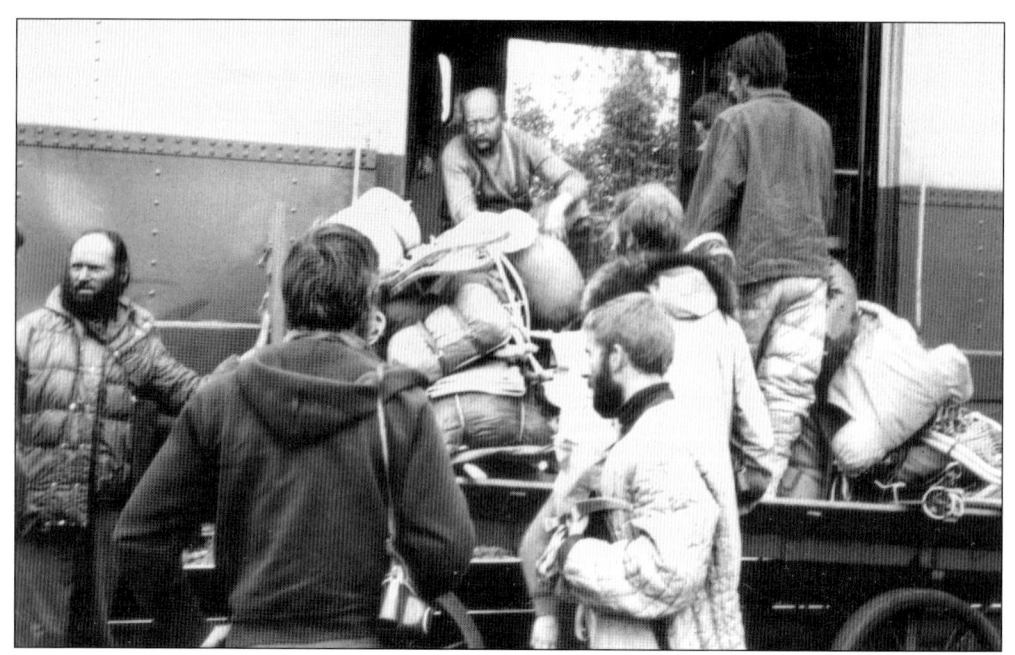

ARRIVING IN TALKEETNA VIA TRAIN. Expedition guide Ray Genet (far left) meets a group of international climbers arriving in the early 1970s. Climbers usually prepare for their Denali summit attempt for more than a year. While not required, climbers often choose to climb with one of the six guide companies approved by the National Park Service (NPS), although more than half go on their own to undertake the arduous Denali expedition. (Courtesy THS.)

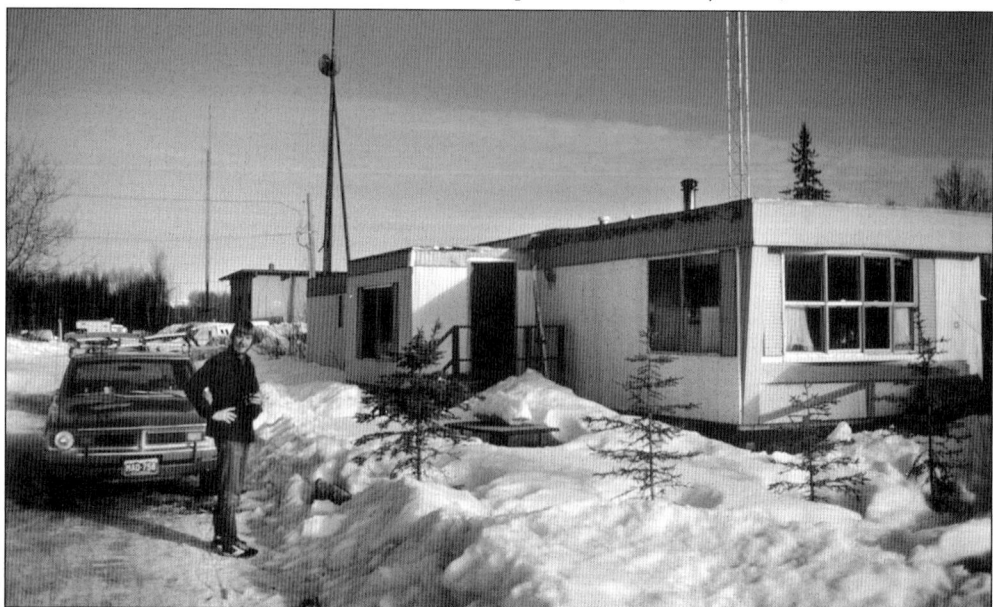

TALKEETNA RANGER STATION. Due to the increasing number of climbers attempting to summit Denali and the subsequent rise in rescues and fatalities, the NPS translated climbing guides into nine languages to communicate requirements and risks to international climbers. A ranger station was established in Talkeetna in 1986. All climbers are required to check in and check out at the station. A mobile home served as the first ranger station. (Courtesy NPS, Roger Robinson.)

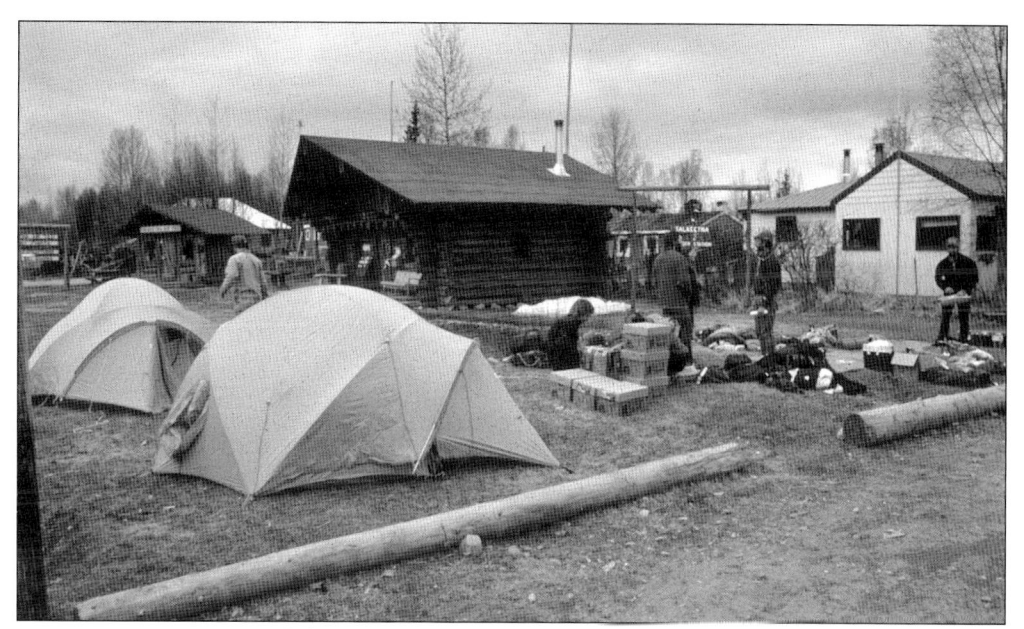

SECOND NPS BUILDING. To better meet the needs of their customers, NPS moved from a mobile home into this log building built by Ray Genet on Main Street in Talkeetna, across from Nagley's and the Fairview Inn and next door to the Sheldon home. Here, each year, hundreds of climbers from around the world registered for their climb and prepared their equipment and supplies for the air taxi service to base camp. (Courtesy NPS, Roger Robinson.)

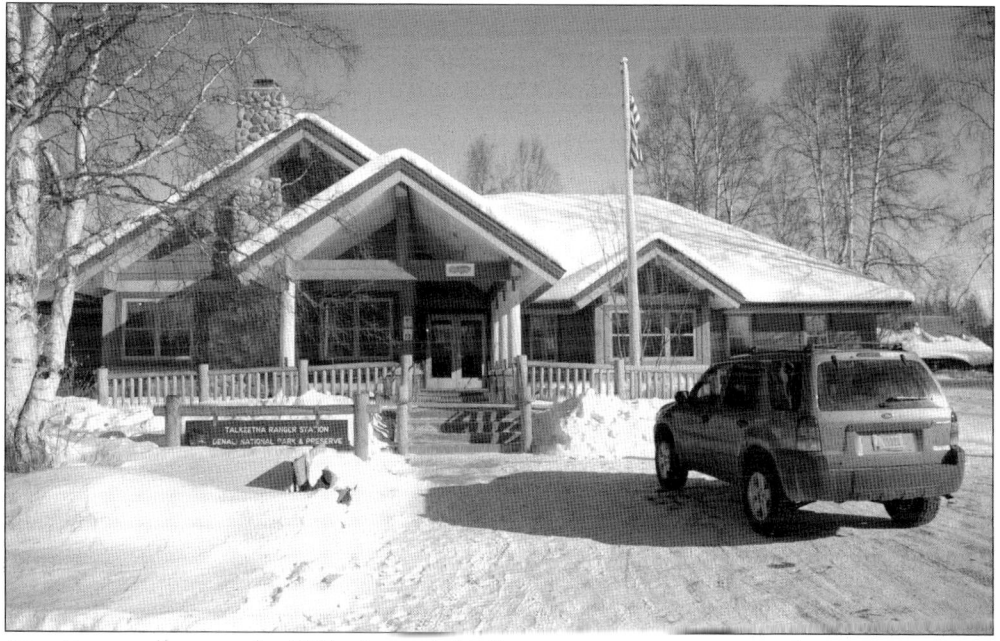

NEW RANGER STATION. In 1997, a beautiful Talkeetna ranger station opened on B Street, across from Belle McDonald's original freight stables. All climbers must register for a permit to climb and attend a mandatory climbing orientation at the ranger station. During this orientation, park rangers provide general information, safety precautions, and communication protocol, and issue a Clean Mountain Can to manage human waste on the mountain. (Courtesy NPS.)

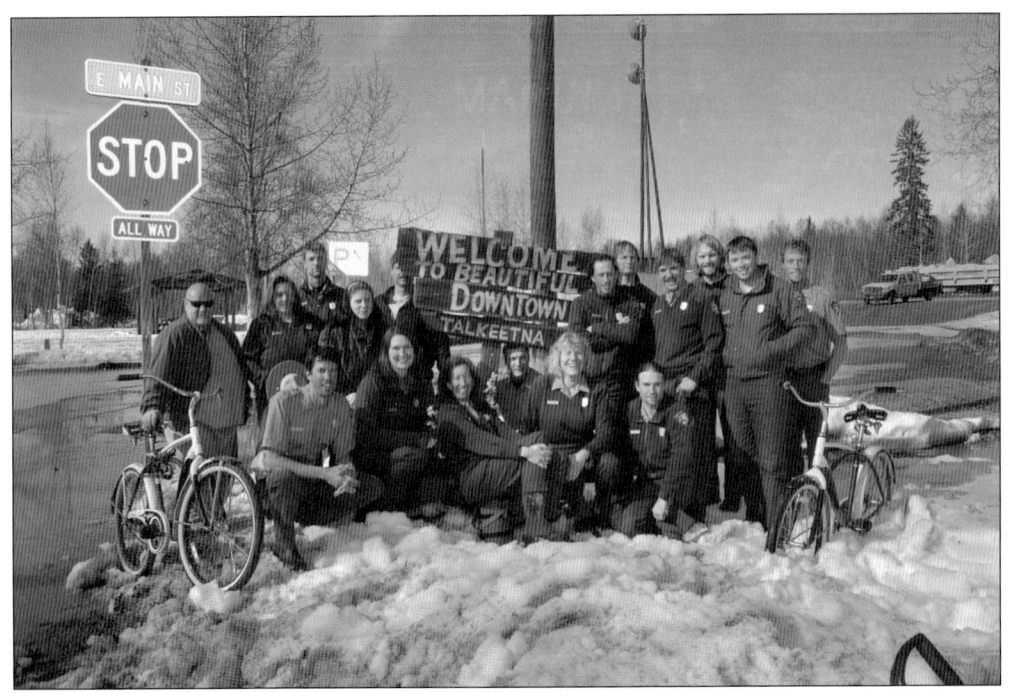

NATIONAL PARK SERVICE STAFF. The NPS staff provides year-round services at the Talkeetna ranger station as well as seasonal services on the mountain at base camp (at 7,200 feet), basin camp (14,200 feet), and high camp (17,200 feet) to assist with communications, coordination, medical, and emergency situations. NPS also provides interpretative services at the Talkeetna Historical Society's mountaineering exhibit. Many NPS employees are specialized high altitude rescue mountain rangers. (Courtesy NPS.)

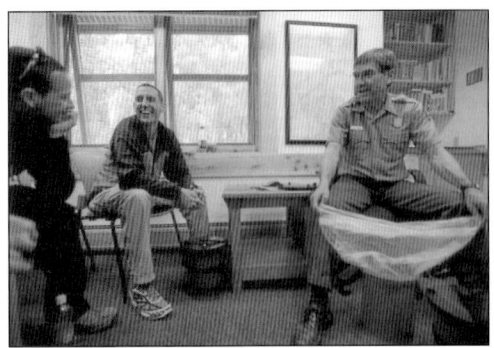

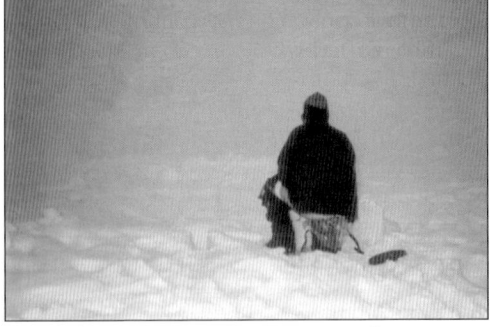

CLEAN MOUNTAIN CAN. At left, NPS ranger Roger Robinson orients two registered mountain climbers on how to use Clean Mountain Cans, which were invented in Talkeetna to help manage the environmental impacts of human waste on Denali from the more than 1,200 climbers who annually attempt to summit North America's tallest peak. In 2008, it became a requirement to carry and use a Clean Mountain Can. (Courtesy NPS.)

CACHE TAGS. Each climber takes approximately 120 to 150 pounds of food and supplies on the mountain. Early expeditions had to take more than 800 pounds of supplies per person. During NPS orientation, each climbing team is issued multiple tags to mark their caches on the mountain. Climbers cache their supplies at several different elevations. Due to problems with ravens raiding climbers' food, NPS recommends each cache be buried three feet deep and marked with wands. (Courtesy Sisul.)

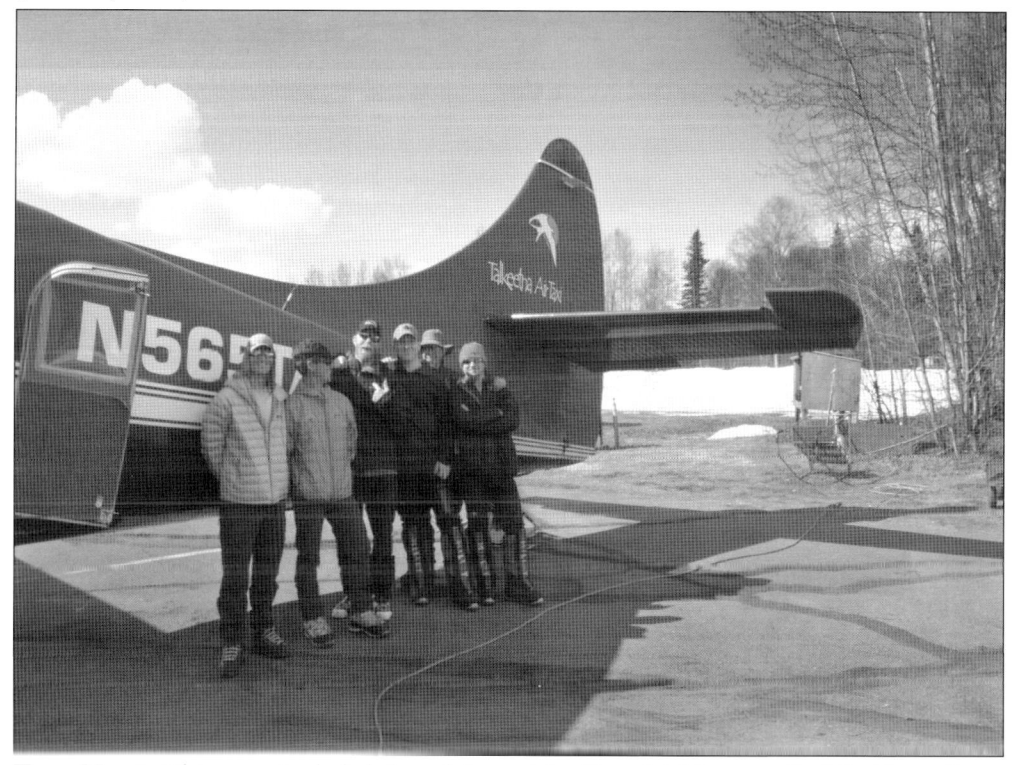

TEAM NO. 3. This team included, from left to right, Sean McManamy, Paul Beddows, Steve Eccles, Steve Graham, Jason Gross, and guide Jack McGee. The climbers were from the United Kingdom, Alaska, and Texas. They posed for this photograph before taking off from Talkeetna. Richard Olmsted was the pilot of their Talkeetna air taxi, which headed for base camp on April 30, 2012. On their first night at base camp, it snowed two feet. (Courtesy THS.)

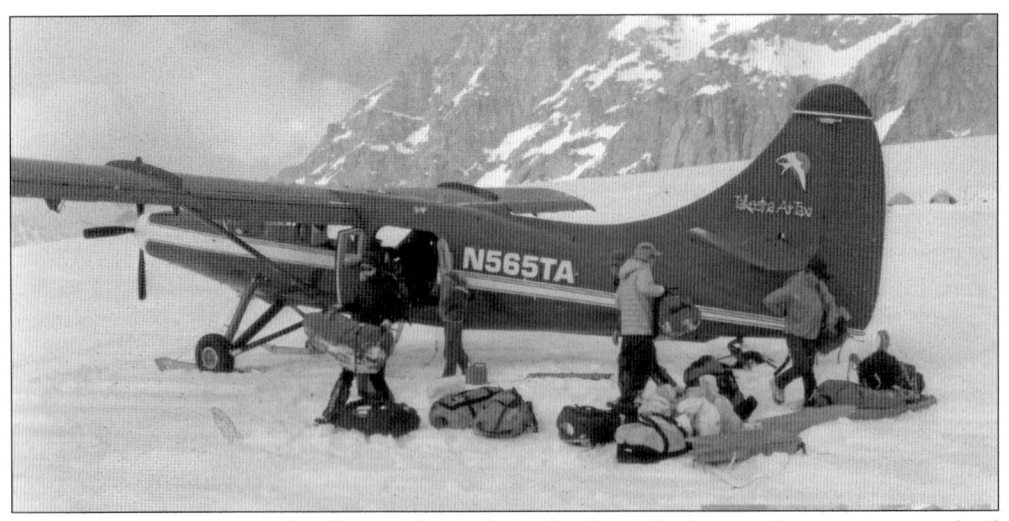

GLACIAL LANDING. Once the plane makes a glacier landing, climbers work as a team to unload their supplies and equipment. Plastic sleds are provided at base camp to assist the climbers to move their supplies. After teams check in with Base Camp Annie—Annie Duquette, who worked at base camp from 1991 to 2001—or Base Camp Lisa Roderick (2002–present), climbers immediately set up camp, as they will remain in base camp for a variable amount of time depending on the weather conditions. (Courtesy THS.)

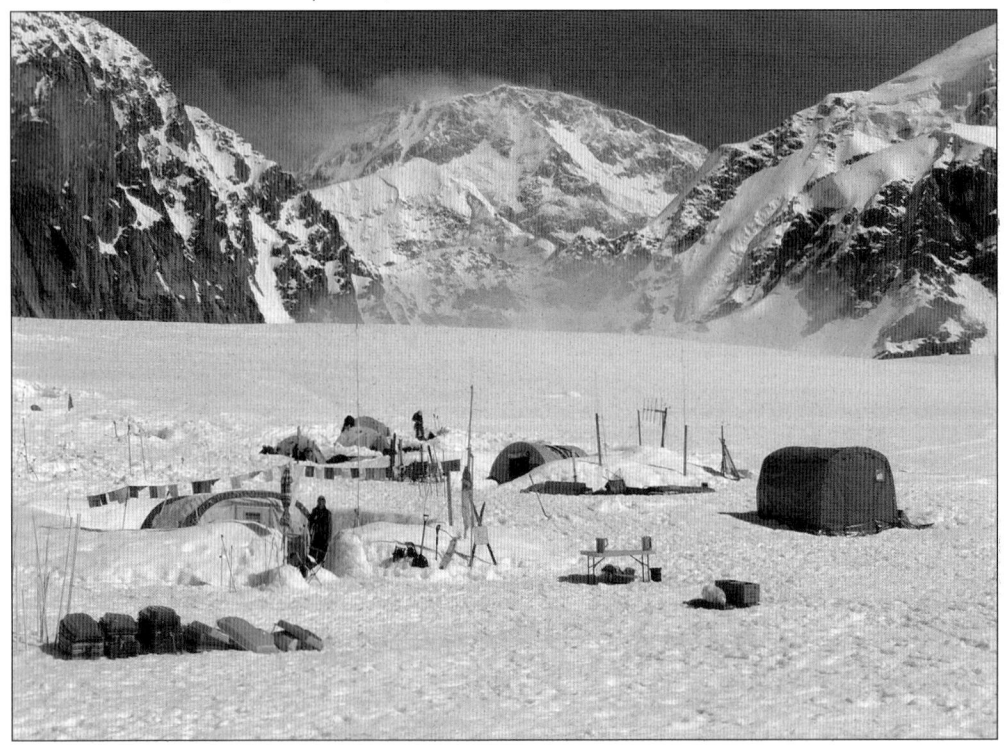

BASE CAMP. The population at base camp varies according to the number of climbers, their schedules, and weather conditions. Base camp is currently staffed seasonally, from May to July. Each climbing team builds snow walls to protect their tents from high winds and frigid temperatures, which get as low as 50 degrees below zero. (Courtesy NPS.)

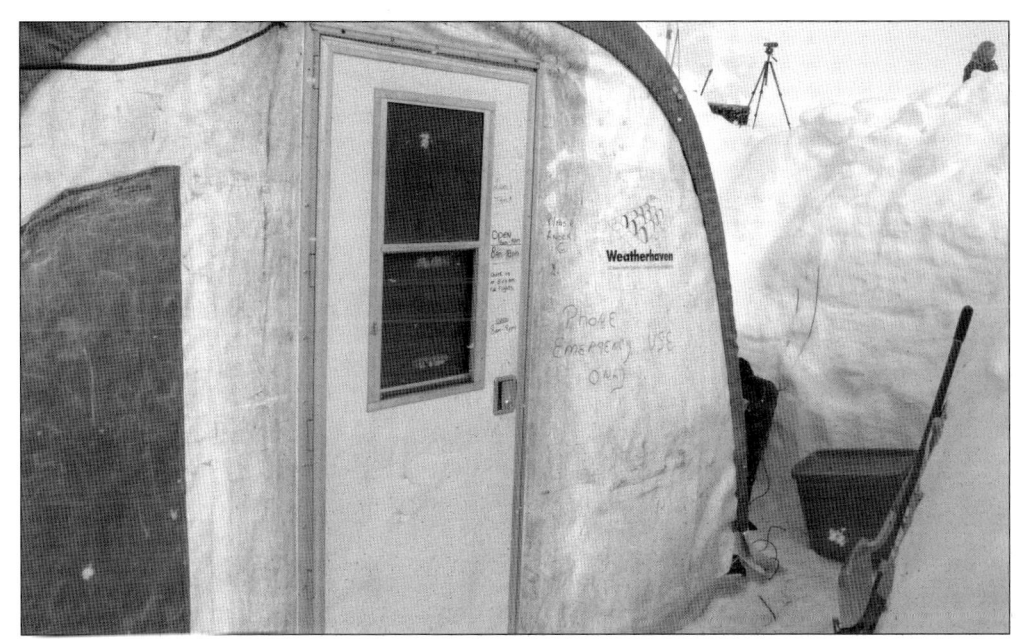

Base Camp Annie. Annie Duquette is seen below on the radio at base camp in the 1990s. Once a team leaves Talkeetna, they are cut off from communications with the rest of the world for weeks. The base camp manager serves as the primary mode of communication between climbers, air taxi service, NPS, and the National Weather Service (NOAA). Each morning, the base camp manager communicates with NOAA to get weather forecasts, communicates with Talkeetna air services to update needs and weather conditions, and provides radio communications to climbers. At times, the base camp manager played a critical role in assisting NPS with search, rescue, recovery efforts, and basic first aid. The manager's tent shelter (above) is established at the beginning of each season in an excavated area approximately three feet deep, offering protection from high winds and elevation changes from glacier melts. (Both courtesy Annie Duquette.)

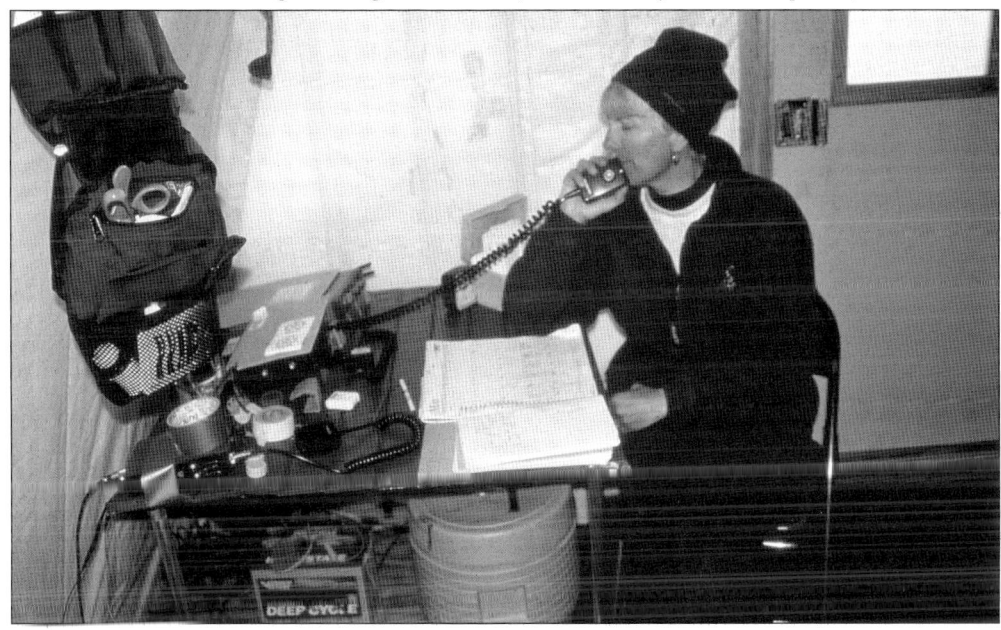

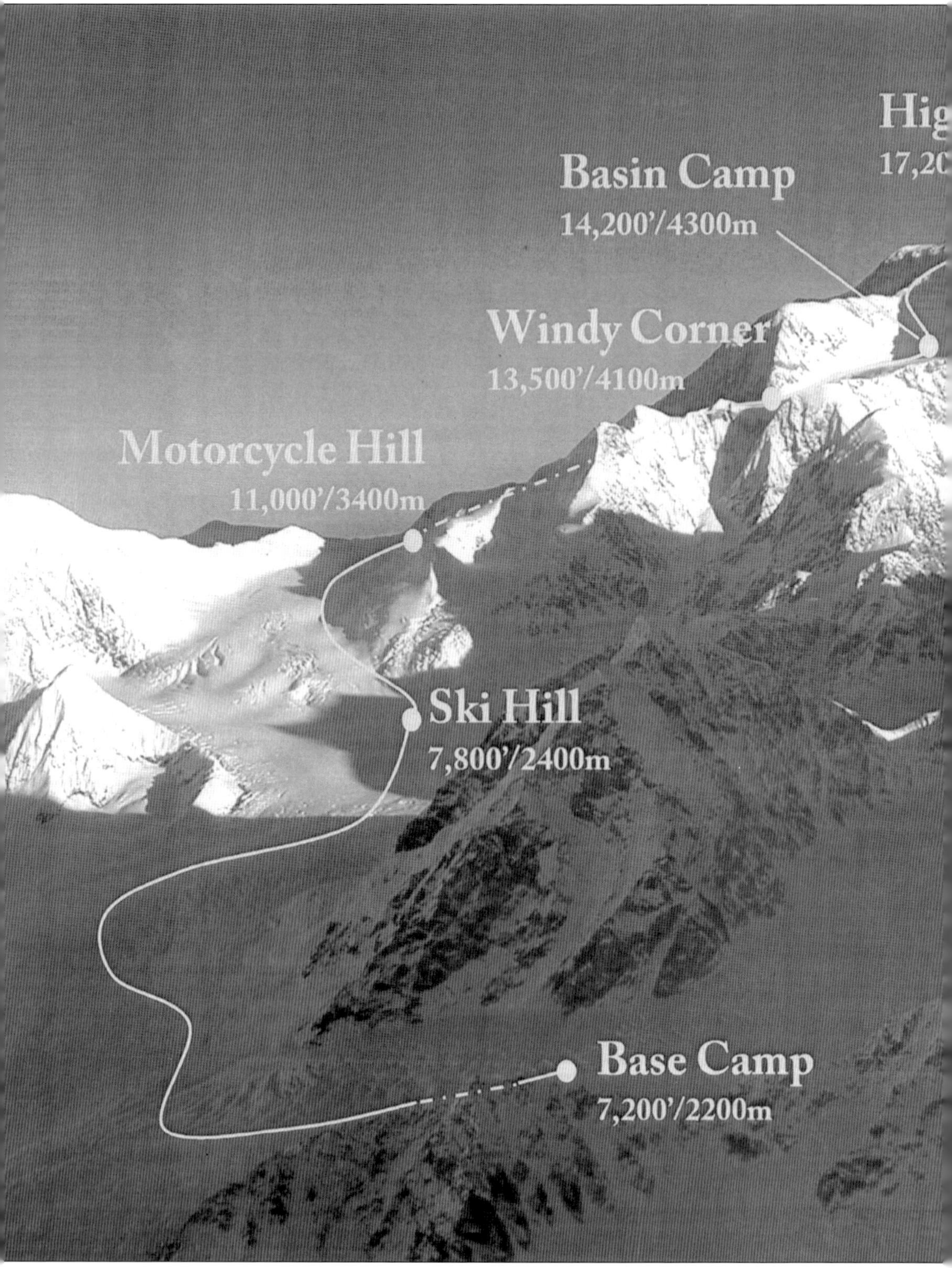
Hig
17,20
Basin Camp
14,200'/4300m
Windy Corner
13,500'/4100m
Motorcycle Hill
11,000'/3400m
Ski Hill
7,800'/2400m
Base Camp
7,200'/2200m

South Peak
20,320'/6194m

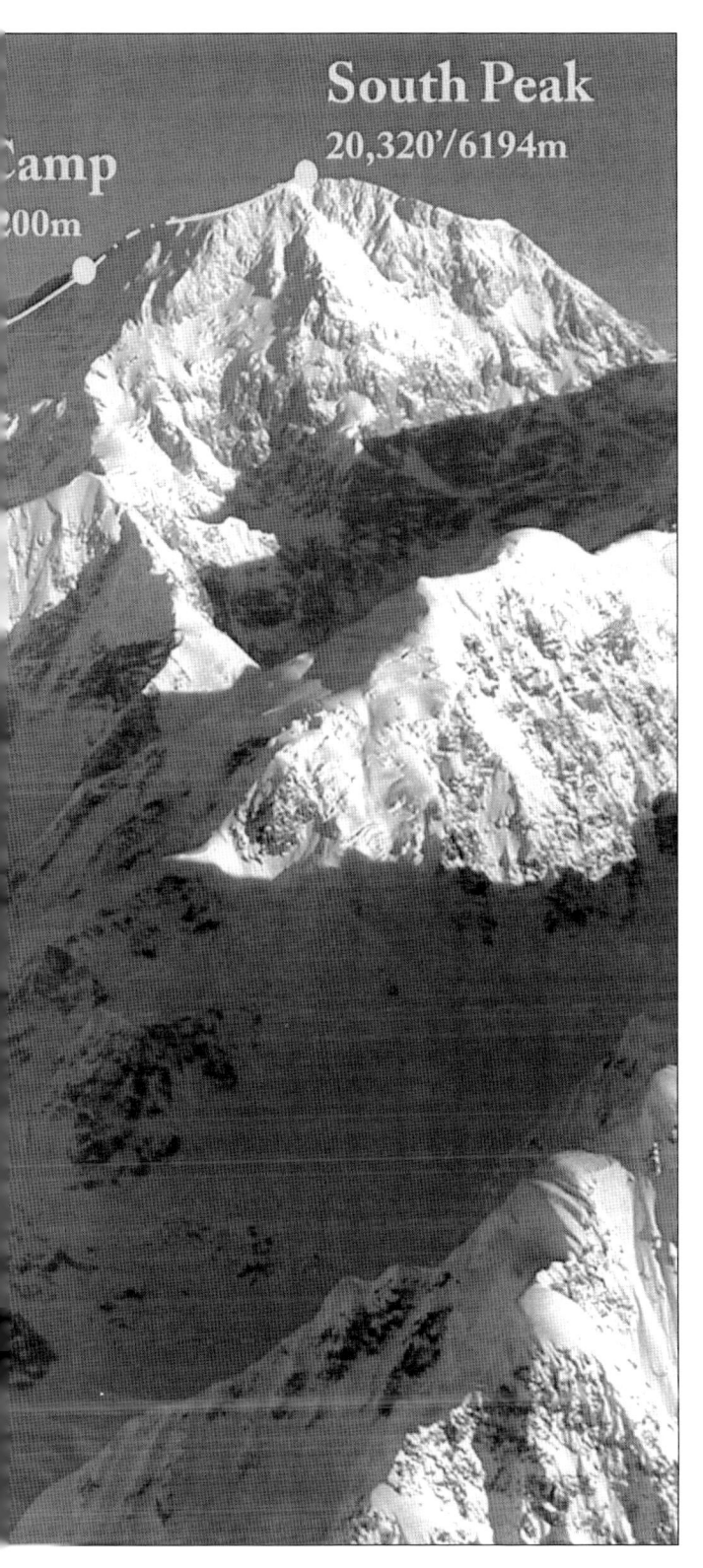

Camp
[2]00m

WEST BUTTRESS ROUTE. The most common route used by climbers seeking to summit Denali's South Peak is the West Buttress Route. The average time to summit the mountain is 19 days; however, it is not unusual to be delayed by weather for several days or even weeks. The climbers must be prepared to acclimate themselves to the lack of oxygen, the potential medical conditions experienced at high altitudes, the risk of exposure to harsh weather elements, and potential injuries from climbing. Climbing teams are expected to be self-sufficient. In the 1990s, the NPS began to staff a medical station at the 14,200-feet-elevation Basin Camp to better assist with rescue and recovery efforts. Volunteer medical professionals and other patrol members assist NPS staff rangers at Basin Camp for one-month shifts, to allow acclimation to the elevation in order to be best prepared for an emergency response. (Courtesy NPS.)

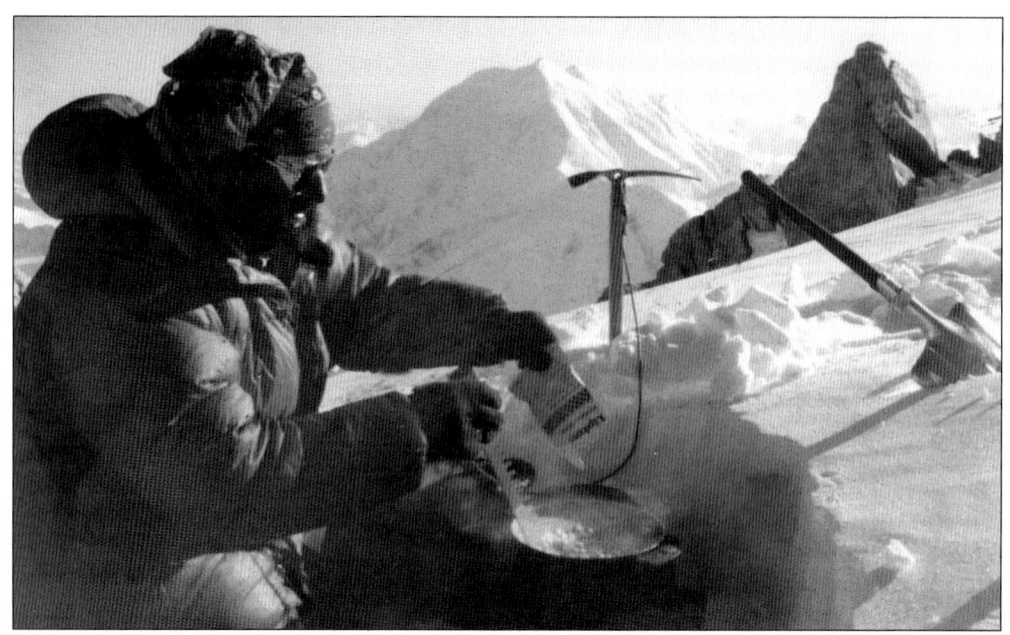

CLIMB HIGH, SLEEP LOW. Bottled oxygen is not used on Denali. "Climb high, sleep low" is the mantra, as climbers typically haul and cache their food and supplies at a higher elevation for future use while making camp at a lower elevation so that their bodies can get used to the altitude. This is repeated several times throughout the climb. At Base Camp, each team is issued fuel tanks, which must be carried and returned to the NPS at the end of the climb. Above, Ray Genet is preparing a meal using an ice axe, melted snow, and dehydrated food. Climbers need to consume as much as possible to keep their strength because they can burn up to 6,000 calories per day. Each climber is required to plan, carry, and prepare their own food. (Courtesy NPS, THS.)

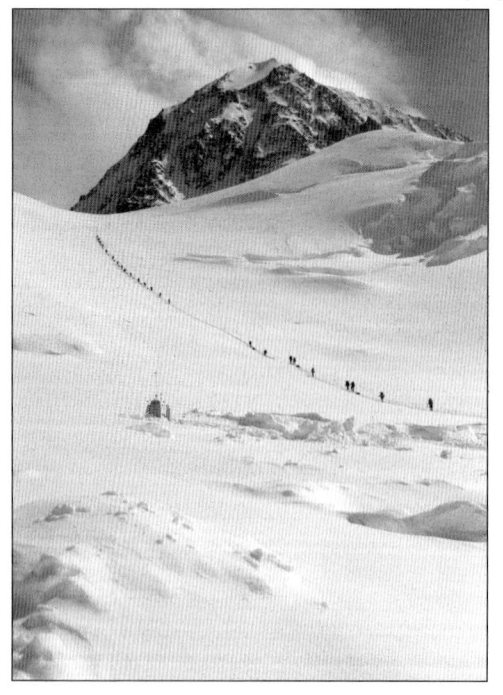

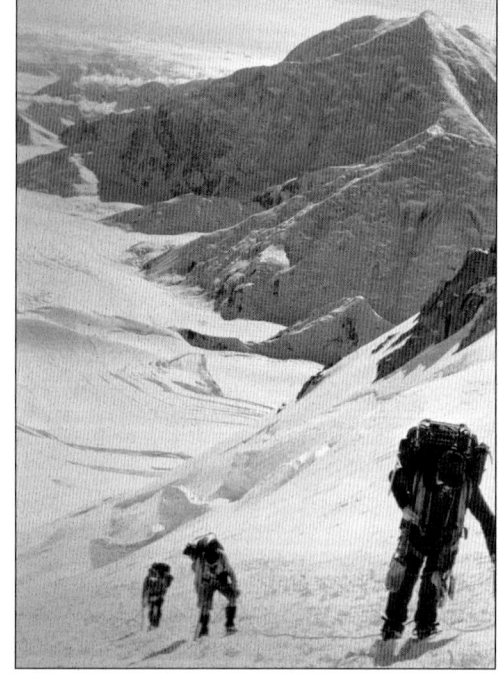

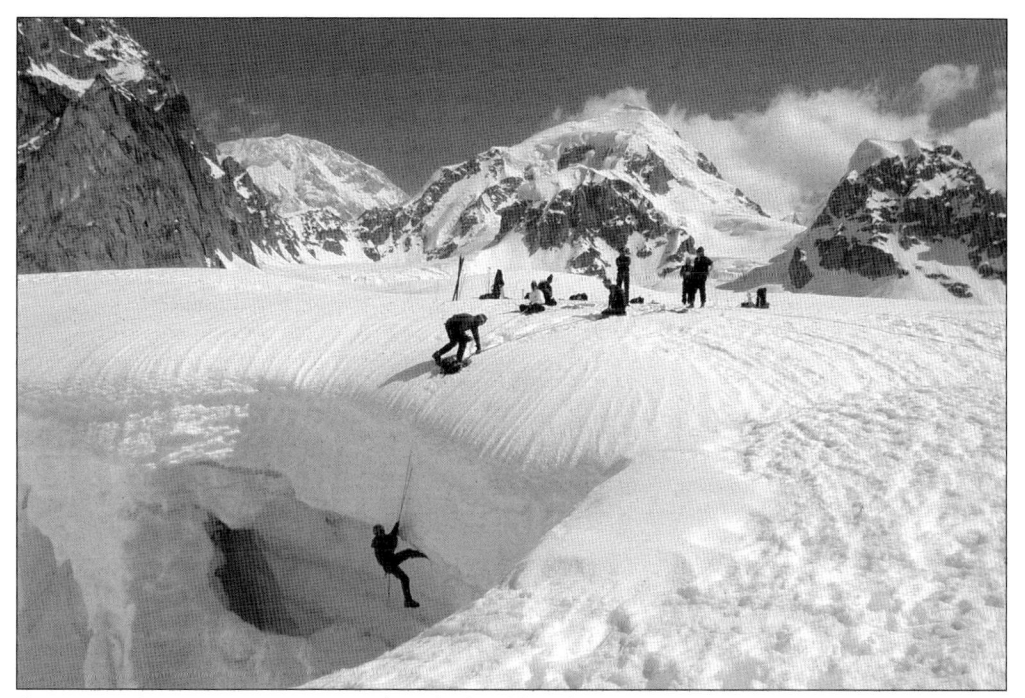

CREVASSE. Crossing crevasses up to hundreds of feet deep, a frequent and highly risky activity, is required when climbing Denali. Here, NPS ranger Mik Shain practices crevasse rescue techniques with volunteer patrol members so they are prepared for emergencies. Approximately eight percent of climbing fatalities on Denali are from falling into crevasses. Several bodies are entombed in ice forever in crevasses on Denali. (Courtesy NPS.)

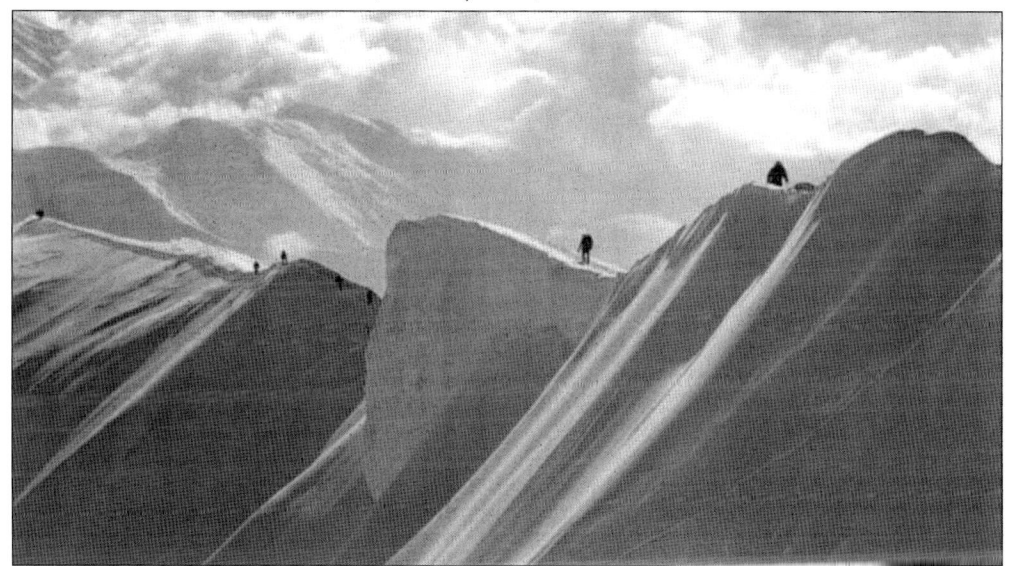

SUMMIT RIDGE. Climbers usually begin their attempt to summit at night; it is light, the snow is harder, and there are fewer chances of stepping through a snow bridge and falling into a crevasse. Weather, a key factor in an attempt to summit Denali, can change rapidly. Climbers need to be prepared for rapid changes and the possibility of bivouacing for days or weeks in extremely cold conditions. (Courtesy NPS.)

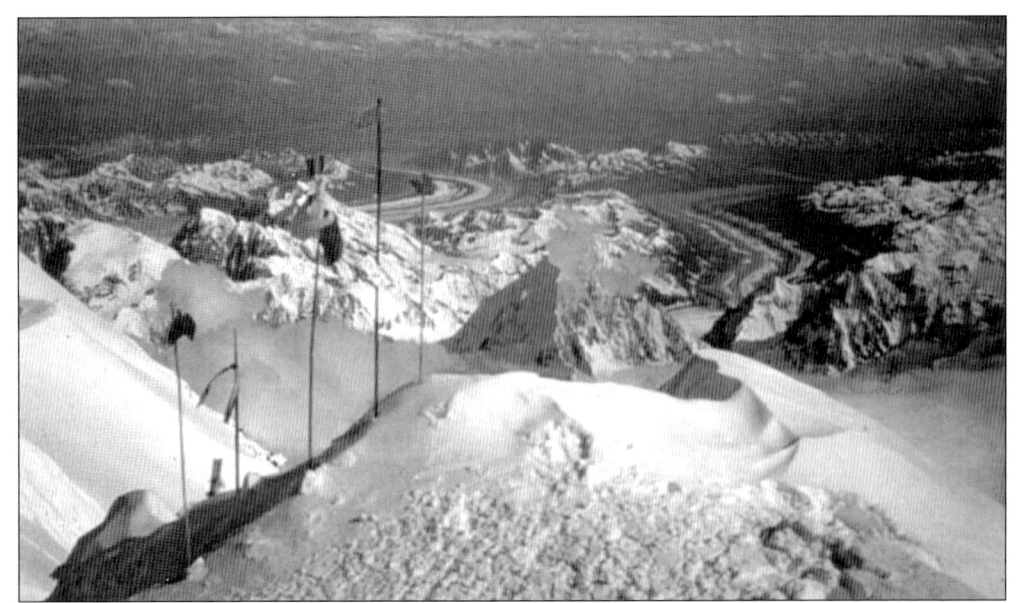

SUMMIT! As of 2012, 38,500 climbers have attempted to climb Denali since 1903. Slightly more than half have successfully summited. After a few minutes enjoying being at the top, climbers begin their descent, which is considered even more difficult. Nearly half the deaths on Denali occur during the descent. (Courtesy NPS.)

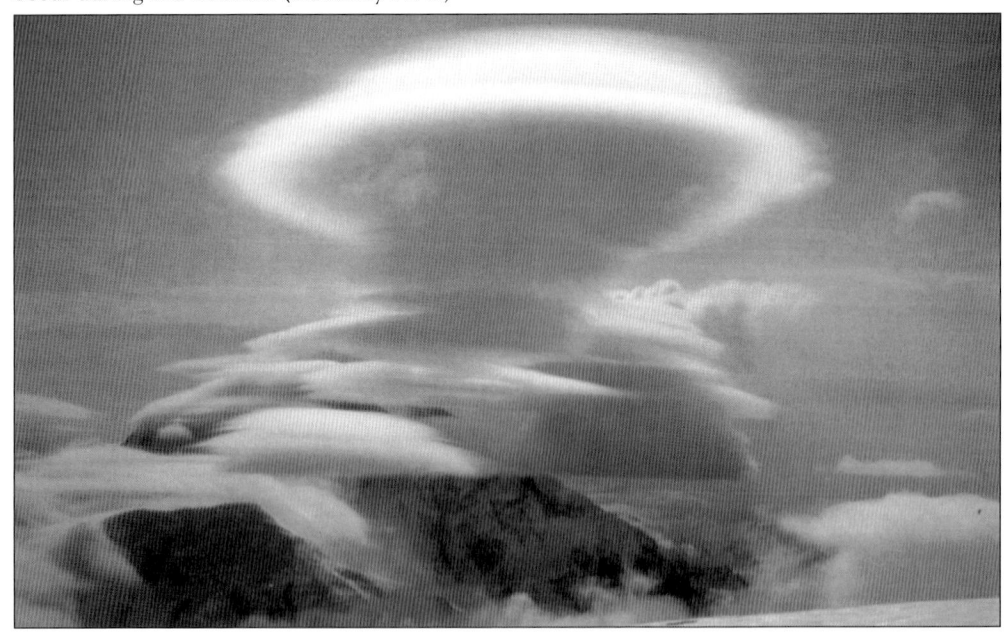

EXTREME WEATHER. This is a lenticular cloud formation over the peak created by high winds. In *Wager with the Wind: The Don Sheldon Story*, author James Greiner writes, "For millions of years, the upper reaches of the mountain have been held in the almost-constant grip of severe coastal storms . . . winds in excess of 100 miles per hour, with accompanying chill factor that exceed 125 degrees below zero during the summertime . . . Due to its tremendous vertical dimension and the accompanying cloud stratification and temperature variation, McKinley is, within itself a veritable weather factory." (Courtesy Annie Duquette.)

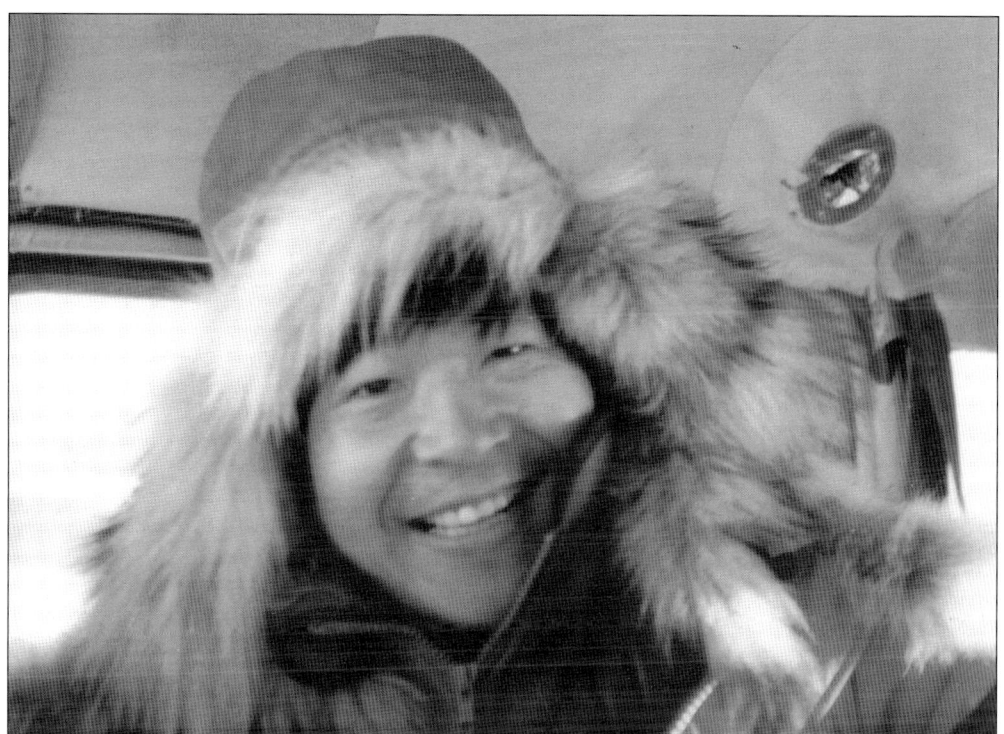

Naomi Uemura. All fatalities on the mountain cause grief for family, friends, and the climbing community. The nation of Japan still grieves for national hero Naomi Uemura, who disappeared on Denali in extreme weather conditions after being the first person in the world to make a successful winter solo ascent of Denali's South Peak on February 12, 1986. He was 44. Pilot Doug Geeting flew over McKinley on February 11, 1986, and spotted a waving Uemura below 17,000 feet. On February 13, 1986, Uemura radioed to request a pickup at base camp in three days. The *Anchorage Daily News* reported, "A storm descended on McKinley that afternoon and lasted four days. The temperature was -40 degrees Fahrenheit . . . winds more than 100 mph. When the storm lifted, there was no sign of Naomi Uemura." Several rescue parties searched for Uemura without success. It is believed the wind may have knocked him off the mountain, but his body was never found. Uemura is entombed forever somewhere on Denali. (Courtesy THS, NPS.)

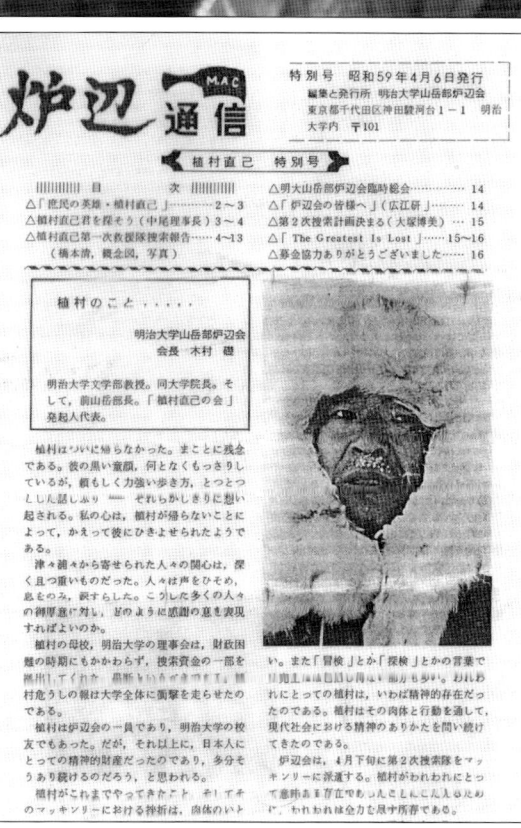

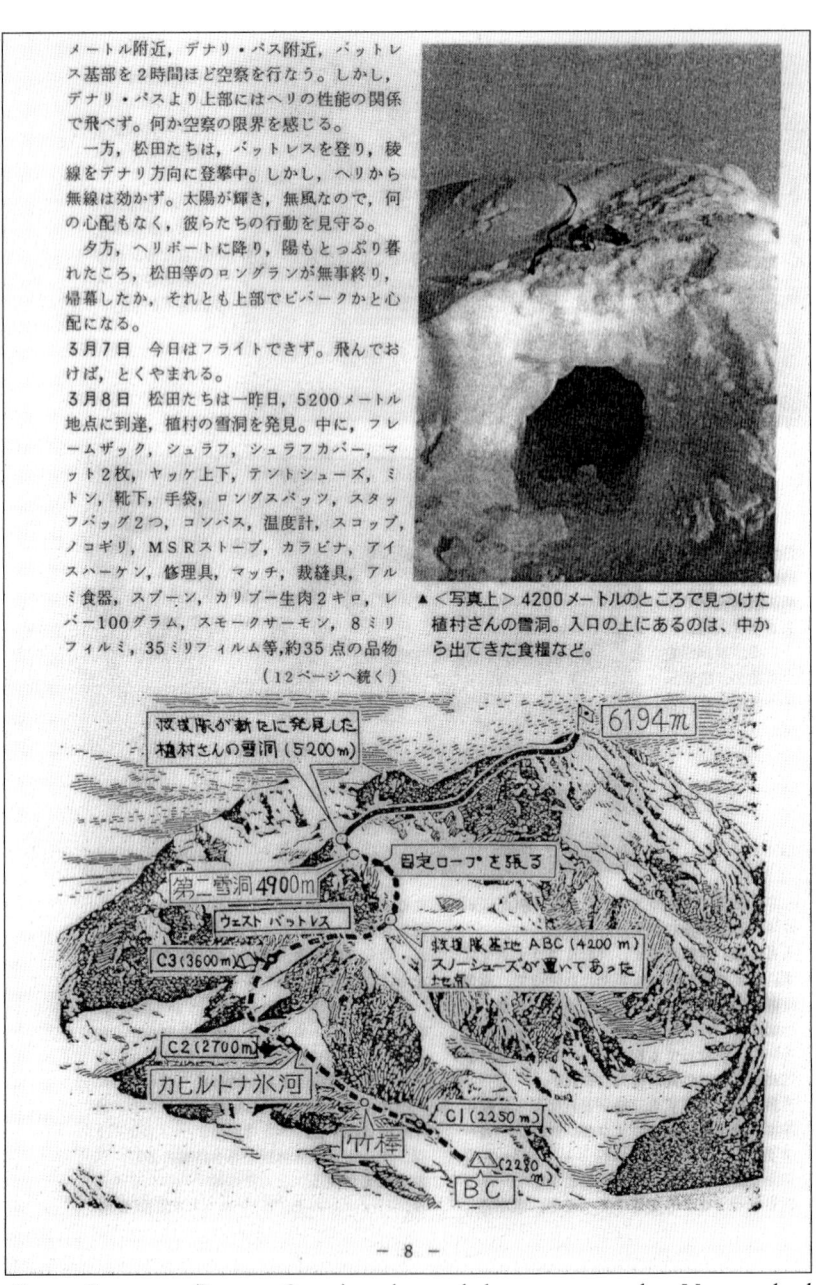

メートル附近，デナリ・パス附近，バットレス基部を2時間ほど空察を行なう。しかし，デナリ・パスより上部にはヘリの性能の関係で飛べず，何か空察の限界を感じる。

一方，松田たちは，バットレスを登り，稜線をデナリ方向に登攀中。しかし，ヘリから無線は効かず。太陽が輝き，無風なので，何の心配もなく，彼らたちの行動を見守る。

夕方，ヘリポートに降り，陽もとっぷり暮れたころ，松田等のロングランが無事終り，帰幕したか，それとも上部でビバークかと心配になる。

3月7日 今日はフライトできず。飛んでおけば，とくやまれる。

3月8日 松田たちは一昨日，5200メートル地点に到達，植村の雪洞を発見。中に，フレームザック，シュラフ，シュラフカバー，マット2枚，ヤッケ上下，テントシューズ，ミトン，靴下，手袋，ロングスパッツ，スタッフバッグ2つ，コンパス，温度計，スコップ，ノコギリ，MSRストーブ，カラビナ，アイスハーケン，修理具，マッチ，裁縫具，アルミ食器，スプーン，カリブー生肉2キロ，レバー100グラム，スモークサーモン，8ミリフィルム，35ミリフィルム等，約35点の品物
（12ページへ続く）

▲＜写真上＞ 4200メートルのところで見つけた植村さんの雪洞。入口の上にあるのは，中から出てきた食糧など。

UEMURA SNOW CAVE AND ROUTE. Searchers located the snow cave that Uemura had made at 17,200 feet to survive the storms that hit during his climb. They found a tent, a sleeping bag, supplies, and a diary, which were left behind to lighten his load before he climbed the West Buttress to summit the South Peak. Uemura described the horrendous weather conditions he faced, noting that due to the heavy load on his sled and the snow conditions, he had to rest for 10 minutes after pulling for just one minute. He was having difficulty with his crampons; the wind was so strong it was difficult to stand; his backpack was nearly blown away; his sleeping bag was frozen from collected moisture from his body; he longed for a warm meal, but had to save fuel, so he used it sparingly, only to melt snow for water; it was dark, but he was determined to reach the summit. (Courtesy THS, NPS.)

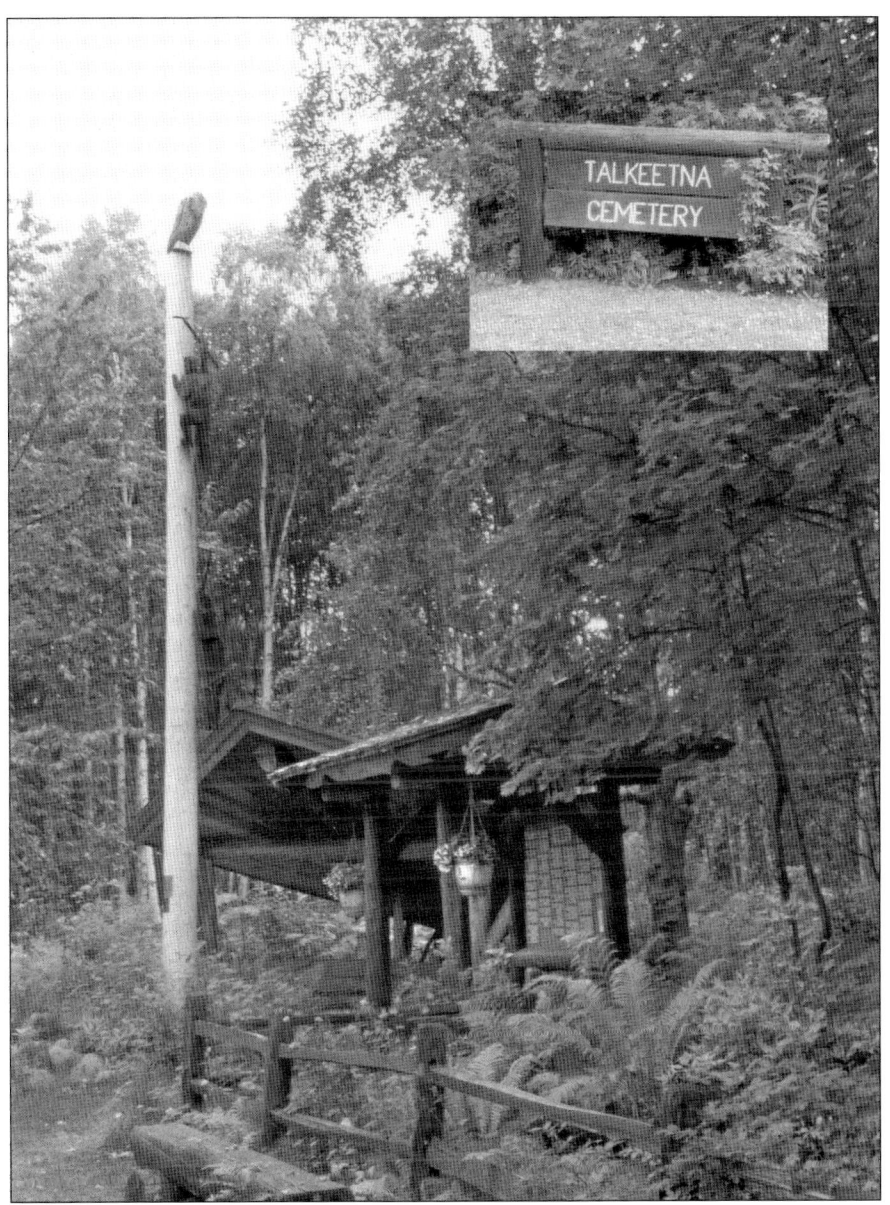

TALKEETNA CEMETERY AND CLIMBERS MEMORIAL. The National Park Service has kept climbing records for the Alaska Range since 1903. Raven crowns the memorial at Talkeetna Cemetery, which honors the climbers who gave their lives in pursuit of their mountaineering dreams. Listed by year, every climber that lost his or her life in the mountains of Denali National Park has their name, age, and country engraved on the memorial. As of 2012, there have been 164 fatalities, with 92 percent male and 59 percent foreign climbers. Climbing falls account for 48 percent of the fatalities, exposure account for 17 percent, crevasse falls account for 9 percent, and avalanches account for 7 percent. The deadliest seasons on record for climbers in the Alaskan Range were 1992, with 13 fatalities; 1976, with 10; 1980, with 10; and 2011, with 9. About 35 percent of bodies are not recovered and remain entombed forever on Denali. The spirit of these climbers is remembered along with Talkeetna's legendary miners, trappers, bush pilots, and freighters at Talkeetna's cemetery and memorial. (Courtesy Sisul.)

109

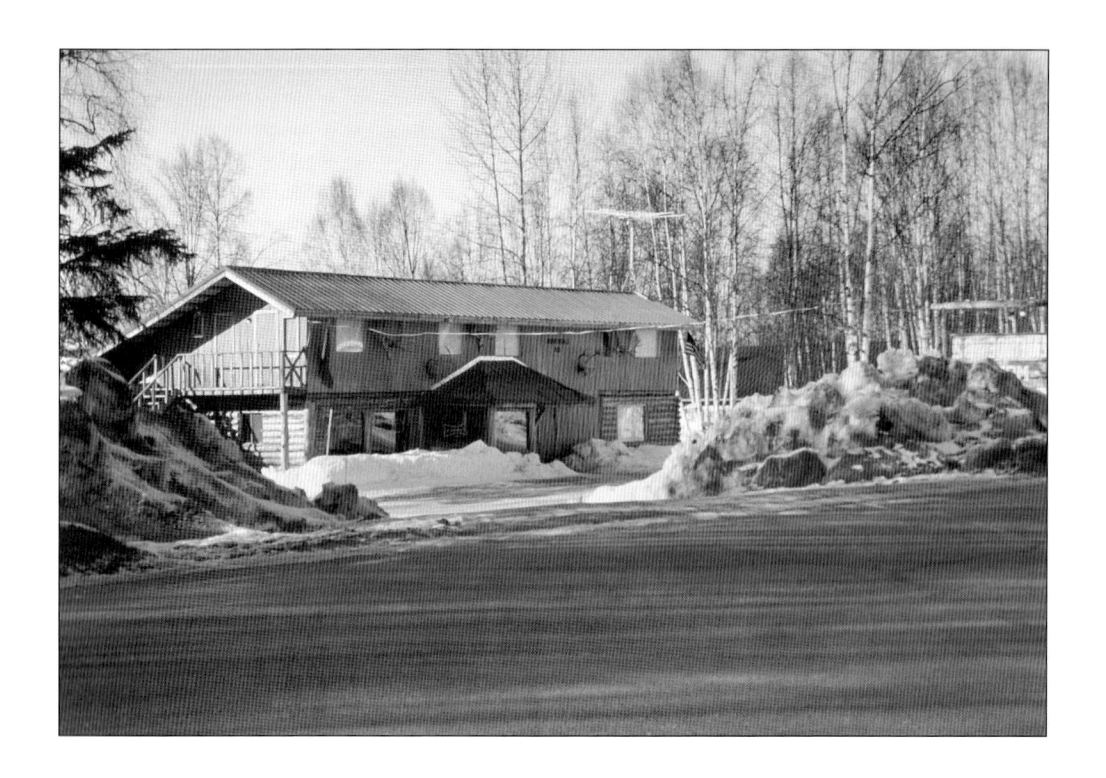

LATITUDE 62. Whether reaching the summit or not, the lucky climbers make it back to Talkeetna, some of them injured, but alive. The first thing climbers generally want after being on the mountain for 20 to 30 days or more is to take a shower and change into clean clothes. Getting some good hot food and a nice cold beer is the next priority. Having a good warm shelter to sleep in, off the snow and out of the elements, is also high on the list. Climbers get all of these things at the Latitude 62 Hotel (above). Room No. 5 (below) at the Latitude 62 is where Naomi Uemura spent his last night in Talkeetna before departing on his final climb. (Both courtesy Sisul.)

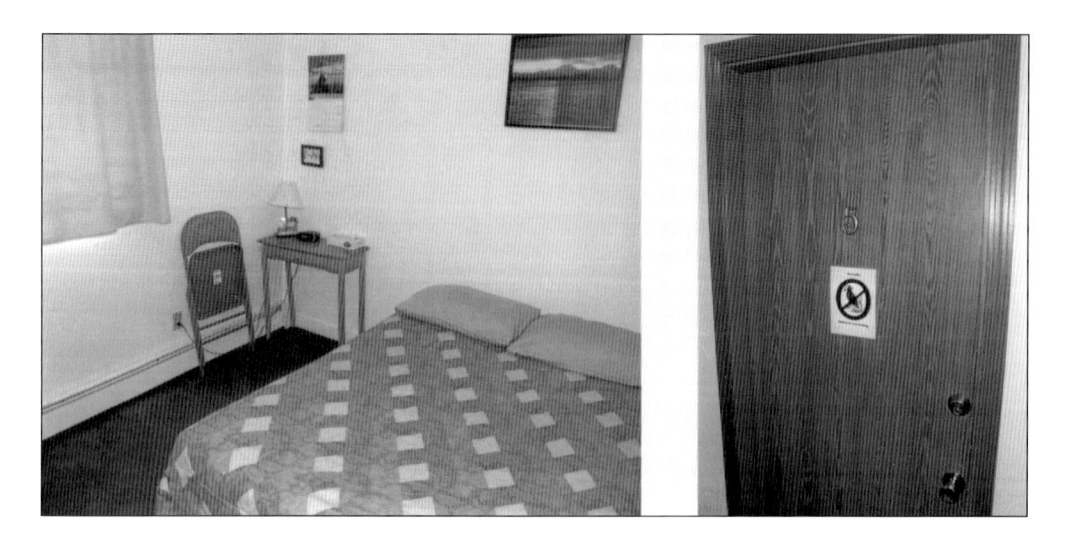

Seven

Fun—Talkeetnan Style

Historically, life in Talkeetna has been challenging due to the weather conditions and the remoteness of the area, which is the very reason many past and current Talkeetnans have chosen this lifestyle and location. People who live here know how to work hard and how to survive the elements. But they also know how to play hard and have good old-fashioned fun. Enjoying the beauty and outdoor recreational activities are ongoing lures for visitors and sources of enjoyment for locals.

Early records indicate that a lottery for the prediction of the exact date and time of the spring breakup of ice on the Talkeetna River was a much-anticipated event. Additionally, the Talkeetna Commercial Club, now the Talkeetna Chamber of Commerce, was instrumental in organizing a number of winter dog races. Animals for pets have provided much joy and entertainment for youngsters through the years.

Activities follow the rhythm of the seasons. Winter boasts snowmobiling, cross-country skiing, ice fishing, and hockey. Once the snow is gone, fishing, hunting, softball, and gardening are enjoyable pastimes. Dancing, music, reading, and socializing at local establishments are enjoyed year-round by Talkeetnans. The Talkeetna Village Park serves as a gathering place for locals and visitors to enjoy picnics, concerts, and hula hoops.

The Talkeetna Historical Society (THS) invented the Moose Dropping Festival in 1973, which continues to be a fundraiser for THS. The festival has been modified to extend throughout the summer season rather than being on a single weekend, and it now includes a Moose on the Loose auction event to help support THS.

Other unique annual celebrations include the Wilderness Woman Contest, Mountain Mama, and the Bachelor Ball. The old Talkeetna Air Service hangar has been transformed into the Sheldon Community Arts Hangar by the Denali Arts Council and provides a venue for concerts, meetings, plays, and numerous other community events. In 2011, Talkeetna premiered its own Denali drama, *How To Make Love Like An Alaskan, or Sleepless in Soldotna*, an improvisational comedy celebrating the myriad absurdities of love and romance, Alaskan style.

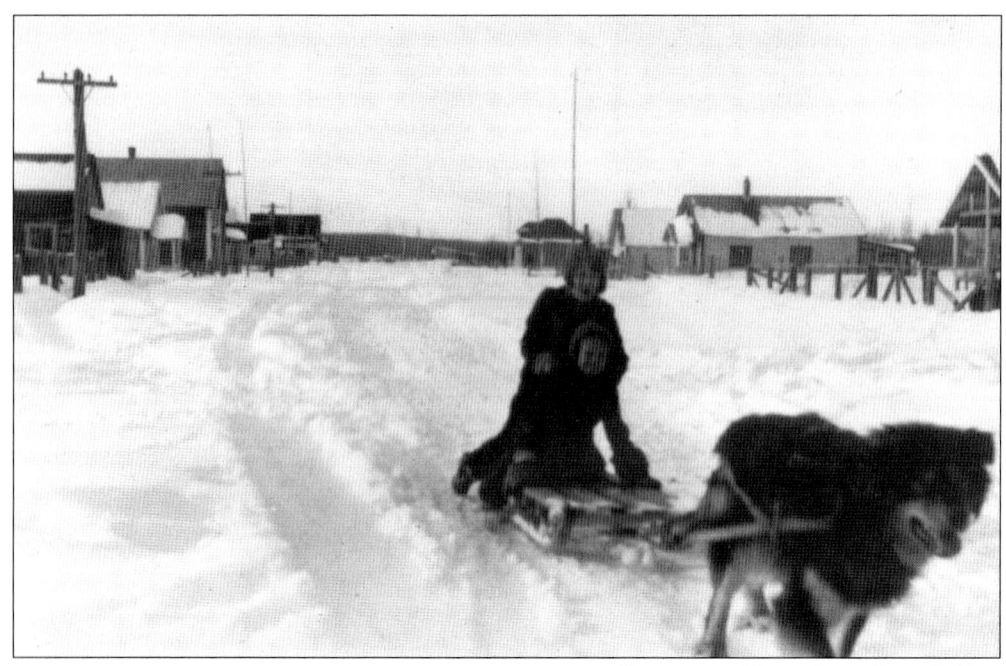

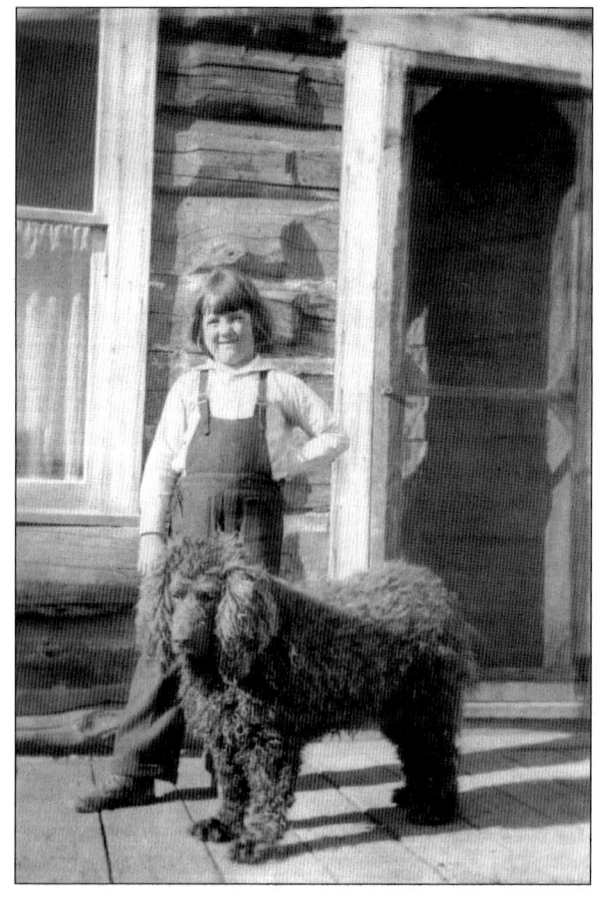

SLEDDING. Above, June Campbell and Betty Mayfield are pulled by Old Wooly down Talkeetna's Main Street in 1939. Old Wooly the dog and this sled belong to Mr. Muir. The Talkeetna Roadhouse is the last building on the left, and Tom Weatherell's old place is across the street on the right. (Courtesy THS.)

BETTY AND DUNK. Pets have always been a source of joy for children in Talkeetna. Here, US commissioner Ben Mayfield's daughter Betty is smiling with her dog Dunk, who was built like a barrel and had curly red hair. (Courtesy Eleanor Trepte.)

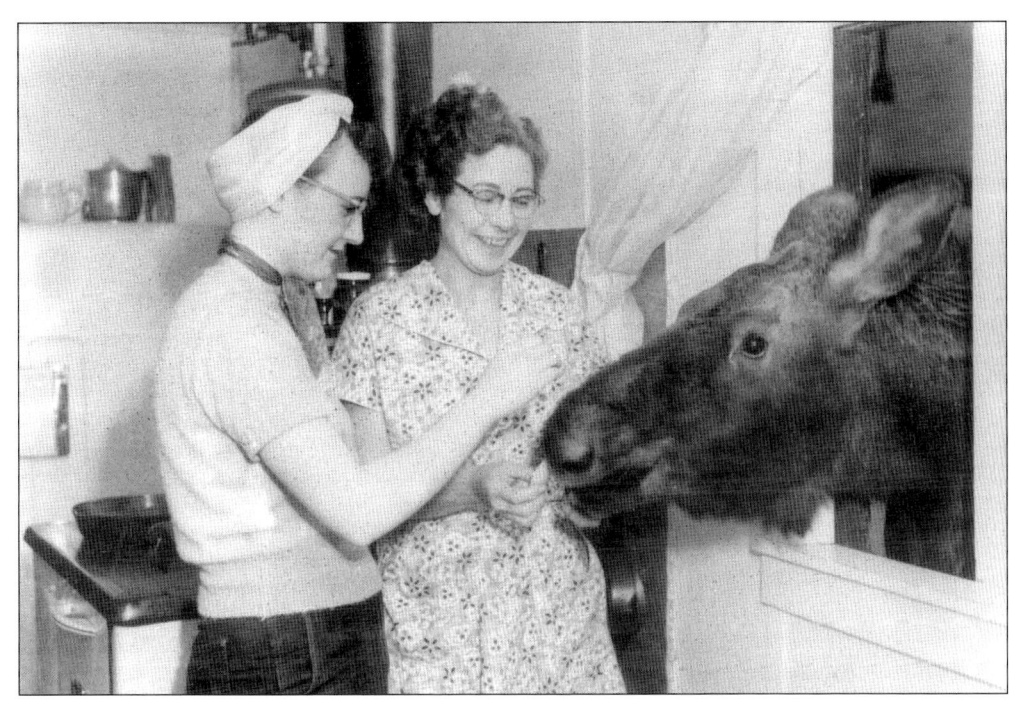

MOOSE ON THE LOOSE? Moose wandering around Talkeetna is not an uncommon occurrence. Above, two unidentified women in the 1950s attempt to pet a moose who has stuck his head inside looking for something to eat. Locals tell stories of feeding pancakes to moose until they can be moved out of the area so they no longer pose a hazard. (Courtesy THS, J. Carlson.)

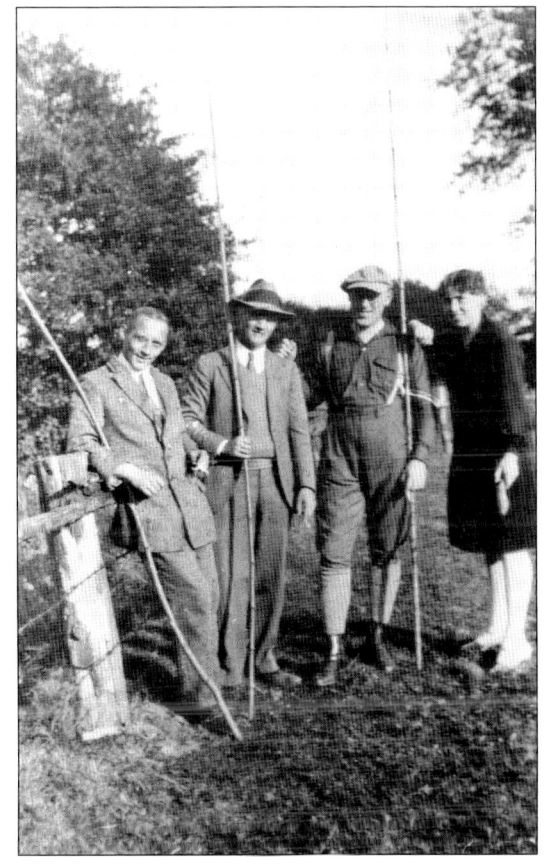

FISHING. Fishing in the area outside Talkeetna has always been a big tourist draw and a source of enjoyment as well as food. These 1940s-era tourists are ready for the local fishing hole. (Courtesy THS.)

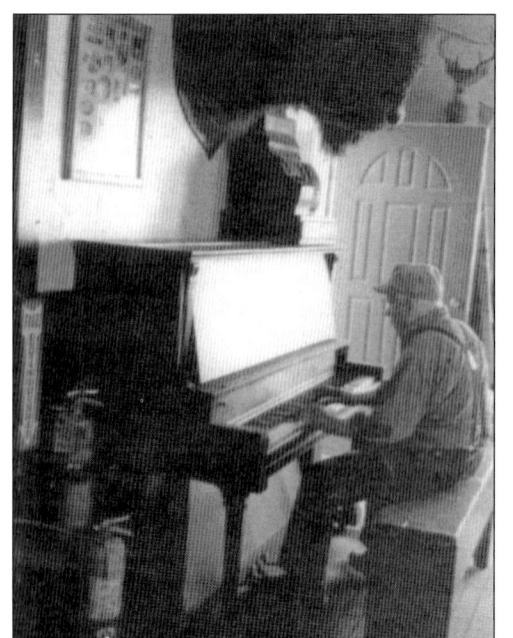

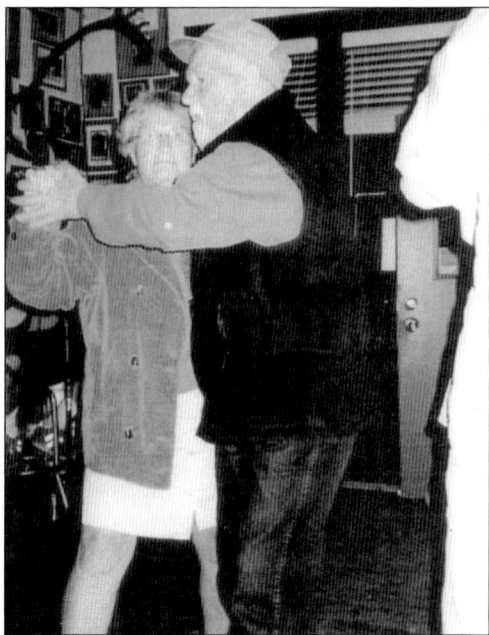

RAGTIME AND DANCING. Talkeetnans have always enjoyed cutting the rug to good music. Although the music and dancing styles have changed, this tradition has carried through to current times. Lynn Twigg, a pilot, trapper, prospector, and fisherman, is pictured above left playing ragtime on the Fairview Inn piano and at right dancing with his wife, Connie, in 1999. (Courtesy Connie Twigg.)

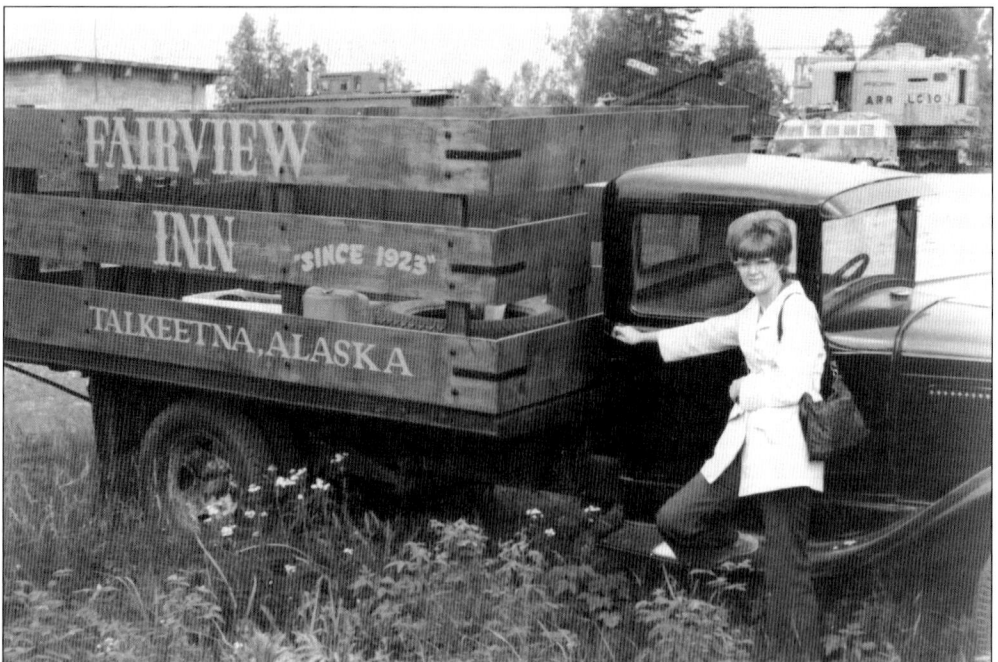

VISITORS. Visiting Talkeetna is fun, and photographic opportunities with local vintage vehicles make for a great backdrop and good memories. This image from the 1960s is dated by the woman's hairstyle, eyeglasses, and clothes, along with the Volkswagen van in the background. (Courtesy THS.)

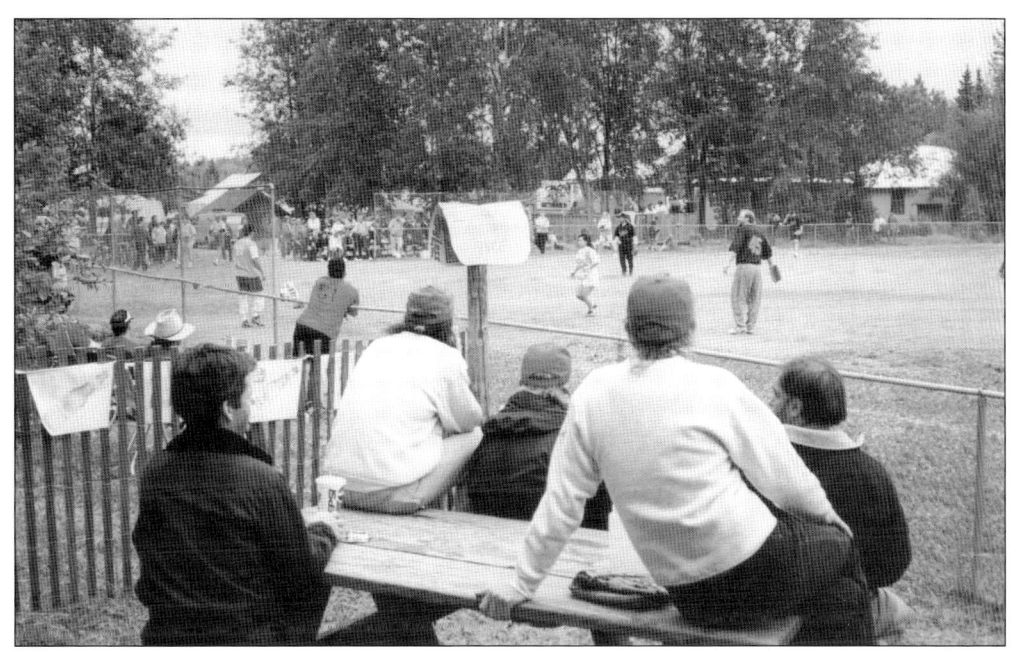

SOFTBALL. Talkeetnans are big softball enthusiasts. The Alaska Railroad sponsored a number of baseball teams during the construction era, and provided transportation via rail for workers to play and watch. This 1980s local softball team is playing at Talkeetna's softball field, located behind the Talkeetna Historical Society and the Talkeetna Roadhouse. Many hours of fun have been had on this field. (Courtesy THS.)

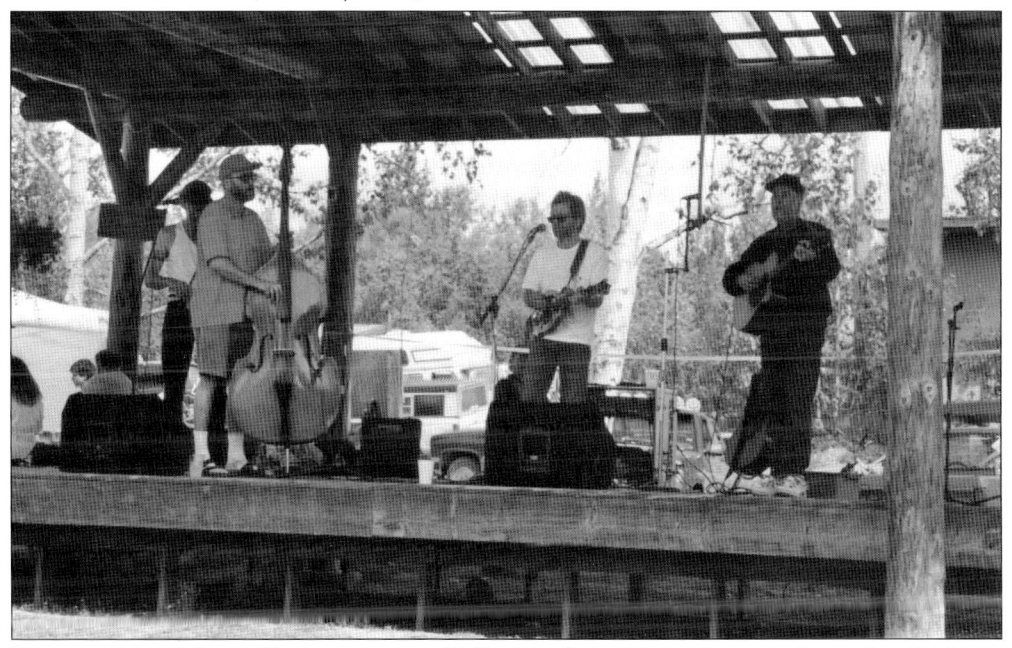

VILLAGE PARK MUSIC. Summertime in Talkeetna features concerts in the park, which are generally held on Friday nights. Local and regional musicians entertain locals and visitors alike with high-quality music. Talkeetna is home to a large number of talented musicians and artists. (Courtesy THS.)

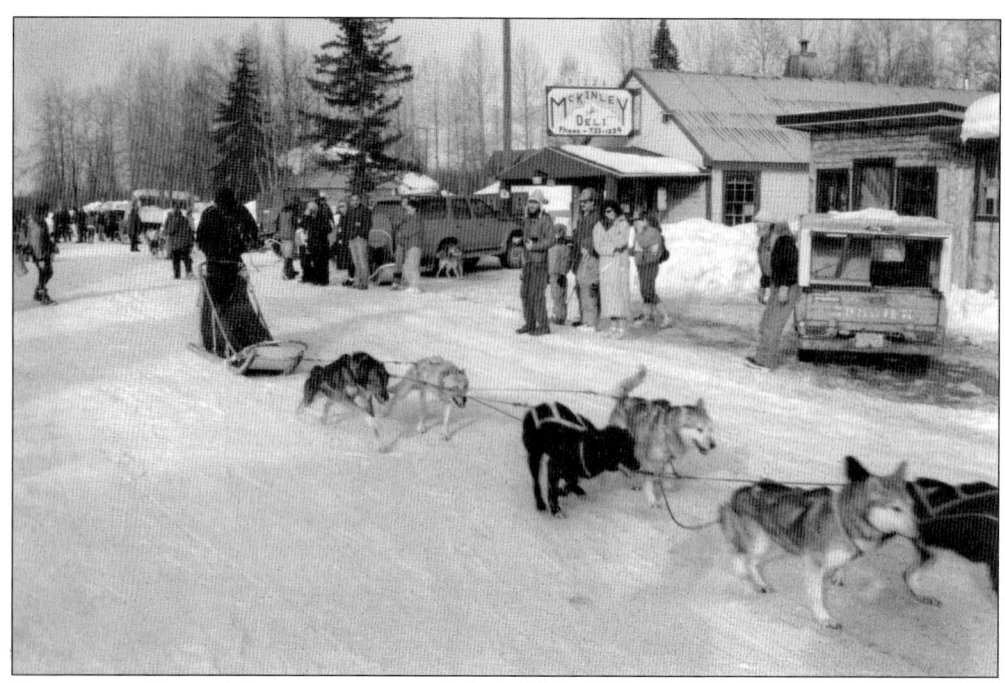

TRADITIONS. Iditarod fever is strong in Alaska. Talkeetnans have always loved their dogs, and still do. This image illustrates the ongoing relationship with man's best friend. Few things are certain—one thing that is certain is change. In this 1980s photograph, the McKinley Deli occupied what is today Mountain High Pizza Pie. (Courtesy Sisul.)

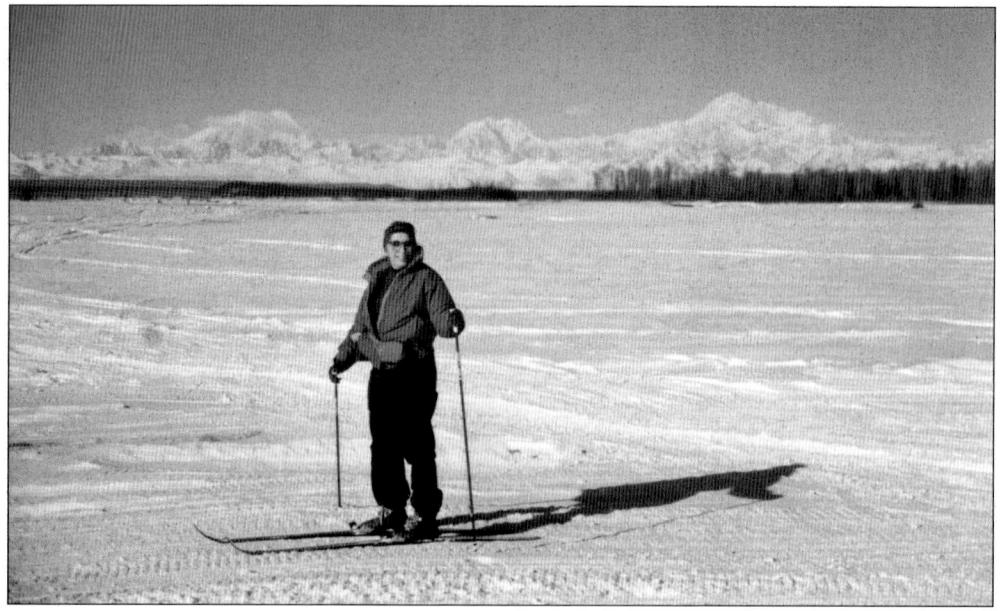

CROSS-COUNTRY SKIING. Seasons dictate recreational activities in Talkeetna. The freezing of the river means it is time to enjoy it in a different way. Here, in the late 1980s, Wasilla resident Meredith Buchman cross-country skis on the Talkeetna River in a beautiful winter wonderland, with Mount Foraker, Mount Hunter, and Denali in the background. Buchman worked for more than 30 years for the Alyeska Pipeline Service Company. (Courtesy Sisul.)

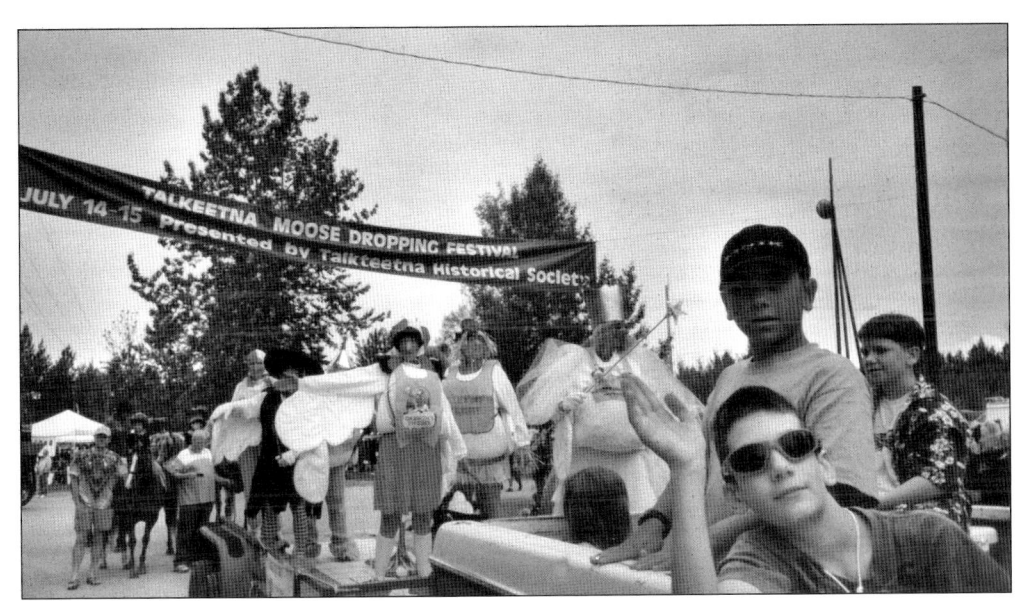

MOOSE DROPPING FESTIVAL. In 1972, the Talkeetna Historical Society (THS), looking to raise funds to support the preservation of local history, invented the Moose Dropping Toss Game, which evolved into the Moose Dropping Festival the next year. In 1997, the Veterans of Foreign Wars (VFW) added a Moose Drop raffle, where volunteers gather, dry, paint, and number authentic moose droppings for the Moose Drop. The numbered droppings are released in the VFW parking lot for prizes. Proceeds support both the VFW and THS. (Courtesy THS.)

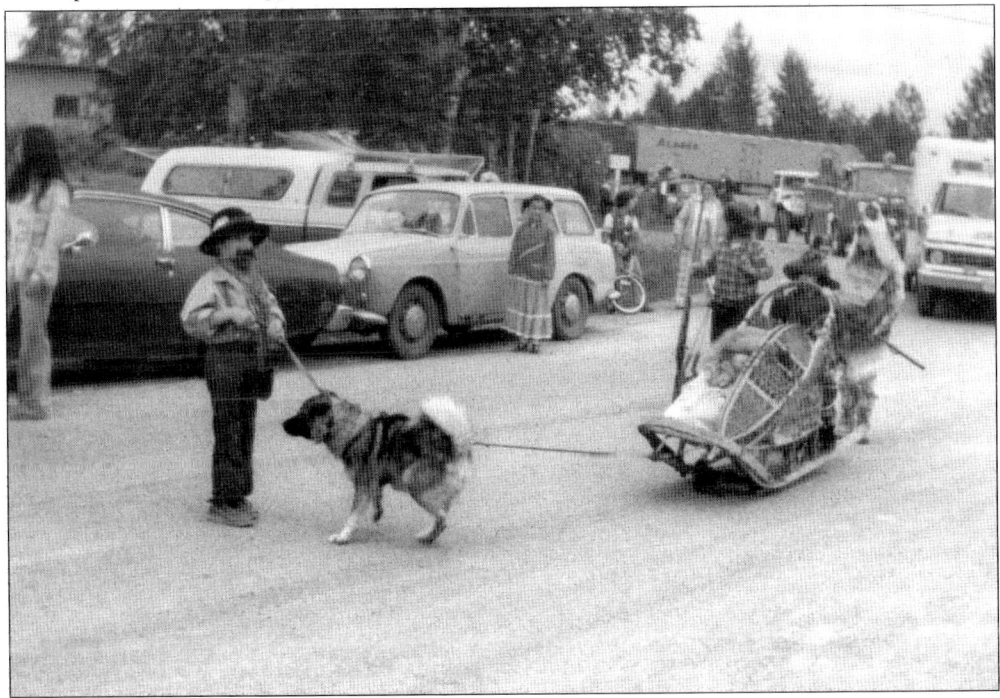

MUSHERS ON PARADE. The weekend-long event featured a parade down Main Street. In honor of Talkeetna's heritage, this child and dog pull a wheeled sled loaded with furs and snowshoes. (Courtesy THS.)

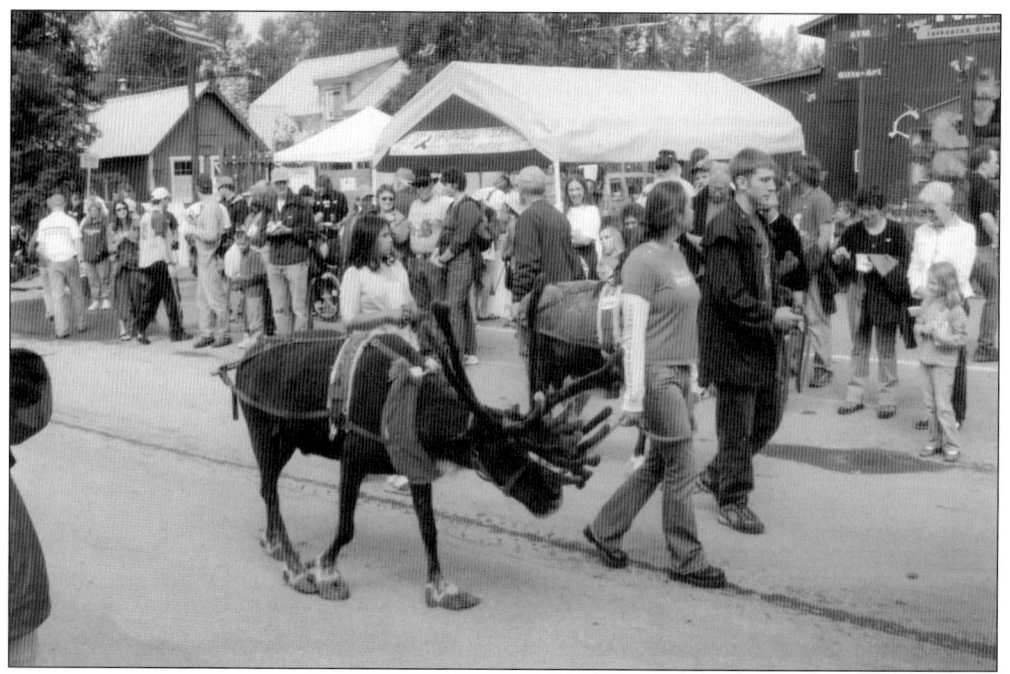

REINDEER. Reindeer owners from Palmer parade with their trained reindeer on Main Street in the 2009 Moose Dropping parade. Music, food, arts, and crafts were all featured events during the weekend-long festival. The festival ran for nearly 40 years, but has recently been revamped into a summer-long series of more informal events. (Courtesy Sisul.)

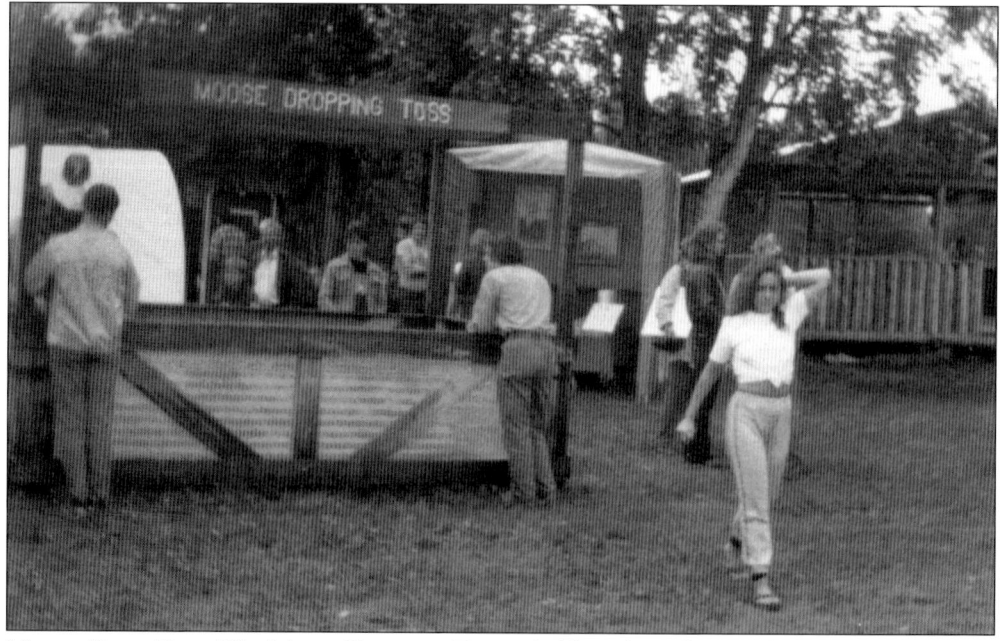

MOOSE DROP TOSS. The Moose Dropping Toss is held in the village park. Painted dry moose droppings are tossed onto a painted moose board with numbers for a chance to split the pot of money, depending on the number of "moose poops" that landed on the board. Proceeds support the Talkeetna Historical Society. (Courtesy THS.)

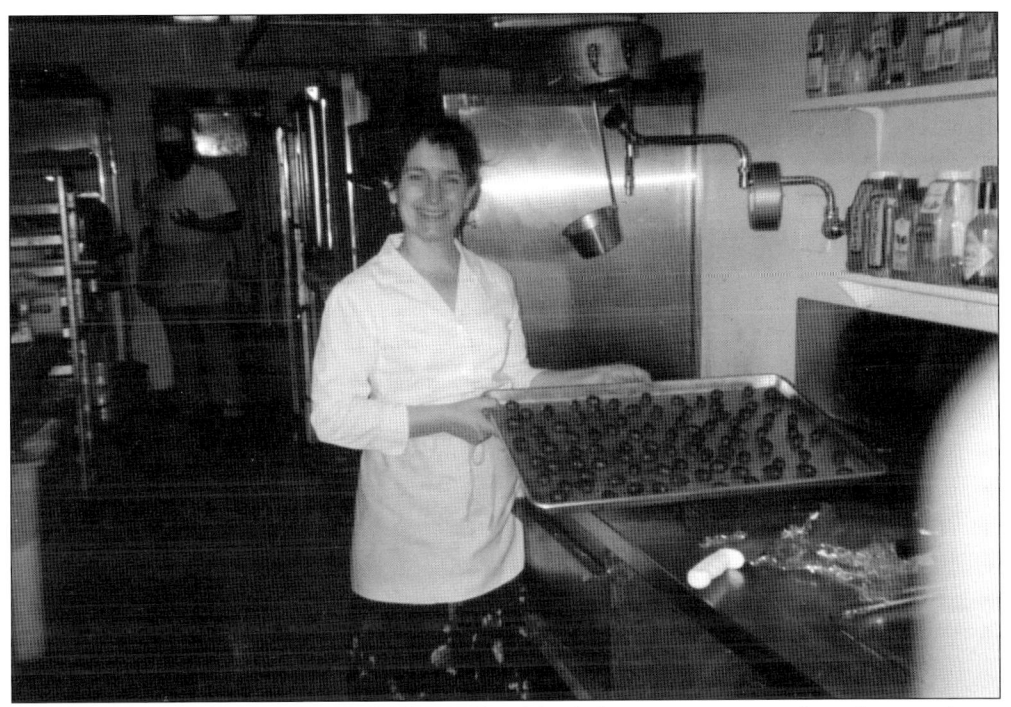

MOOSE DROP COOKIES. A variety of delicious local foods from restaurants and vendors are always featured at the Moose Dropping Festival. Here, Trisha Costello of the Talkeetna Roadhouse holds a pan full of edible cookies shaped to look like moose droppings, which of course are much tastier than the real things. (Courtesy THS.)

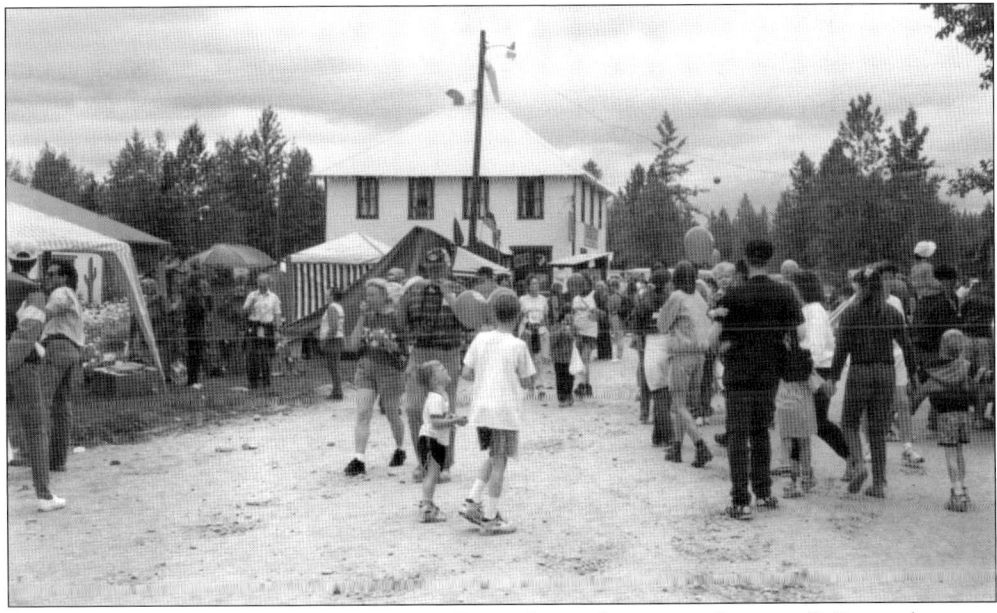

PEOPLE ON THE STREET. Moose Dropping Festival crowds are seen here on D Street, between Talkeetna Historical Society, Nagley's, West Rib, and the Fairview Inn in the 1980s. People are walking, talking, mingling, and enjoying corn on the cob, balloons, arts and crafts, and many other activities. The Fairview Inn, forever a village icon, is in the background. (Courtesy THS.)

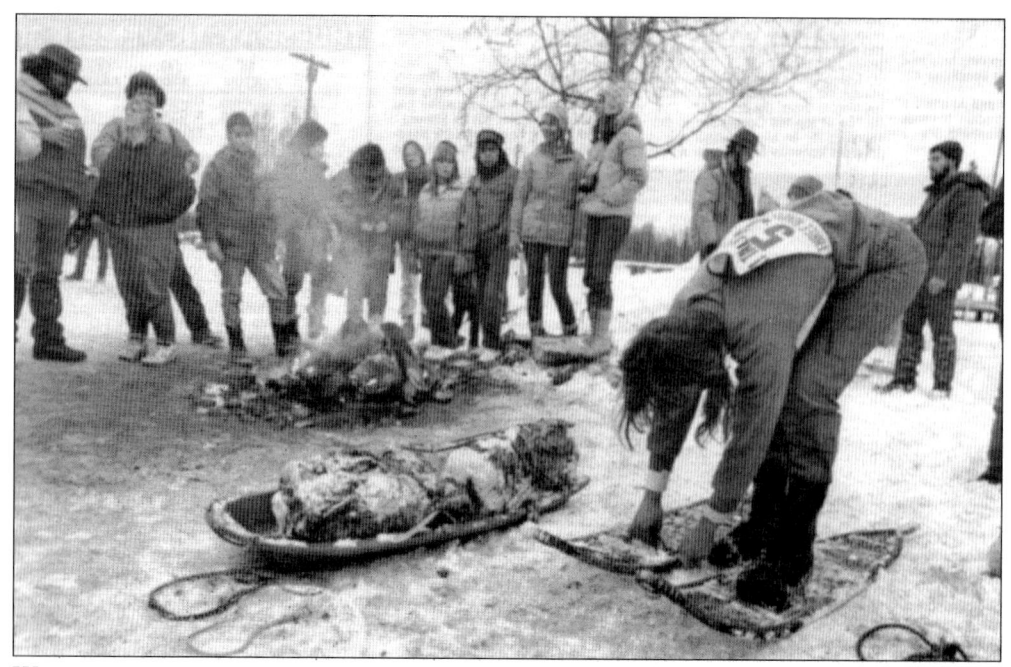

WILDERNESS WOMAN CONTEST. Frontier fun is had each December at the Wilderness Woman Contest. Open only to unmarried women, contestants challenge each other in a variety of frontier activities including snowshoeing, hauling water, stacking wood, building fires, and snowmobiling. The Wilderness Woman winner is crowned at the annual Bachelor Ball, historically held at the Fairview Inn, and more recently, at the Sheldon Community Arts Hangar. (Courtesy VN, THS.)

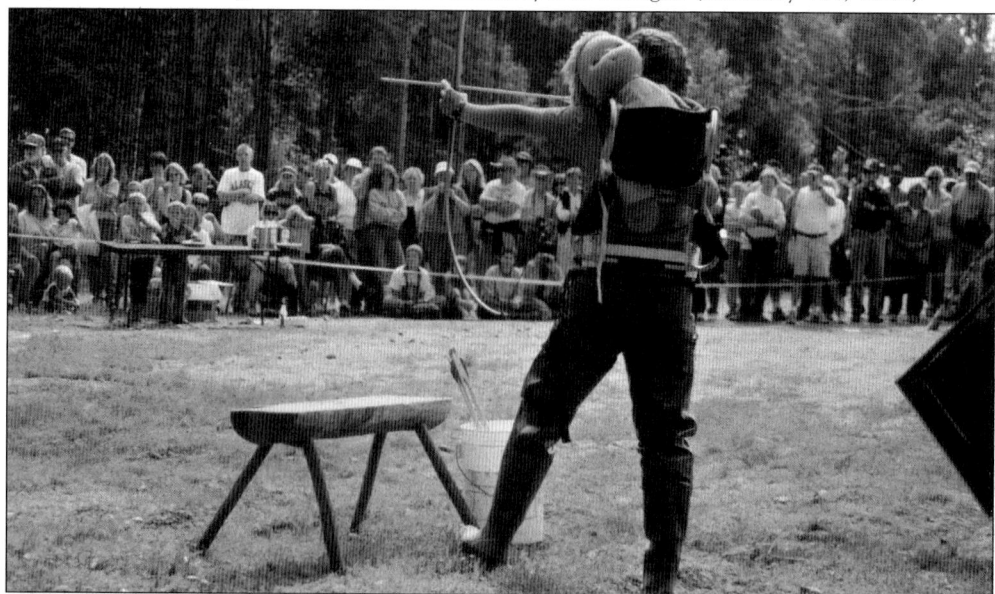

MOUNTAIN MAMA CONTEST. Each summer, a Mountain Mama contest is held. Seen here with a doll-baby in her backpack, this Mountain Mama contestant aims her arrow at the target set up on the village airstrip. Spectators enjoy watching women compete in these fun activities. The only prerequisite to enter into the competition is that you must be a mother. The Talkeetna Historical Society sponsors the contest. (Courtesy THS.)

WOOD CHOPPING WITH BABY DOLL. Chopping wood is an activity that has not ceased for the last 100 years in Talkeetna, as wood is still used to cook and heat homes. Frontier women need to be able to chop wood and use it to survive. The Mountain Mama contest is a fun event that makes light of the tough living conditions Talkeetnans experienced in the past and continue to experience today. (Courtesy THS.)

TALKEETNA CAN-CAN GIRLS. To celebrate the opening of the *Don Sheldon Experience* film, the Talkeetna can-can girls below performed the can-can at the premiere performance in 2004. The group includes, from left to right, (kneeling) Chris Mahay; (standing) Sarah Crepeau, Marne Gunderson, Rowana Wick, Lisa Drumm, Khalishka Russell, and Kristie Seay. Their image hangs in a place of honor under the musk ox in the corner of the Fairview Inn. (Courtesy Fairview Inn.)

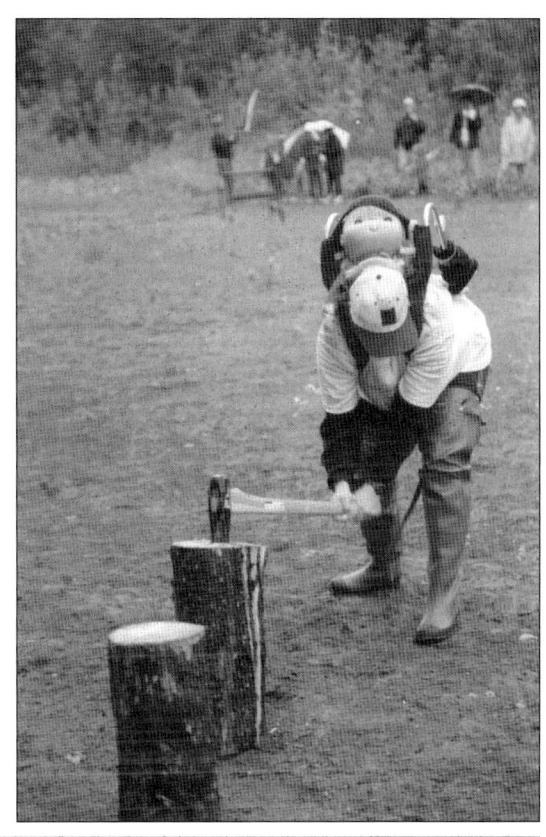

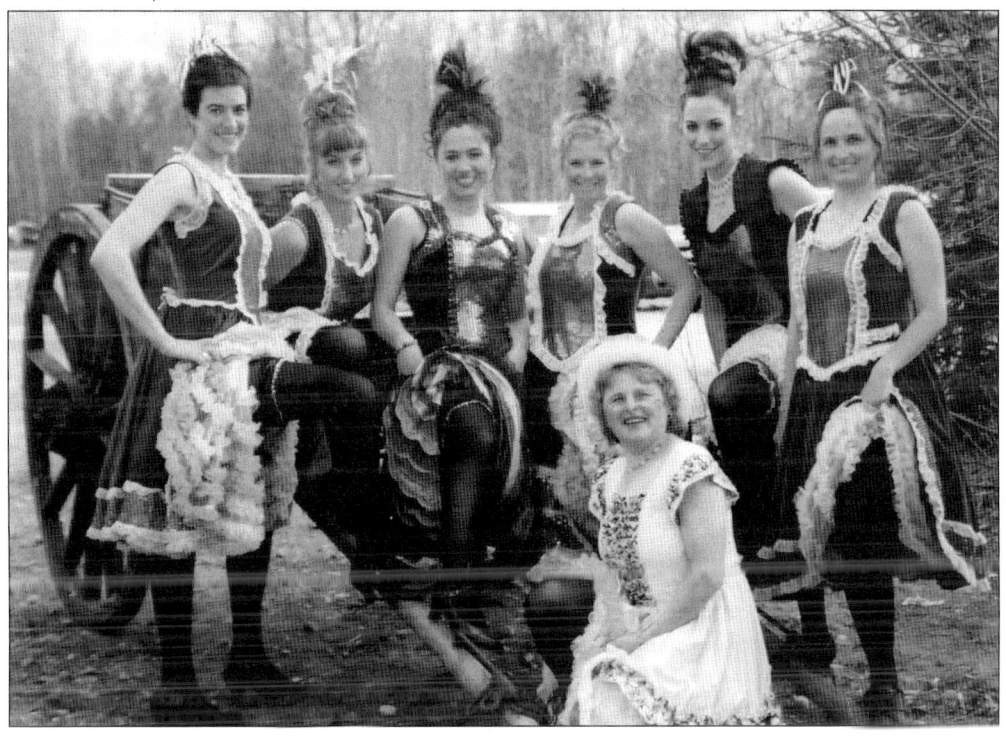

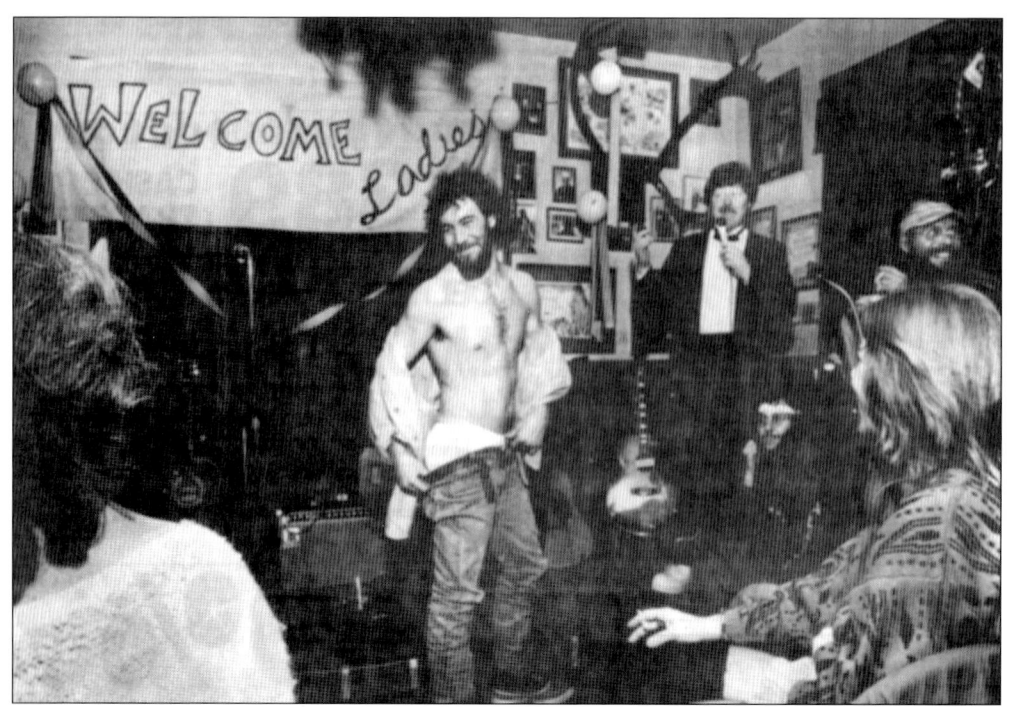

BACHELOR BALL. Talkeetna has a skewed gender ratio, with 20 males to every one female. The *Anchorage Daily News* once reported, "It happens every winter. After the last tourist heads south and the Susitna River starts to freeze, the bachelors of Talkeetna lift their gazes from the bottom of their beer mugs and look around their dormant little town. What they see is the disheveled faces of other burly bachelors. It's a sorry sight . . . The annual Talkeetna Bachelors Ball is the towns solution to the social drought." Women bid on a bachelor, with the winner entitled to a drink and a dance. There is a $100 fine if the auction results in marriage. Talkeetna women also have a saying: "The odds are good, but the goods are odd." (Courtesy ADN.)

SLEEPLESS. Based on the Wilderness Woman contest and the Bachelor Ball, it appears that Talkeetnans are hopeless romantics. What better way to combine these talents than with an improvisational sketch comedy celebrating love and romance, Alaskan style, in the local production *How to Make Love Like an Alaskan, or Sleepless in Soldotna?* The Denali Arts Council promotes, creates, and nurtures community-based opportunities for artistic expression like this one. (Courtesy DAC.)

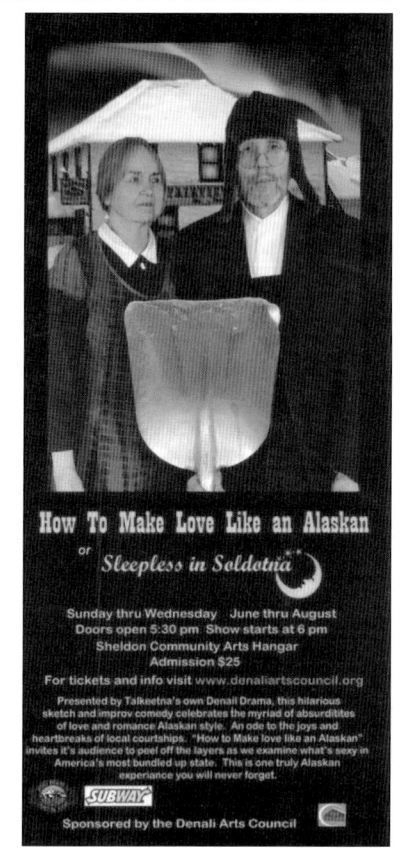

Eight
FUTURE LEGACY

Talkeetna remains an authentic, historic, semirural Alaskan village. Prior to 1964, there were no access roads between the rest of the world and Talkeetna. The railroad served as the lifeline to Anchorage and beyond. In 1964, the 14-mile dirt Talkeetna Spur Road was built, connecting Talkeetna to the Parks Highway, which leads north to Fairbanks via the Denali National Park and Preserve, and south to Anchorage. It was paved in the 1970s. The relatively long period of isolation from vehicular traffic helped Talkeetna preserve its special, rural Alaskan character, which is one of the great attractions of Talkeetna today. Its location, 60 air miles from Denali, attracts climbers from around the world to stage for summit attempts on the highest peak in North America and adds an international flavor to the village.

With its many original log buildings from the earliest days of the railroad era still intact, local Talkeetnans realized the importance of preserving these unique historic qualities, and in 1972, the community pulled together to form the Talkeetna Historical Society. After considerable work by local volunteers, Talkeetna was listed in the National Register of Historic Places in 1993. In the 1990s, the tourism industry discovered Talkeetna, and began to bring thousands of visitors to the historic village each year.

In the 1990s, Talkeetna also began the long, hard process of developing a comprehensive plan to better guide its future. After six years of dedicated work by its citizens, the Talkeetna Comprehensive Land Plan was adopted in 1998. Talkeetnans articulated their vision to ensure that Talkeetna continued to be an "end of the road" village, maintaining its small-town atmosphere, sense of community, and high quality of life. Protecting and preserving the wilderness and natural resources while maintaining recreation and an ecologically sound tourism economy are also key values. Talkeetna's goal is to respect, preserve, and enhance the historic essence of Talkeetna to ensure that the special sense of place remains an integral part of Talkeetna for future generations.

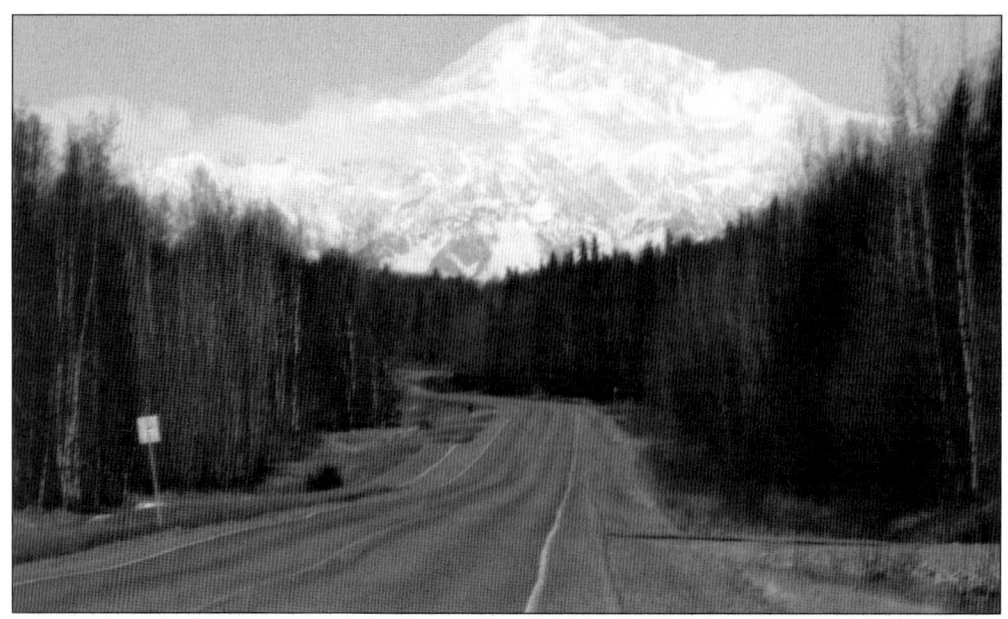

ROAD TO DENALI. Retaining Talkeetna's rural historic village characteristics has not always been easy. Talkeetna fought the government in the 1960s when the state proposed to put the Parks Highway through Talkeetna. Miraculously, Talkeetna was victorious in rejecting the high-speed highway near their town. Talkeetnans won a second three-year battle against the federal government when a proposal to build a mega National Park Service (NPS) facility next to Talkeetna was defeated after the town insisted that the NPS follow the National Environmental Policy Act and complete an environmental impact statement. Talkeetna flatly refused federal money from Congressman Ted Stevens for an unwanted project—instead, Talkeetna was able to redirect the appropriation to mitigate tourist impacts in town. Another hotly contested debate took place in the 1980s over the paving of Talkeetna's streets. A compromise was reached, which reluctantly allowed the paving of Main Street to prevent dust clouds, but left the rest of the village roads "pavement free." (Both courtesy Sisul.)

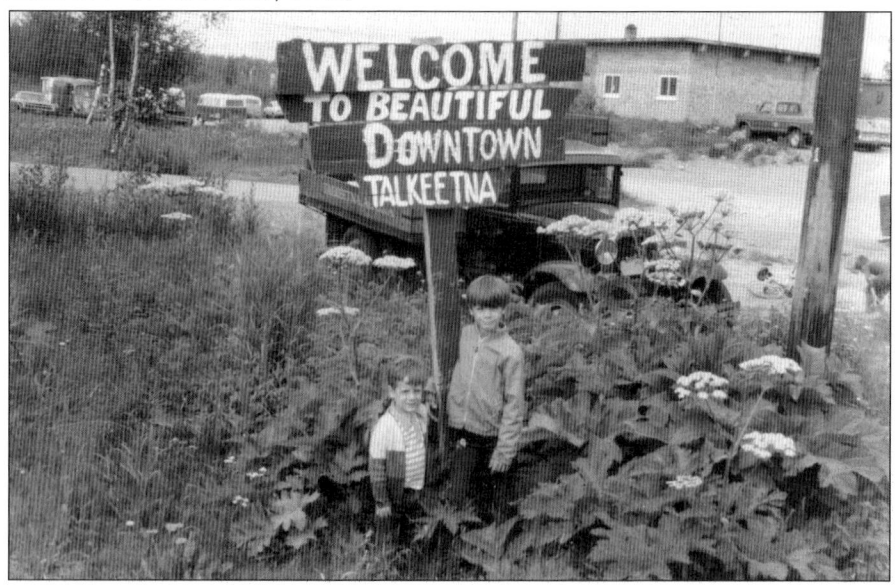

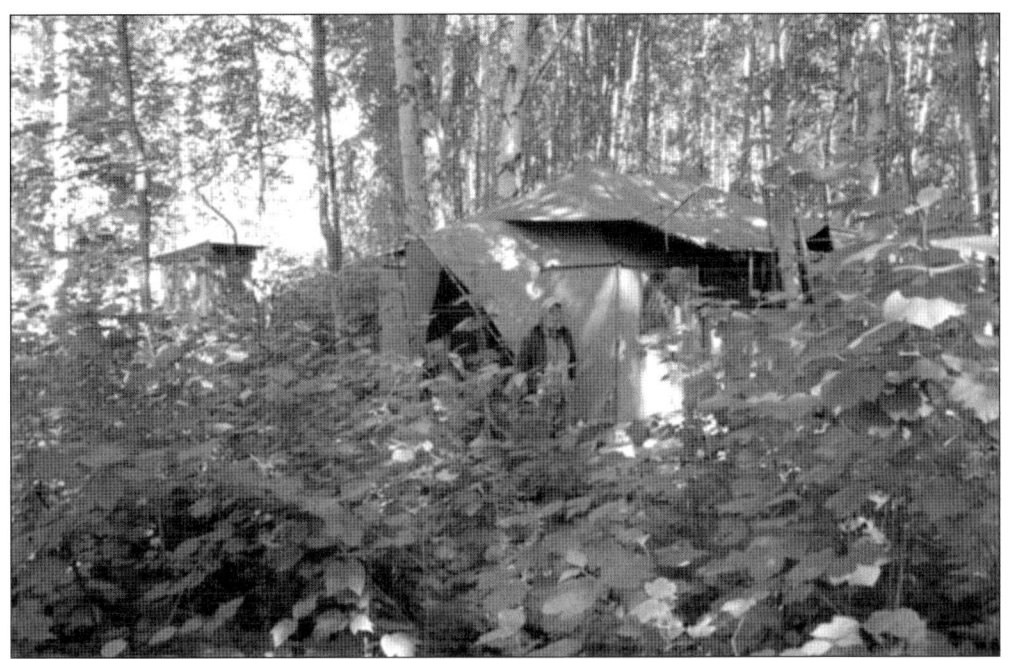

LIVING OFF THE GRID. Many people in Talkeetna have made a conscious choice to live their chosen lifestyle off the grid. Frank O'Brien, for example, arrived in Alaska in 1960 from Massachusetts, worked on the North Slope and on the railroad, and has chosen to live off the grid in a tent year-round without running water, electricity, or central heating. Others in the area live in totally self-sufficient log cabins in the woods, using solar panels and other sustainable methods to live the 21st-century lifestyle, with central heating, internet connections, telecommuting with the global community while living off the grid in wet or dry cabins—wet meaning running water, dry meaning no running water. (Courtesy Sisul.)

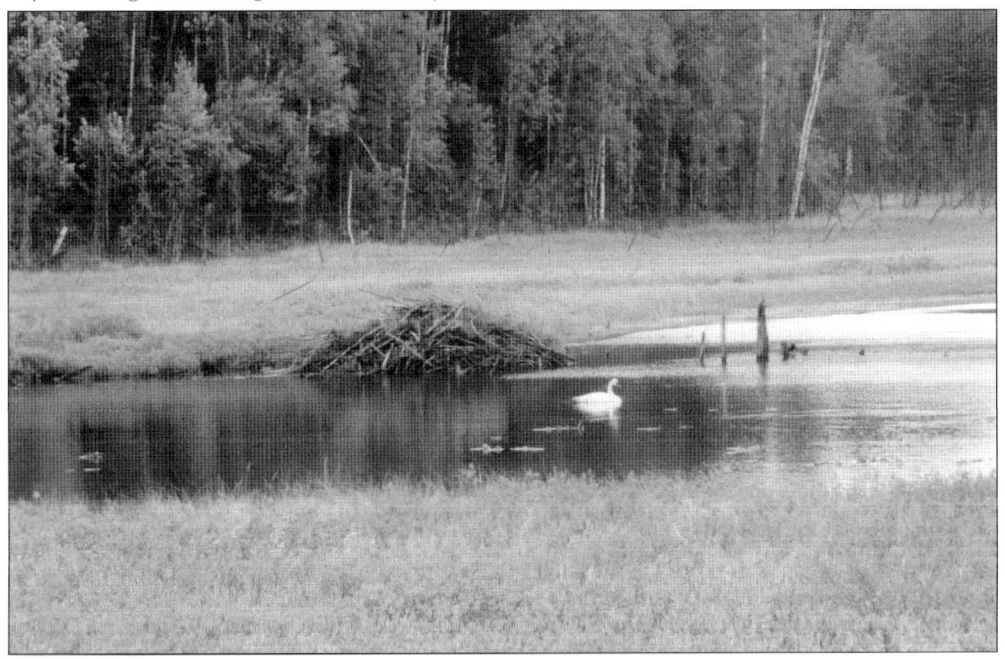

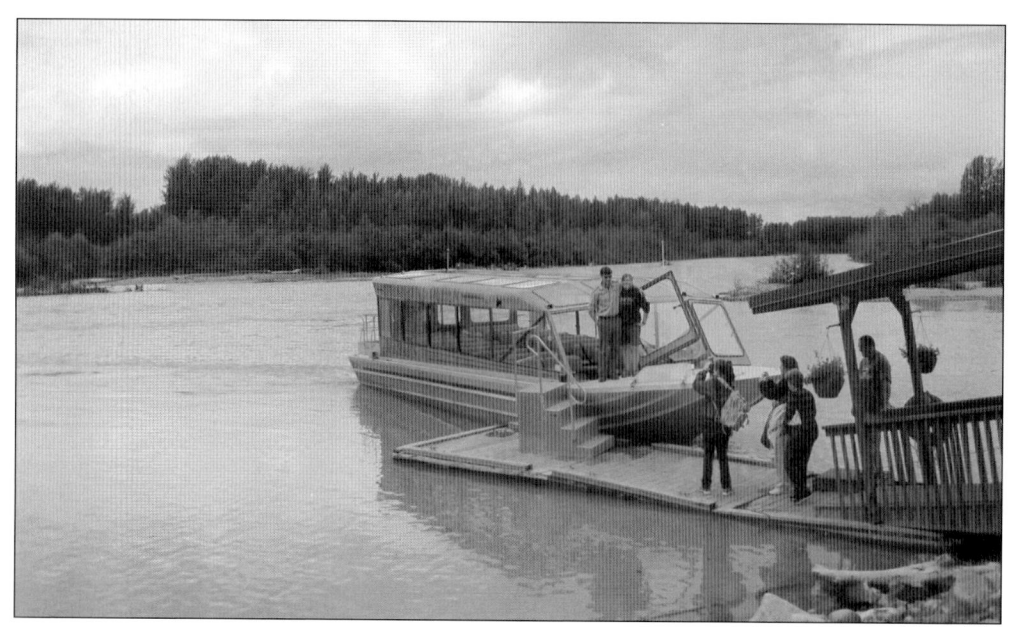

ECOTOURISM. Nurturing a habitat that supports fish, game, and beautiful scenery is a belief that has been strong in the Talkeetna region since the Dena'ina roamed these lands thousands of years ago. The severe weather conditions and challenges it brings still exist, however. These elements add to the charm and draw of Talkeetna. Denali and Talkeetna are national treasures. Over the years, there has been a shift in the Talkeetna area from a resource extraction focus to a resource protection approach, ensuring sustainable resources today and tomorrow. Ecotourism, mountain climbing, and flight-seeing are activities that follow the same seasonal rhythm that has defined Talkeetna life for centuries. (Both courtesy Sisul.)

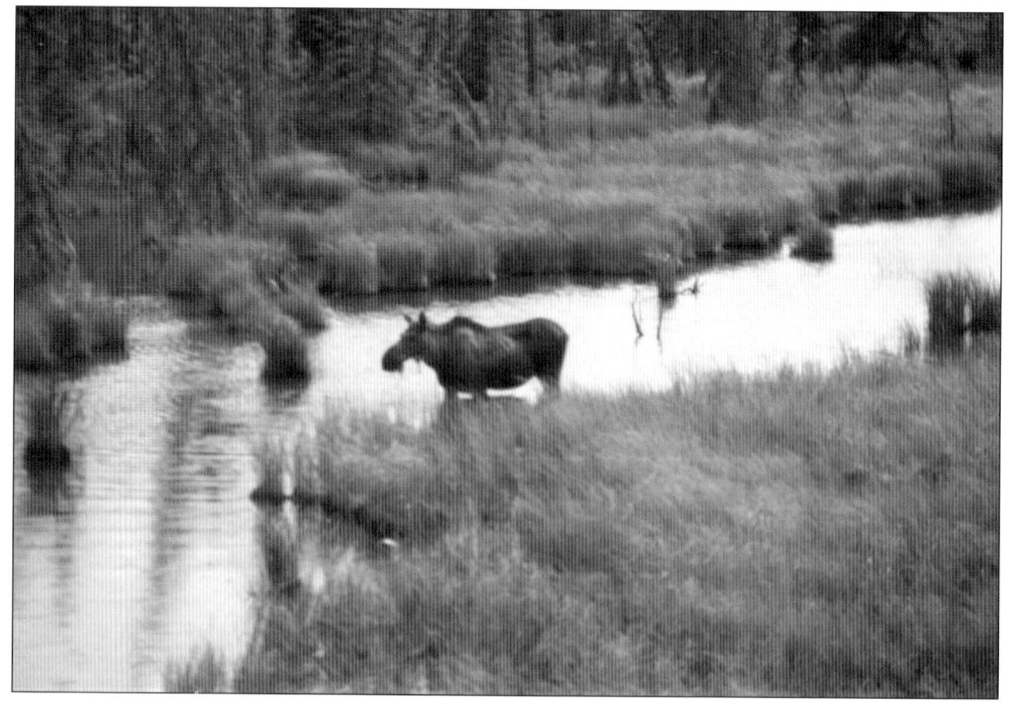

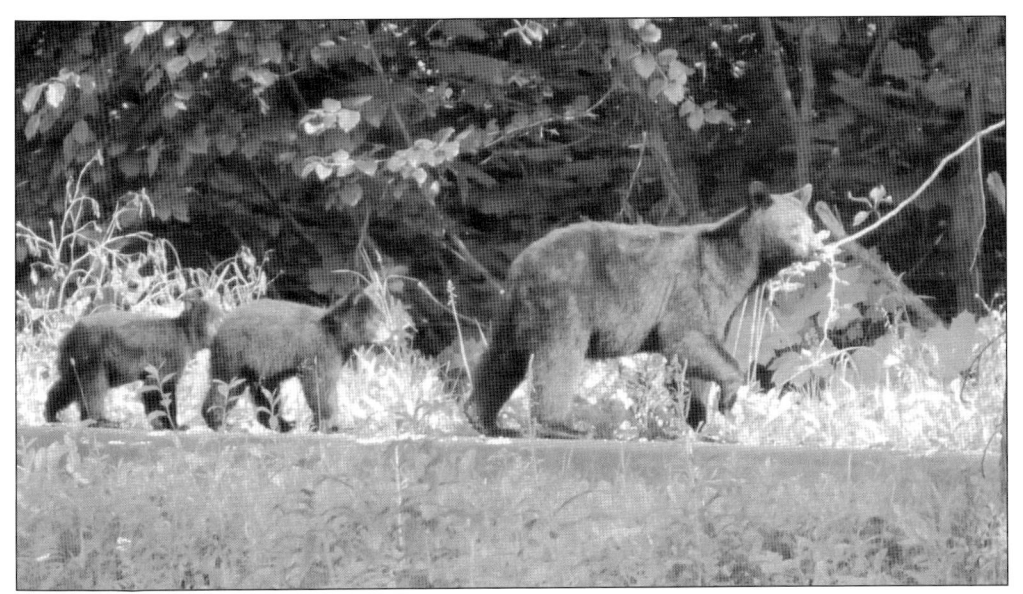

FUTURE LEGACY. The three bears above symbolize the cycle of life, which is dependent on a healthy habitat and the sustainable use of natural resources. Locals and visitors experience the thrill of seeing magnificent wildlife in their natural habitat. As population increases and tourism remains strong, the challenge will be how best to balance progress with protection to ensure the historical treasure survives for future generations. Just as the original inhabitants of Talkeetna, the Dena'ina, had core values of sustainability and leaving their environment better than when they arrived, Talkeetnans today share that same vision. Denali is considered to be a spiritual place, which extends to K'dalkitnu (Talkeetna), 60 miles as the raven flies from Denali. Talkeetnans are working hard to ensure that the legacy they leave will be even better for those who venture to this very special place, where the three rivers meet in the shadow of "The Great One," Denali. (Both courtesy Joe Scarlett.)

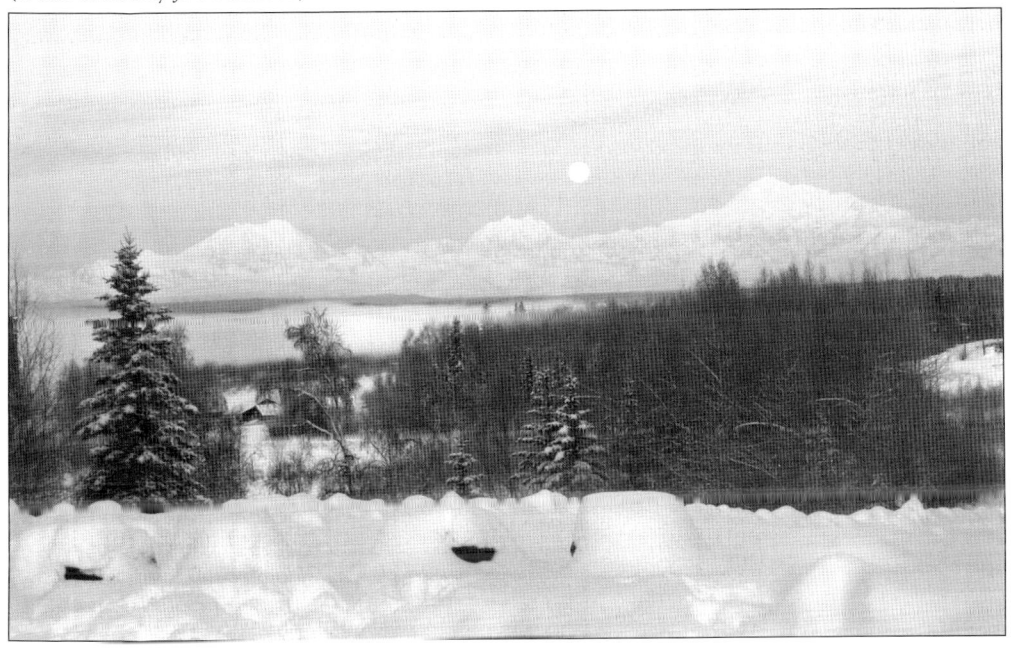

Discover Thousands of Local History Books
Featuring Millions of Vintage Images

Arcadia Publishing, the leading local history publisher in the United States, is committed to making history accessible and meaningful through publishing books that celebrate and preserve the heritage of America's people and places.

Find more books like this at
www.arcadiapublishing.com

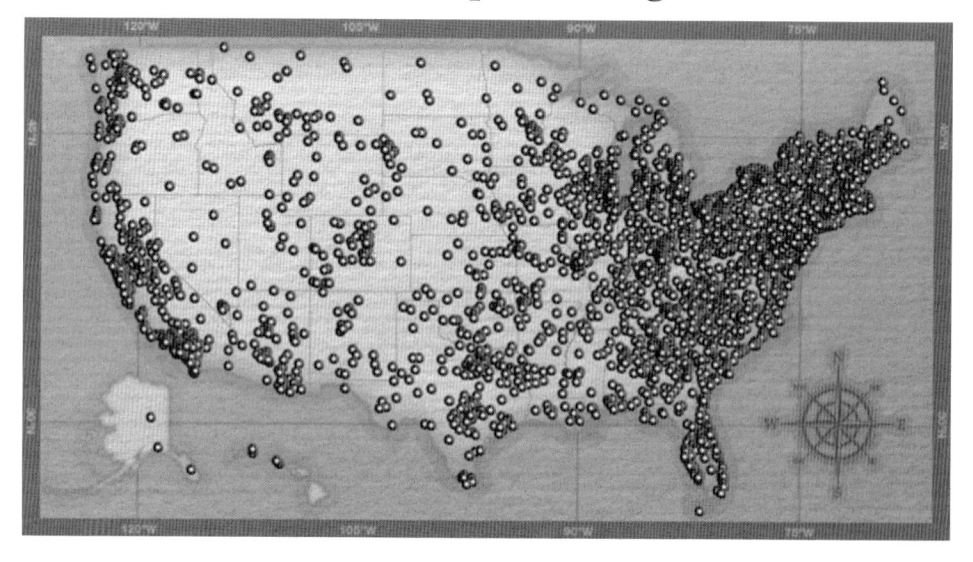

Search for your hometown history, your old stomping grounds, and even your favorite sports team.

Consistent with our mission to preserve history on a local level, this book was printed in South Carolina on American-made paper and manufactured entirely in the United States. Products carrying the accredited Forest Stewardship Council (FSC) label are printed on 100 percent FSC-certified paper.

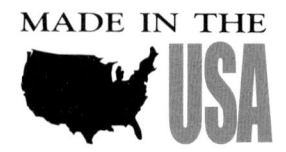

MADE IN THE USA